T0393777

Play and Wellbeing

In an era of increasingly patient-centered healthcare, understanding how health and illness play out in social context is vital. This volume opens a unique window on the role of play in health and wellbeing in widely varied contexts, from the work of Patch Adams as a hospital clown, to an Australian facility for dementia treatment, to a New Zealand preschool after an earthquake, to a housing complex where Irish children play near home. Across these and other featured studies, play is shown to be shaman-like in its transformative dynamics, marshalling symbolic resources to re-align how patients construe and experience illness. Even when illness is not an issue, play promotes wellbeing by its power to reimagine, invigorate, enliven and renew through sensory engagement, physical activity, and symbolism. Play levels social barriers and increases flexible response, facilitating both shared social support and creative reassessment.

This book challenges assumptions that play is inefficient and unproductive, with highly relevant evidence that playful processes actually work hard to dislodge unproductive approaches and thereby aid resilience. Solid research evidence in this book charts the course and opens the agenda for taking play seriously, for the sake of health.

This book was originally published as a special issue of the *International Journal of Play*.

Cindy Dell Clark is Associate Professor of Anthropology at Rutgers University-Camden, USA. She has studied children's vantage points within families and culture, both as an applied research consultant and as a scholar. She is the author of *In A Younger Voice: Doing Child-Centered Qualitative Research* (2010), *In Sickness and In Play: Children Coping with Chronic Illness* (2003), and *Flights of Fancy, Leaps of Faith: Children's Myths in Contemporary America* (1998).

Play and Wellbeing

Edited by
Cindy Dell Clark

LONDON AND NEW YORK

First published 2016
by Routledge
2 Park Square, Milton Park, Abingdon, Oxon, OX14 4RN, UK

and by Routledge
711 Third Avenue, New York, NY 10017, USA

Routledge is an imprint of the Taylor & Francis Group, an informa business

© 2016 Taylor & Francis

All rights reserved. No part of this book may be reprinted or reproduced
or utilised in any form or by any electronic, mechanical, or other means,
now known or hereafter invented, including photocopying and recording,
or in any information storage or retrieval system, without permission in
writing from the publishers.

Trademark notice: Product or corporate names may be trademarks or
registered trademarks, and are used only for identification and
explanation without intent to infringe.

British Library Cataloguing in Publication Data
A catalogue record for this book is available from the British Library

ISBN 13: 978-1-138-11958-1

Typeset in Times
by RefineCatch Limited, Bungay, Suffolk

Publisher's Note
The publisher accepts responsibility for any inconsistencies that may have
arisen during the conversion of this book from journal articles to book chapters,
namely the possible inclusion of journal terminology.

Disclaimer
Every effort has been made to contact copyright holders for their permission to
reprint material in this book. The publishers would be grateful to hear from any
copyright holder who is not here acknowledged and will undertake to rectify
any errors or omissions in future editions of this book.

Contents

Citation Information	vii
Notes on Contributors	ix
Preface *Michael M. Patte*	1
1. The state of play *Cindy Dell Clark*	3
2. A clown most serious: Patch Adams *Cindy Dell Clark*	5
3. Playfully engaging people living with dementia: searching for Yum Cha moments *Julie Dunn, Michael Balfour, Wendy Moyle, Marie Cooke, Kirsty Martin,* *Clark Crystal and Anna Yen*	16
4. From playground to patient: reflections on a traditional games project in a pædiatric hospital *Judy McKinty*	29
5. Living in a broken world: how young children's well-being is supported through playing out their earthquake experiences *Amanda Bateman, Susan Danby and Justine Howard*	44
6. Physical activity play in local housing estates and child wellness in Ireland *Carol Barron*	62
7. Playfulness of children at home and in the hospital *Katherine Ryan-Bloomer and Catherine Candler*	79
8. Family play and leisure activities: correlates of parents' and children's socio-emotional well-being *Diana D. Coyl-Shepherd and Colleen Hanlon*	96

CONTENTS

9. Using playfulness to cope with psychological stress: taking into account both positive and negative emotions
Po-Ju Chang, Xinyi Qian and Careen Yarnal
115

10. Books worth (re-)reading: *The act of creation* by Arthur Koestler (1969)
Cindy Dell Clark
139

Index
143

Citation Information

The chapters in this book were originally published in the *International Journal of Play*, volume 2, issue 3 (December 2013). When citing this material, please use the original page numbering for each article, as follows:

Editorial
Editorial
Michael P. Patte
International Journal of Play, volume 2, issue 3 (December 2013) pp. 159–160

Chapter 1
The state of play
Cindy Dell Clark
International Journal of Play, volume 2, issue 3 (December 2013) pp. 161–162

Chapter 2
A clown most serious: Patch Adams
Cindy Dell Clark
International Journal of Play, volume 2, issue 3 (December 2013) pp. 163–173

Chapter 3
Playfully engaging people living with dementia: searching for Yum Cha moments
Julie Dunn, Michael Balfour, Wendy Moyle, Marie Cooke, Kirsty Martin, Clark Crystal and Anna Yen
International Journal of Play, volume 2, issue 3 (December 2013) pp. 174–186

Chapter 4
From playground to patient: reflections on a traditional games project in a pædiatric hospital
Judy McKinty
International Journal of Play, volume 2, issue 3 (December 2013) pp. 187–201

Chapter 5
Living in a broken world: how young children's well-being is supported through playing out their earthquake experiences
Amanda Bateman, Susan Danby and Justine Howard
International Journal of Play, volume 2, issue 3 (December 2013) pp. 202–219

CITATION INFORMATION

Chapter 6
Physical activity play in local housing estates and child wellness in Ireland
Carol Barron
International Journal of Play, volume 2, issue 3 (December 2013) pp. 220–236

Chapter 7
Playfulness of children at home and in the hospital
Katherine Ryan-Bloomer and Catherine Candler
International Journal of Play, volume 2, issue 3 (December 2013) pp. 237–253

Chapter 8
Family play and leisure activities: correlates of parents' and children's socio-emotional well-being
Diana D. Coyl-Shepherd and Colleen Hanlon
International Journal of Play, volume 2, issue 3 (December 2013) pp. 254–272

Chapter 9
Using playfulness to cope with psychological stress: taking into account both positive and negative emotions
Po-Ju Chang, Xinyi Qian and Careen Yarnal
International Journal of Play, volume 2, issue 3 (December 2013) pp. 273–296

Chapter 10
Books worth (re-)reading: The act of creation *by Arthur Koestler (1969)*
Cindy Dell Clark
International Journal of Play, volume 2, issue 3 (December 2013) pp. 297–300

For any permission-related enquiries please visit:
http://www.tandfonline.com/page/help/permissions

Notes on Contributors

Michael Balfour is Chair of Applied Theatre at Griffith University, Brisbane, Australia. His research expertise is in the social applications of theatre, specifically in social institutions and contexts of conflict and war.

Carol Barron is an anthropologist and lecturer in the School of Nursing and Human Science at Dublin City University, Republic of Ireland. Her research interests are children and play, and research methodologies with children and young people. She is the chairperson of Súgradh, which is the National organization which promotes play in Ireland. She is currently widening her studies, undertaking a course in folklore, focusing on children's oral narratives in play.

Amanda Bateman is a Lecturer in Early Childhood Education and is a member of the Early Years Research Centre at the University of Waikato, New Zealand. She has published in the area of early childhood peer interactions and teacher–child interactions. She has led a Teaching and Learning Research Initiative-funded project investigating pedagogical intersubjectivity in the early years in New Zealand, and an international collaborative project investigating the impact of the Christchurch earthquakes on the children living there.

Catherine Candler is Associate Professor and Director of the School of Occupational Therapy at Texas Woman's University, Denton, TX, USA. She is a Board Certified Paediatric Therapist, and her research interests are in evidence-based practice for the simple intervention techniques which therapists use. Examples of these are the use of headphones for children with auditory sensitivity, attention to spatial organization in handwriting remediation, the use of ASL poetry in fostering more sign imitation, and using a multisensory environment for children with profound disabilities.

Po-Ju Chang holds a doctorate from the Department of Recreation, Park, and Tourism Management at Pennsylvania State University, State College, PA, USA. Her research interests are playfulness and resilience, positive aging, and women's leisure. She is Assistant Professor of Landscape and Recreation at the National Chung Hsing University, Taichung, Taiwan.

Cindy Dell Clark is Associate Professor of Anthropology at Rutgers University-Camden, USA. She has studied children's vantage points within families and culture, both as an applied research consultant and as a scholar. She is the author of *In A Younger Voice: Doing Child-Centered Qualitative Research* (2010), *In Sickness and In Play: Children Coping with Chronic Illness* (2003), and *Flights of Fancy, Leaps of Faith: Children's Myths in Contemporary America* (1998).

NOTES ON CONTRIBUTORS

Marie Cooke is Deputy Director of the Centre for Health Practice Innovation at Griffith University, Brisbane, Australia. Her research interests are complementary and alternative medicine.

Diana D. Coyl-Shepherd is an Associate Professor in the Department of Child Development, within the College of Behavioral and Social Sciences at California State University, Chico, CA, USA. She teaches courses in adolescent development, global perspectives of children, family relations, and research methods and statistics. Her research interests include attachment relationships across the lifespan, couple and parent–child relations, and fathering.

Clark Crystal is the Artistic Director of Blue Roo Theatre Company, based in Brisbane, Australia, and a freelance Applied Theatre artist working in a range of community settings.

Susan Danby is a Professor of Early Childhood at Queensland University of Technology, Brisbane, Australia, where she is also Program Leader of the Health, Wellbeing and Happiness strand within the Children and Youth Research Centre. Her areas of expertise are in early-years language and social interaction in home and school settings, helpline talk, childhood studies, and qualitative methodologies, including ethnomethodology and conversation analysis.

Julie Dunn is an Associate Professor, and a member of the Applied Theatre team at Griffith University, Brisbane, Australia. She is involved in a range of play, drama education, and applied theatre projects.

Colleen Hanlon is an honor's student in Child Development at California State University, Chico, CA, USA. She contributed to data collection, data entry, analysis of the parent and child qualitative data, and to writing the manuscript for her chapter. Her professional plans include graduate studies in human development and early childhood education. Her current research interests include emotion development in young children and attachment relationships across the lifespan.

Justine Howard is an Associate Professor and postgraduate programme manager in the Centre for Children and Young People's Health and Wellbeing at Swansea University, UK. She is a chartered psychologist specializing in play and child development. She has published widely in the field of play, and is regularly invited to speak on the topic both nationally and internationally.

Kirsty Martin has a PhD in Anthropology and Sociology. She is currently employed as a researcher on the playful engagement project at Griffith University, Brisbane, Australia.

Judy McKinty is an independent children's play researcher based in Melbourne, Australia. She is an Honorary Associate of Museum Victoria and a co-editor (with June Factor and Gwenda Beed Davey) of the online publication *Play and Folklore*, published twice-yearly by Museum Victoria.

Wendy Moyle is the Director of the Centre for Health Practice Innovation at Griffith University, Brisbane, Australia. Her research interests are dementia care and quality of life.

Xinyi Qian is a tourism specialist in the Tourism Center at University of Minnesota-Twin Cities, USA. One line of her research is focused on the contributions of leisure and recreation to well-being across the life span. She is also interested in how personal and psychological factors interact to influence behaviours that can have significant effect on the environment.

NOTES ON CONTRIBUTORS

Katherine Ryan-Bloomer received her PhD from Texas Woman's University, Denton, TX, USA, in Occupational Therapy, with an emphasis in child development and advanced paediatric practice. She has worked at Baylor Specialty Hospital and at Our Children's House at Baylor, the paediatric rehabilitation hospital of Dallas, TX, USA. In 2009, she became an Assistant Professor of Occupational Therapy at Rockhurst University, Kansas City, MO, USA; she is also a staff occupational therapist at the Rehabilitation Institute of Kansas City. Among her research and publication interests are sensorimotor assessment, autism, constraint induced movement therapy, and hand-arm bimanual intensive therapy.

Careen Yarnal is Associate Professor in the Department of Recreation, Park, and Tourism Management at Pennsylvania State University, State College, PA, USA. Her research interests include adult play and playfulness, college students' use of leisure time and excess alcohol consumption, and academic approaches to addressing college student excess alcohol consumption.

Anna Yen is an Applied Theatre artist and Feldenkrais Method practitioner who explores playfulness through 'presence, pleasure and complicity'.

PREFACE

The editors of the *International Journal of Play* (*IJP*) have decided to produce one special issue each year to spark debate and reflection on play policy, practice, and theory from around the world. The inaugural special issue of *IJP* focuses on the role of play in human wellbeing and on ways in which play is connected to biological or physical health, mental health, spiritual health, or to the healthy shared relationships of people across the lifespan. This topic is of great interest to the editors of *IJP* as we continue to be concerned about the marginalized status of play in the lives of children and adults in modern times and the implications this stance may have on human wellbeing. We are also inspired by the volume and quality of multi-disciplinary research articles we received in response to our call for papers on this topic.

This special issue is being guest edited by Cindy Dell Clark, a visiting associate professor of Anthropology from Rutgers University, Camden. Dr Clark teaches and conducts research on health-related issues with a special focus on the perspectives of children. She has published four books including a child-centered ethnography on how children and their families cope with asthma and diabetes, *In sickness and in play: Children coping with chronic illness*; a child-centered ethnography on the place of popular imaginary figures in a skeptical society, *Flights of fancy, leaps of faith: Children's myths in contemporary America*; a handbook on child-centered research, *In a younger voice: Doing children's qualitative research*; and an edited book on the processes of play, *Transactions at play*. Dr Clark is a Fellow of the Society for Applied Anthropology and an editorial board member of *Medical Anthropology Quarterly*.

One of the features of our inaugural special issue is an interview with Patch Adams, the prominent American physician, social activist, clown, and author. The interview sheds light on Adams' 50-year career advocating for treating the patient and not just the illness, and offers glimpses of his life's work – the inspiration of a 1998 Hollywood movie starring Robin Williams.

In the postmodern world, play is often viewed as frivolous, impractical, and unproductive (Patte, 2009). Elkind (2007) characterizes the individualistic and competitive nature of modern society as a breeding ground for anxious adults who consider play a luxury that their children cannot afford. Yet others attribute negative outcomes to diminished opportunities for play including underdeveloped social skills (Kaboom, 2009); poor health (Robert Wood Johnson Foundation, 2009); low levels of creativity (Pink, 2005); and an inability to assess and manage risk (Gill, 2007). The prominent twentieth century play scholar Brian Sutton-Smith found 'the opposite of play – if redefined in terms which stress its reinforcing optimism and excitement – is not work, it is depression' (1999, p. 254).

The contributions to our inaugural special issue of *IJP* reveal that play does indeed impact human wellbeing through stimulating the senses, invigorating the spirit, and enlivening the soul.

References

Elkind, D. (2007). *The power of play: How spontaneous, imaginative activities lead to happier healthier children*. Cambridge, MA: Da Capo Press.

PLAY AND WELLBEING

Gill, T. (2007). *No risk: Growing up in a risk adverse society.* London: Gulbenkian Foundation.

Kaboom. (2009). *Play matters: A study of best practices to inform local policy and process in support of children's play.* Washington, DC: Author.

Patte, M. M. (2009). The state of recess in Pennsylvania elementary schools: A continuing tradition or distant memory? In C. Dell-Clark (Ed.), *Play and culture studies, transactions at play, 9* (pp. 147–165). Lanham, MD: University Press of America.

Pink, D. H. (2005). *A whole new mind: Why right-brainers will rule the future.* New York, NY: Riverhead Books.

Robert Wood Johnson Foundation. (2009). *Active education: Physical education, physical activity, and academic performance.* San Diego, CA: Robert Wood Johnson Foundation.

Sutton-Smith, B. (1999). Evolving a consilience of play definitions: Playfully. In S. Reifel (Ed.), *Play and culture studies, 2* (pp. 239–256). Stamford, CT: Ablex.

Michael M. Patte
Bloomsburg University of Pennsylvania, USA

The state of play

Cindy Dell Clark

Department of Sociology, Anthropology and Criminal Justice, Rutgers University (Camden), Villanova, USA

It's Time to Put Fun Back into Fundamental Ways of Viewing Health and Well-being.

Kristin Alexander (Alexander, Miller & Hengst, 2001) has remarked that children's involvement in fictional or oral narratives (so-called 'story attachments') constitute a 'homeless phenomenon'. By that she means, story attachments are ever-present in real children's lives, yet as a topic have not carved out much space for intense study within the bounds of any one social science discipline. In many respects, play similarly is a homeless phenomenon, neither the central province of anthropology nor psychology nor education nor therapy, but rather a visitor to all these fields, borrowing space at the edges of disciplines rather than occupying the central space of any given field.

Academic behavioral research tends to be more prosaic than poetic, of course, which may explain why play – fraught with slippery references of meaning and side-stepping dexterity of action – has remained at the margins of established fields. Play, like a moonbeam that resists being held in one's hand, is a problem hard to solve with fixed, linear conceptions. Play is often more a matter of process or tone than a singular behavior. Play is flux, not stasis. Play cannot be coerced to an ultimate form, but rather emerges from creative associations and sensitive non-directive social engagement.

The inquiries into play and well-being contained in this volume suggest that the very ambiguity and morphing dynamism of play is what makes it instrumental to human functioning and coping. Play is tailor-made for unfixing what needs fixing, for adapting and adopting new ways of signifying when the old approaches are stale, unsatisfactory, dysfunctional or unhealthy. Put another way, play has just the creative stuff needed to reframe what is possible and to conjure new possibilities, when the old ones become inadequate. Playfulness opens us to bisociation, Koestler's term for the human capacity to reach across domains of meaning and thereby to forge new conceptual connections leading to creative insight or cathartic release (see Clark, page 139 for a review of Koestler's *The act of creation*).

The authors whose work appears in this volume have set forth multiple contexts in which playfulness brings an eruption of adaptable, flexible meaning-making. Their work demonstrates that play processes are crucial underpinnings of well-being.

- Clowning is explored by Dunn and her colleagues, as a means for engaging Australian elders living with dementia (Dunn, Balfour, Moyle, Cooke, Martin, Crystal and Yen, page 16). In a separate piece profiling Patch Adams the clown-physician, clowning is shown to have particular suitability for catalyzing new frames of reference, even when this is a life and death matter (Clark, page 5).

- In everyday home settings, American families who jointly engage in leisurely fun activities are shown to score higher on some measures of socio-emotional well-being (Coyl-Shepherd and Hanlon, page 96). In Ireland, homes and neighborhoods are significant sites for children's improvisational fun; as children use lampposts, trees and streets for their own spontaneous play, public space provides them with a lion's share of their physical activity, a self-powered buffer against obesity, with impact beyond that of school-based exercise (Barron, page 62).
- In a preschool-based case study from New Zealand – conducted months after a damaging earthquake had punctured children's and teachers' school day – children continued to use play as a means to reframe and make sense of their shared traumatic experience (Bateman, Danby and Howard, page 44).
- A study of American college students (coping with the inevitable stress that circulates prior to exams) suggests that playfulness can be a resource in two ways: It is mathematically associated with increased levels of positive emotions, while also being associated with fewer negative emotions (Chang, Qian, and Yarnal, page 115).
- Last but not least, play is a significant resource for children and families dealing with hospitalization. Children who are playful at home continue to use play as a resource when hospitalized, Ryan-Bloomer and Candler's US-based study (page 79) finds. While hospitalized, children's playfulness increases between admission and discharge, as kids use playfulness to adapt to a particularly stressful environment. Along similar lines, everyday play approaches that traditionally had been parts of child lore were exhibited and available for use in a children's hospital ward in Australia, as part of an intriguing case of clinical application described by McKinty (page 29). These ordinary, traditional games produced an exceptional hospital experience, not only among young patients but also among the adults with whom patients interacted. Parents, physicians and hired tradesmen alike responded with enthusiasm to playing with the traditional play materials, bringing about a valued sense of hierarchy-leveling enjoyment and supportive social sharing for young and old.

Perhaps in part because play generally lurks only on the margins of academic disciplines, too many implicit models of playfulness view fun and games as non-essential, a sort of curiosity free of substantive weight in serious human existence. The work of the researchers in this volume puts the lie to that prosaic oversight.

Although admittedly playfulness is a bisociative and dynamic force that can evade being pinned down with reductionist inquiry, the many varieties of play are, at root, essential to social and emotional life. Contemporary humans navigate an unpredictable and often stressful world. Under duress, persons find that selfhood is in need of maintenance, repair, and remaking. It is high time to take clowns, child lore, neighborhood play and family leisure more seriously, within the main corridors where theories and policies form.

A clown most serious: Patch Adams

Cindy Dell Clark

Department of Sociology, Anthropology & Criminal Justice, Rutgers University, Camden, USA

Patch Adams is profiled, based on an interview in his home conducted in December 2012. Adams' contribution to therapeutic clowning is discussed and analyzed.

Michael Patte and I visited Patch Adams, the renowned clown and physician, during December 2012 in his Illinois home (Figure 1 shows Patch at home during the interview.). The home he shares with composer and playwright Susan Parenti is charming inside and out, full of objects made by human hands that exude color, creativity, and human warmth. Their welcoming home is cozily reminiscent of the Crosby, Stills, Nash and Young song lyrics 'our house, is a very very very fine house' complete with – as mentioned in the song – two cats, who on the day we visited were away being spayed. In the living room where we had the interview, high-tech equipment was out of sight. The computer used by Adams' assistant was in a basement office. (He writes his own correspondence by hand, not computer.) The large-screen TV (which Patch used to show us videos) was kept under cover by a lovely handmade quilt.

Amidst the genial homespun touches were omnipresent shelves of books. Patch Adams' huge library, recently moved to this residence, encroached on the scene, with shelves placed into every nook and cranny of the ground floor, and tucked into every available pocket of the living room. The books added a special presence of their own, akin to my favorite old crammed bookstores in Chicago's Hyde Park neighborhood. On shelves freshly built of clean new wood were all my favorite books and thousands more. The books were serious tomes on a host of issues in the medical sciences, social sciences, and social policy, some solemn to the point of irony, such as a case filled by more publications on the folklore of fart jokes than I knew existed. Adams lives in a bibliophile's paradise. Not that he spends much time there.

Patch Adams returned from an out-of-country trip the night before our morning visit on a bright winter day. Michael Patte had traveled in, by chance, on the same plane as Patch Adams and Susan, the previous evening. Michael caught sight of Dr Adams, dressed in his trademark clown attire, sitting among the other passengers in business suits and street clothes. Dressed full clown as Patch was, it would have been hard to miss him. Dr Adams had just returned from an event in Italy. In two days' time he would leave home again for another trip abroad. Patch wears his signature clown attire all waking hours of every day, we learned upon meeting him. Aside from 70 or 80 days a year, Patch travels endlessly. But he does not usually go to glamorous

Figure 1. Patch Adams, during our December 2012 interview (Photo by Michael Patte).

locales in Italy. Adams goes wherever there is trauma, starvation, disaster, poverty, wherever human suffering is in extremis.

The Global Outreach program of his Gesundheit Institute has sent Dr Adams on clowning missions to post-tsunami Sri Lanka, post-earthquake Haiti, refugee camps in Kosovo and northern Africa, and among the dire needy in El Salvador, Cambodia, Peru, Romania, and points far and wide. He goes wherever misery is dire, not as a doctor without borders, but as a clown without borders, an authentic American shaman one might say, who confronts the most desperate human suffering and brings playfulness to bear on it. He has made cheering up into an art form, judging from videos of Adams in action, some of which I had seen before meeting him and some of which he showed us during our interview. I will say more about one or two of those videos later.

Born with the name Hunter Doherty in 1945, Patch Adams's life story is well known. His biography was the basis for a hit 1998 movie starring Robin Williams. Adams' childhood was marred by his father's alcoholism, and as a teen he at one point became actively suicidal. After three psychiatric hospitalizations in one year, he decided to live, but differently. He became an activist for humanist values, eventually going to medical school; upon graduation in 1971, he operated a free community hospital for the next 12 years. After meeting Patch Adams, there can be no mistake that Patch is an ardent activist. During our interview, Dr Adams made critical assessments of many aspects of society, including psychiatric treatment by drugs. As a physician in practice, he has refrained from ever applying a psychiatric diagnosis, for he disagrees that mental illness is reducible to a biological disorder. Adams endorses Freud's contention from *Civilization and its discontents* that mental illness is 'a healthy response to a messed up society'. In American society, Patch Adams reminded, loneliness is rampant and capitalism regularly trumps compassion. He began to wear colorful clothes because they act as an antidote to separation and loneliness. Pointing to the loose and large balloon pants of his costume, he proclaimed 'I just walk around like this in an airport or on the street [and] people smile.' He continued, 'With the blue hair and the fork earring, I was looking for a way that whoever stood next to me couldn't resist starting a conversation.' 'Does it work?' I asked. His reply was assured: 'Everywhere. Everywhere … whether it's a refugee camp or a dark alley.'

Clowning

Patch Adams is not the first clown I have met offstage, I am fortunate to say. As a public speaker I appeared twice before audiences of hundreds of clowns, many of them veterans of professional circuses. These attendees were attending meetings for clowns who had the job to role play

Ronald McDonald, the McDonald's spokesclown and namesake of Ronald McDonald House. Ronald McDonald House is a non-profit charity that provides hostels near hospitals that are havens for the families of hospitalized children. After speaking to this unique audience about my research on chronically ill kids, a number of clown-attendees approached me to converse, describing how special it is to be a clown visiting the sick. By their testimony (which was in line with scholarly research about clown healers) clowning in hospitals can be patently transformative for the patient. A clown who worked at Toronto's Hospital for Sick Children, Gryski (2003) introspected and wrote about the special way that clowns stand at a threshold between reality and fiction; in the process, they make hospital rooms into 'sanctuaries for wounded psyches and souls'. Therapeutic clowning brings an enacted force of life upon a threatened existence. Clowns are counterforces to trauma and threat. They do this by creating a play-space that flattens hierarchy, while remaining open, liminal, and patient responsive. Within the zone of clowning they establish, attention stays fully in the moment. Accompanying this state of mind there is a sense of undivided connection between clown and patient, as they together co-create meaningful play.

Perhaps it is the dropping of interpersonal boundaries that makes for clowns' reputations of being unfathomable or unsettling. Clowns creep some people out, as horror movies have exploited for profit. But another common response to clowns is that they convey a sense of potent enchantment, a sacred presence, even magic. Swedish scholar Linge (2012) has written that clowns 'unfix' literal reality in order to accommodate a patient's urgent need to remake meaning. Clowns fulfill the role of merry tricksters, who violate taboos and undo hierarchical structure, mocking doctors and nurses and poking fun at onerous medical treatments. Clowns help patients to cope, not through drugs but through play and imagination. Anthropologists have theorized that therapeutic clowns are versions of healing shamans, for whom jocularity is a force of transformation no matter how irreverent (Makarius, 1970; Van Blerkom, 1995).

Patch Adams' fame undoubtedly has given a major boost to the field of therapeutic clowning, currently flourishing in many countries with solid community support. Dr Adams remarked to us that he regularly trains aspiring clowns, taking them on his travels or teaching newcomers at clown camps. Patch Adams has been a collaborator with other clown programs such as New York's Big Apple Circus Clown Care Unit, operating since the mid-1980s. Mr Stubs, an early clown from the Clown Care Unit, is known for a widely reported story of his quick wit in the face of a doubting physician. Confronting Mr Stubs on his rounds in a pediatric unit, a medically trained doctor criticized therapeutic clowning to Mr Stubs' painted face. 'Clowns don't belong in hospitals,' he said tactlessly. Mr Stubs snapped in response, 'Neither do children.'

Patch Adams, who clowns with patients old and young alike, did not spend much time in our interview analyzing the process of clowning step by step, despite my vain hope to coax him to consciously decode play's therapeutic workings for the sake of future research. Patch Adams is a doctor and a doer, an expert practitioner. He keeps notes daily, which allow him to reflect on what he did on each clowning occasion and how well it seemed to work. But he is not given to analytical abstraction or meta-reflection about the workings of therapeutic clowning. 'I see the edges [of pain] in people,' he answered me when I pressed him to reflect on his own clowning. 'It's the job of a clown and a doctor to walk towards suffering … I want to help. I care.' When asked, he agreed with anthropological theorists who say clowns are shamans; indeed, he went a step further to say that *all* healers are shamans, both clowns and professionals in health care. But he did not dwell on what he does, as a scholar might. Patch Adams' preference is for practice, not analysis. As he put it to me, 'It would be fun to hear how academics talk about [it], because you're studying it and you hear all good things for it. Why aren't you doing it all the time?'

It is the compassion inherent in clowning that centers Dr Adams' view of his practice, which he regards as a vehicle for social change, a form of political activism. In his writings, Dr Adams has argued that medicine is also a vehicle for societal change, when practiced lovingly (Adams, 2005). Compassion, joy, and love were ever-present themes in Adams' conversation about what clowns do. Clowning, he argued, has power to change society because playful sharing at a deep level can spill over to enhance human connection more generally. But Adams added a caveat: the spillover of compassion works only when institutions do not cordon off expressive healing as exceptional and separate from the rest of behavior. In a journal essay, Patch Adams considered his many decades of experience and remarked:

> If we allow our strategic love to remain a therapy, we are implying that there are times when it isn't necessary. But if we commit to growing love as a context, we are called to continually create an atmosphere of joy, love, and laughter. There are so many simple ways to do it; I often feel like the clown costume is a trick to get love really close to patients. As soon as we see a health context that is joyous, loving, and funny … we can decide to contribute a context of love and fun every day. This makes our communities healthier, and helps to bring a peaceful and loving society. (Adams, 2002, 447)

The motivation to heal society and the idea that clowning is activism were themes that resounded again and again that day in Patch Adams' living room. From childhood, he knew clownish behavior had power, for as a youth he played the fool to survive bullying:

> When I grew up, I first clowned because it was protection against bullies. I was a very skinny, sissy boy and I found if I made the bully laugh, they didn't hit their fool. (Interview)

In his years of medical practice, Dr Adams observed that his patients were unfortunately restricted in expressions of joy, radiance, or connectedness. 'I assume a person is bored, lonely, and afraid until they show me otherwise' was how he summed up the state of patients. Playfulness, in his view, is a form of rapture that opens up a situation to relieve the boredom, loneliness, and fear.

To illustrate how he does it, Patch Adams chose to show us videos of himself clowning with patients. He also peppered his comments with show and tell, reaching into his costume's endless pockets and pulling out props. A personal favorite of Adams is his Dr Fart brand fart machine/ sound effect, explained as a surefire way to lighten the mood on elevators when riding with strangers. The Dr Fart brand sound effect was superior, he said, since it has six different settings for different sounding farts, and could be adapted to personal tastes. He also showed us a fabric belt that he wore by the bedside when accompanying dying patients. The belt was full of hidden pouches with trinkets to distract the pain-ridden. One panel contained a variety of scent potions; he said the choice of which potion to use became clear in his interaction with the patient.

Dr Adams talked about his props and scents as able to be customized, a sign of how much he takes patients' responses into consideration in his clowning. Therapeutic clowning is not a rehearsed performance; it is a transformation in conjunction with the patient, explaining why scents or fart sound effects are ideally customized to the particular audience.

Patch Adams has been outspoken on political issues that, to him, have bearing on whether compassion in the world expands or contracts. The week the USA invaded Iraq in March 2003, he and Susan walked around Venice (where they were staying), with Patch in costume – not dressed as a clown exactly, but dressed as a literal asshole. 'It's authentic, the whole thing,' he smiled describing his asshole suit, 'my eyeball sits right in the hole.' Over the sound of Michael and I giggling, he continued: 'The costume had a big sign over it, reading "a typical supporter of George Bush."' On another occasion during the Reagan presidency,

Dr Adams initiated a clown trip to Russia intended to be 'peace work' in the midst of the cold war; he has returned to Russia to clown every year since then.

When Patch Adams gives lectures, he calls out political issues as he sees them. For example, he said he has not been hesitant to say that 'the United States is the number one terrorist nation,' given its militarism and intelligence practices. Dr Adams has had threats to his life in response to his political views, revealing that there may be social limits to the protection that comes from playing the fool to speak freely. Patch Adams is pro-choice, pro-euthanasia, anti-psychiatry, and anti-racist. He has been anti-racist since youth, and was bullied repeatedly when calling out racist behavior in his school days.

The current lack of total well-being among Americans is a profound issue to Adams, as he made clear. 'I think people in their late 20s start feeling like their life is over,' he said. 'We're a Prozac nation. You have everything, and you're bitching and moaning.' Without skipping a beat, he enunciated aloud the needed intervention: 'So. Clowning'.

Clowning's metaphysics

As I have said, Patch Adams did not parse or analyze clowning explicitly in our interview. When asked to cite the best evidence for play's benefits, he said 'the experience of it'. To convey this, he showed us videos of himself in action either at play or during clowning. Implicit in each video, without much need of explication, was a pattern of practice that maps fairly well to current conceptions of how clowning works. Patch Adams does sublimely well what academics in multiple disciplines have said clowns do. Clowns are persons who cross thresholds to respond to the patient in the moment, creating a supra-normal sense of unity through playfulness and flaunting taboos at every possibility.

Across 1971–1984, when Patch Adams operated a free community clinic in rural West Virginia, Dr Adams had plenty of opportunities to hone the skills needed for clowning through practice. One of the videos he showed us was taken in his home at that time, a 12-acre communal farm. The farm hosted hundreds and hundreds of visitors over a dozen or so years. A visitor at the time of the film had symptoms of the eating disorder now known as bulimia. The group residing at the farm had assembled to make a film with her, in which everyone would throw up simultaneously in solidarity with the woman. She had lived among the community for about 10 days, but until this film, had kept isolated from others, in her room. As the film was being planned, the mood was playful and inclusive of everyone. During preparations, new visitors joined the scene, including a group of motorcyclists from the Hell's Angels gang. They were invited to be part of the film, too. Another visitor brought a birthday cake along with him, for he was lonely and wanted company to help him celebrate his birthday. 'And we stopped everything to have a birthday party,' Patch recalled.

Using a term of the era, the film documented a 'happening'. One guy drank beer from a hole in the side of a can, to prepare himself to vomit. A dead dog, brought to the house by the ex-lover of a resident, was filmed too. Some of those assembled were, like Patch Adams, trained physicians or nurses, although they did not wear medical garb in daily life. It turns out, when the time came to vomit, none of the physicians in the film were able to throw up on cue. But everyone else did vomit as a group, copiously, laughing and smiling at the act. 'It was the ultimate catharsis,' I commented to Adams after the video played. He nodded agreement.

During those years in West Virginia, fun was a staple of life. They staged elaborate weddings, including for two male friends, Ozzie and Leo. The group staged plays, often based on history. They had all-night rock-and-roll parties three nights a week. But the fun was not all consuming. In addition to seeing patients, there was a communal farm to operate, which they also did successfully, despite being novice farmers.

PLAY AND WELLBEING

It is likely that Patch's experience, living communally and partaking daily in socially shared play, fine-tuned his ability to read people and to manipulate symbolic content extemporaneously. Certainly, the clinic/farm era left him an unabashed breaker of taboos (vomiting and dead dogs included) with an accompanying sense that defying taboos leads to new possibilities and affective transformation. Even when Michael and I were about to leave, Adams playfully suggested that we pose for our souvenir photos while either mooning or putting fingers up our noses. (Michael and I both picked the nose option).

The best way to explore how, as a clown healer today, Patch Adams' clowning unfolds step by step is to closely examine a contemporary video. He showed us a video recorded in a hospital in Guatemala during one of Adams' 'spring break' forays done annually with college students. As is his usual habit, Patch Adams arrived at the hospital and asked to be taken to the person in the hospital who was suffering the most. He was escorted to the adult ward, where he met an older mother and her severely ill adult son. Both of them were pacing the floor in a state of panic. Obvious to anyone was the large scar on the male patient's chest, from recent open-heart surgery. The surgery had been a failure. The man would be 'going under the knife' again soon, and both the patient and his mother did not expect him to survive the next round of surgery. They were absolutely sure he was going to die. This was the situation, as Patch Adams crossed the threshold to their room.

Dr Adams spoke to the family through an interpreter. As the video's first scene began, Patch talked over the film for our benefit to explain 'I'm constructing it all based on response.' In other words, his actions were improvised, in the moment, in response to the despairing patient and mother.

Patch Adams	Buenas dias. Buenas dias. [Turning to the mother] I thought it was his sister. No, sister. Doctor, he's crazy. This is not the mother, he's hallucinating. [To the doctor:] What medications are you on? [Patch Adams gestures for the son and his mother to play as if they were brother and sister, and they hold hands and act out Patch's narrative.] This is your sister. You were skipping along, holding her hand. And skipping along. Looking at the birds. And staying out late and missed lunch. And your mother was a little upset. But your sister put a good word to the mother. And she forgave you. I think you should kiss your sister, she saved your life. [Patch Adams gestures a change of roles:] Here's your mother. Oh that was nice. [He praises them as they embrace.] Maybe the other one is lonely. Oh, it's a private thing. Kiss. Oh boy, yes.

As we watched the video, Patch Adams reminded Michael and me that these were the very people in the hospital identified as being in the worse condition.

Patch Adams	When a boy has a good mother, you turn out well. What a gift your mother gives you.
Patient	A good education.
Patch Adams	Different than the teacher. [The patient nods in agreement.] And your mother taught you to be a good man. A kind man. Not macho. Not a macho man. No a loving man. Loving man. Loving kiss. [Patch Adams takes off his hat for a gesture of warmth, and turns to the mother.] Now what did he give you?

As the video gave her response in Spanish, Adams remarked to Michael and me that the man had been, at the time, too weak even to sit in his mother's lap.

Patch Adams	[Singing, to the tune of Braham's lullaby:] Rockaby baby, in the tree top, when the wind blows, the cradle will rock.
Mother	[Began to sing a Guatemalan cradle song, in Spanish.]
Patch Adams	This is the most beautiful moment I can remember. She needs to be president, you understand. Every country in the world needs mamas for president. Because if every country had her for president no one would be hungry. Armies would build houses for poor people. The whole world will be in peace. Let's hold hands. The world will be in peace, oh mamas as presidents everywhere. [To the translator:] Can you explain that to them? [The crowd in the room had been growing, with some 15 hospital staff members now standing alongside the patient and his mother. The assemblage grasped hands, and formed a circle.] …

Patch Adams	We have a song in English that came from John Lennon, from the Beatles, a very simple song. [Beginning to sing:] All we are saying is give peace a chance. [Others join in, singing in English with him:] All we are saying is give peace a chance. [The interpreter translated the lyrics into Spanish, as Patch continued:] So let's just rock [in place] and go [singing again, as the assemblage began to sway in place:] All we are saying is give peace a chance. All we are saying is give peace a chance. [Patch Adams encouraged all to sing:] 'Everybody!' [The singing resumed:] All we are saying is give peace a chance. All we are saying is give peace a chance.
Patient	[Although looking very ill, showed his active involvement by suggesting another song he knows in English, '"We are the World" by Michael Jackson.' All continued to hold hands, and sang the chorus of the Jackson song together, smiling:] We are the world, we are the children, we are the ones to make a better place so let's start giving. It's a choice we're making. We're saving our own lives. It's true we'll make a better day, just you and me. [When they finished this song, there was applause, laughing and smiling, including the mother and son no longer desperately anxious, but smiling.]
Patch Adams	All that for a beautiful mother. [The applause continued.] I'm so glad you and your mother were here, and you, you are in remission soon?
Patient	Yeah that's right.
Patch Adams	You are going to recover, yes? Yes absolutely. But you recover because your mother will give you hell if you don't, okay, so you better recover. [The patient, his mother and Patch Adams posed together for photographs.]

Hitting the stop button on the video player, Patch Adams commented to Michael and me, 'They did all the work.'

Taking this episode of clowning as a continuous co-constructed narration to be interpreted dynamically, we can begin with lines 241–247. In this segment, Patch framed a separate as-if reality, in which the patient's mother played the part of his sister. As Adams set the scene for this pretense, he referred to the presiding doctor as 'crazy', 'hallucinating', or on 'drugs' because he did not realize that the mother was (in the play) the patient's sister. This was a joking way to put the mother at ease, as if she was not an elderly mother but a more youthful person, the patient's sister. It also served to level hierarchy, not only as a put down to the usually dominant doctor, but also placing son and mother on a parallel level of fictitious kinship. Adams then introduced a lighter, uplifting context, looking at the birds together and staying out past curfew. As mother and son pretended to be sister and brother, the mood percept-ibly shifted out of high anxiety. In the role of the sister, the mother-as-sister bid herself (the actual mother) to forgive the son's transgression of as-if tardiness, after Adams suggested that the as-if sister should 'put a good word to the mother'. Mother and son seemed to carry forward the sense of shared forgiveness and acceptance after completing the role play, embracing each other at length in their real roles as mother and son.

In lines 250–254, Patch leveraged the affection between mother and son to elicit their expressions of mutual gratitude: first, the son's gratefulness to the mother, which he tied to his ability to get an education and, second, the mother's own thanks to her son, praised by Adams as a kind, loving man able to show his affection (not 'macho'). The mother's point of gratitude was not translated aloud, but the son warmly accepted her expression.

The clowning then built further on the established tone of mother–son acceptance and affec-tion, which by this point had banished all hint of the initial intensely fearful mood. The tender serenity between mother and son was amplified in lines 256–258, when Adams invoked Braham's lullaby as a soothing cradle song normally sung by a parent to a child. This hit a respon-sive cord in the mother, who reciprocated by singing her own cradle song, in Spanish.

In lines 259–264, Adams pivoted to a broader way of framing love. He spoke to equate mother-love with a world-impactful force, stating that if mothers were world leaders, mamas would lead a more generous and peaceful world. He invited the assemblage of onlookers to

PLAY AND WELLBEING

join him in this vision of mama/world love. The mother–son pair were, in effect, joined by others in the world when the assemblage joined hands and sang 'All we are saying is give peace a chance.' Patch invited all to sing along as they swayed in a rocking motion, recalling the rocking of a lullaby. It is hard to deny that the words of the song took on a degree of double-meaning: on the level of the world, a plea for world peace, but simultaneously, on the level of the patient and mother, a call for reinforcing shared inner peace and solace.

It is interesting to note that the mother volunteered her own lullaby after Patch Adams sang a lullaby. In parallel with this interplay, her son (in lines 271–276) offered his own song to be sung by the assembled group, after Patch had led the singing of 'All we are saying is give peace a chance.' The patient's request was Michael Jackson's 'We are the world,' a song associated with children, but reiterating the theme of universal peace. The lyrics are 'We are the world/we are the children/we are the ones to make a better place so let's start giving/it's a choice we're making/*we're saving our own lives/It's true we'll make a better day just you and me.*' Just as was true for the previous song, these words held solace-giving significance on a personal level along with the literally stated words of world unity. The song was a call to action to 'save our own lives' and a reinforcement that compassion on a personal level holds value for a 'better day'. The son, by choice of song, took the lead in agreeing that the love between individuals (such as his mother and himself) holds broad meaning for the sort of world they inhabit.

Patch Adams reiterated and reinforced the wider significance of a mother's love in lines 277–280. 'All that for a beautiful mother' he concluded after the singing of lullabies and shared songs of peace. He seemed to speak for everyone present, who applauded together, at length. Adams then pivoted back to the personal situation of the patient and his mother. He asked the patient if he expected to be in remission and recovery. His comments tied remission and recovery to the mother–son relationship, by stating that the mother would be angry ('give you hell') if he failed to recover (and, although this is not directly stated, succumbed to death). Adams' word choice, that the mother would 'give him hell', makes a joke of what they feared most, that the son might soon depart for the afterlife. The clowning process ended, as Adams, the patient, and the mother posed for pictures together.

Adams, commenting after the video finished that 'They did all the work,' credited the patient and his mother with providing the transformative impact. But clearly, Adams was a sensitive, creative, and strategic catalyst for the transformation. Therapeutic play, even when done by a play therapist with a child, is optimum when self-directed so as to propel a shift in the individual's system of meanings (Clark, 2007). Even when no therapist is present, children use make-believe and story on their own to remake meaning and regain resilience (Clark, 2003). So if, old or young, it is the patients who empower their own renewal of meaning, how are we to characterize the clown's role in the process?

First, a clown masked in face paint or fake nose, whether Patch Adams or another clown, unleashes a kind of irony that unmasks and underscores that there are layers of meaning below the surface, such as the emotional strain of possible death within a mother–son relationship. A clown inherently symbolizes that outside appearances are not what they seem, and that inversion might be an option to undo threats on the surface, uncovering deeper resilience. Gifted clowns, and Patch Adams is truly gifted, have strategic sensitivity and choose activities that symbolically speak to the socio-emotional issues sensed. For instance, a child anticipating death might be engaged, in clowning, in a game of hide-and-seek, a game that plays on the theme of people no longer seeing one another (Koller & Gryski, 2008). Dr Adams clowned so as to highlight mother–son love, at a time when fear of death and separation had clouded the mother–son connection.

Second, clowns share with shamans the ability to catalyze emotional release, by mediating between opposed symbolic meanings. As the Patch Adams clowning segment illustrates, clowns are expected and licensed to deal in double-meanings, such as puns, jokes, poetic lyrics, and playful turnabouts. This marks clown interactions as a distinctive modality, inconsistent with literal, reductionist simplicity. An audience expects to experience clown narratives and tricks on simultaneous, opposed planes of meaning rather than as uncomplicated or fundamentalist singularity. Clowns engineer a kind of positive duplicity and multivocality through humor and narration. Doctors, who stick to single-minded empiricism in much of medical practice, are shown by clowns to be fools. Silly acts, such as using medical gloves for balloons or a stethoscope to listen to the patient's leg, convey that things taken seriously in a hospital can be made light of through mockery. In the video segment, Patch Adams deftly turned the shared fear of mother and son to its flip side, in which the deep value of the mutual love between them could serve as a counterforce to anxiety. Once he had put into play a fear-to-love inversion, he employed another figurative trick, accentuating a mother's love as powerful even on a global basis, when singing 'All we are saying is give peace a chance.' A hostile world, with so little hope, could be flipped into a place of solace by keeping love in prominent view, singing about a world of peace. To be sure, the validation and reinforcement of these mediated meanings came from the mother and son, who followed Patch's lead by singing, first, a lullaby and later, a peace-themed song of their own choosing.

Levi-Strauss (1963) believed that shamans help sufferers to express the inexpressible paradoxical logic of illness, such as the need to rediscover order in a disordering experience. A therapeutic clown-expert such as Patch Adams is a mediator of opposed, double-meanings. In Guatemala, Adams brought a skillful, healing duplicity through symbolic mediation. Engaged with persons caught in the iron fixed grip of fear, he invited them to join him in the tensile malleability of poetics and playfulness – introducing a tone of flux and creativity. Clowns can quickstart this sort of mutual limbo, aided by their ironic, clownish role. Therapeutic clowning at its best, however, involves emotionally strategic mediation. Through indirect, double-edged symbolism, a therapeutic clown can invite a patient(s) to take advantage of symbolic distancing (through playfulness) and put to use the elastic flexibility of story, pun, sleight of hand, and affective metaphor. This dynamic has potential to transform and reframe troubled feelings or relations. It was the Guatemala patient and mother who found renewal for themselves through transformed significance, but it was a sensitive clown catalyst, Dr Adams, who set the dynamics for this healing in motion through his symbolic adeptness.

Pediatric clowns sometimes make regular, repeated visits to the same patient. In such cases, the young patient often takes a proactive role in shaping what happens, asking the clown to revisit the jokes or tricks that were especially cathartic in past sessions. Clowns generally encourage child patients to play an empowered role in laughing themselves silly. They enter a child's room, only if the child wants them to enter. They increase a child's confidence by placing the child in high status, above doctors or above themselves. One clown, for instance, asked a very sick child for his autograph while acting out the part of a subservient fan (Ford, Courtney-Pratt, Tesch, & Johnson, 2013). Clowns make silly mistakes for the child to correct. To connect with a child, the best clowns use a high degree of creativity to tailor-make their double-edged tricks. A clown who could not enter a child's room, due to risk of infecting the child, devised a way to show connection at a distance; he stood on a stepladder, outside the child's hospital window, evoking the child's hearty laughter (Linge, 2011). Another wrapped a child's parent in toilet paper, to simulate the parent having the same injuries, at the same bodily sites, as the child. Clowns introduce frivolity in every possible way, from dancing with the hospital curtains to getting the doctors to ineptly dress in the gowns and gloves needed to enter protective isolation (Ford et al., 2013).

Interviewing Patch Adams, who sees clowning as a serious enterprise with political impact, brought home the sense that clowns make waves when their audiences become ready to see double. By seeing double I mean the perception of mediated meanings, the flexibility to consider multiple sides of an issue. In an era of polarized politics, Patch Adams has a point that clowns may be particularly adept political mediators. The tropes, tricks, stories, games, and puns used by clowns have particular potential to bring people into flexibility and dialogue, above and beyond a person's single-minded fixedness or fear.

Without doubt, one must honor the courage and wit of clowns-as-shamans to engage liminality and intersubjectivity in order to mediate pain and suffering. Patch Adams has taken a path to playfulness, taking on the attire and role of a clown in order to face down human suffering. And in his life he has inspired, trained, and in my view legitimated this path for others.

Conclusion

For play scholars looking to theorize about therapeutic play and clowning, perhaps the most important thing learned in our interview was that Patch Adams is a meticulous keeper of written records, recording all his clown activity and how patients have reacted on each occasion he clowns. This could make up an invaluable qualitative database for analysis by play scholars, in the present or future. I suggest that the Association for the Study of Play or another scholarly organization should pursue the idea of arranging now, for these records to one day have a permanent home in a facility where scholars would have access.

Patch Adams has demonstrated, by implication of his work, that human society needs symbolic flexibility to achieve and maintain compassion, and that playfulness is a guise for providing it. Anthropologists, who regularly ponder dynamic, multivalent, cultural processes, have held that dialogic, mediated, and poetic modes of meaning are crucial for the sharing of social reality and the maintenance of socially appropriate personhood.

Scholars who may have overlooked the human capacity for double-meaning would do well to take clowning as seriously as Patch Adams. Clown therapy, on a psychological level, seemingly involves a complex juxtaposition and interplay of mediated symbolism. That humans think in multiple symbolic planes is not a new idea, of course. Within the literature on creativity, the capacity to mediate between one plane of meaning and another plane of meaning is a long-standing theme. Creativity is, after all, a way of breaking the walls of fixed thinking, through a mental leap across frameworks or contexts not usually related. A classic theorist of creativity is Koestler (1969), the twentieth-century intellectual and author. Elsewhere in this volume, I discuss Koestler's classic book on creativity, *The act of creation*. Koestler wrote about humor and satire in that book, remarking that these are experiences of 'bisociation', his term for thinking simultaneously on multiple planes. 'The comic effect of … satire is derived from the simultaneous presence, in the reader's mind, of the social reality with which he is familiar, and its reflection in the distorting mirror of the satirist,' he wrote. The satirist introduces as a 'mirror' a plane of meaning separate from the habitual one, a mirror that reflects characteristic features so as to highlight those features and refocus attention. Patch Adams, in Guatemala, employed a kind of looking glass constructed out of song and pretense, a mirrored plane that refocused attention on relatedness, compassion, mutual support or, as Adams might put it, love. Dr Adams' clowning brings about therapeutic resilience through a kind of fun-house mirroring, through double-edged antics, metaphor, and irony. But make no mistake; the frivolity is serious stuff indeed.

References

Adams, P. (2002). Humour and love: The origination of clown therapy. *Postgraduate Medical Journal, 78,* 447–448.

Adams, P. (2005). Medicine as a vehicle for social change. *The Journal of Alternative and Complementary Medicine, 11*(4), 578–582.

Clark, C. D. (2003). *In sickness and in play: Children coping with chronic illness.* New Brunswick: Rutgers University Press.

Clark, C. D. (2007). Therapeutic advantages of play. In A. Goncu & S. Gaskins (Eds.), *Play and development: Evolutionary, sociocultural, and functional perspectives* (pp. 275–293). Mahway, NJ: Lawrence Erlbaum.

Ford, K., Courtney-Pratt, H., Tesch, L., & Johnson, C. (2013). More than just clowns – clown doctor rounds and their impact for children, families, and staff. *Journal of Child Health Care,* 1–11. (Pre-publication version)

Gryski, C. (2003). Stepping over thresholds: A personal meditation on the work and play of a therapeutic clown. *POIESIS: A Journal of the Arts and Communicaton, 5,* 94–99.

Koestler, A. (1969). *The act of creation.* London: Picador Press.

Koller, D., & Gryski, C. (2008). The life threatened child and the life enhancing clown: Towards a model of therapeutic clowning. *eCAM: Evidence-Based Complementary and Alternative Medicine, 5*(1), 15–17.

Levi-Strauss, C. (1963). *Structural anthropology.* New York, NY: Basic Books.

Linge, L. (2011). Joy without demands: Hospital clowns in the world of ailing children. *International Journal of Qualitative Studies of Health and Well-Being, 6*(1). Retrieved from http://www.ijqhw.net/index.php/qhw/article/view/5899

Linge, L. (2012). Magical attachment: Children in magical relations with hospital clowns. *International Journal of Qualitative Studies of Health and Well-Being, 7.* Retrieved from http://www.ijqhw.net/index.php/qhw/article/view/11862

Makarius, L. (1970). Ritual clowns and symbolic behavior. *Diogenes, 69,* 44–73.

Van Blerkom, L. M. (1995). Clown doctors: Shamanic healers of Western medicine. *Medical Anthropology Quarterly, 9*(4), 462–476.

Playfully engaging people living with dementia: searching for Yum Cha moments

Julie Dunn, Michael Balfour, Wendy Moyle, Marie Cooke, Kirsty Martin, Clark Crystal and Anna Yen

Griffith Institute for Educational Research and the Griffith Health Institute, Griffith University, Nathan, Australia

In the absence of a cure for dementia, there is an increasing recognition of the need to develop approaches that address its key impacts of social isolation, depressed mood, and quality of life. In response to these issues, a three-year research project entitled *Playful Engagement and Dementia: assessing the efficacy of applied theatre practices for people with dementia in residential aged care facilities* was developed in partnership with Wesley Mission Brisbane. The paper reports on data collected within the pilot phase of this project, offering an analysis of the play vocabularies used by two applied theatre artists who interacted, using a relational clowning approach, with 17 residents with mid- to late-stage dementia. The analysis, based on two complementary frameworks, reveals useful insights into the key features of the approach, noting those that were effective in generating 'moments' of engagement and mutual recognition. How the applied theatre artists spontaneously, reflexively, and sensitively applied these vocabularies, tailoring them to each individual's play preferences, interests, and stage of dementia is also examined.

It's our third visit with Tom, a resident of an aged care facility who is living with dementia. Tom's room is light, airy and very comfortable. He smiles as Tiny Lamington and his 'identical twin sister' Dumpling arrive at his door. They are wearing red noses and clothes reminiscent of the 1950s. Tom immediately announces, 'I was just thinking of you'.

From this opening, the visit flows into one that is not as overtly playful as might be expected, for the two artists wearing red noses are not tripping over each other, juggling objects or making jokes. However, close attention to the interactions occurring reveal that there is significant playfulness in their use of language and status.

This session is in striking contrast to Tiny and Dumpling's first visit with Tom a couple of weeks earlier. At that session Tom was staring straight ahead and seemed unaware of anything happening around him. To initiate engagement, Tiny and Dumpling sang and brought out various props including a small percussion instrument. Eventually the repetition and rhythm of the music generated a response, with Tom reaching for Dumpling's hand. At the end of the session Tom tentatively offered his first words to them saying, 'That was a lovely trip'.

For the second visit, the research team is provided with Tom's biographical notes, and in response, attempt to engage him by focusing on his childhood in Hong Kong. Able to speak Cantonese, Dumpling begins playing with basic aspects of that language, before gently asking Tom if he remembers any Cantonese words. An extended but deliberate silence is created as Tiny and Dumpling wait for a response. Suddenly Tom speaks, 'Yum Cha!' This is a powerful moment.

Now, as visit three progresses there is lots of laughter as Tom attempts to teach Tiny how to count in Cantonese. Within this encounter, Tiny drops his status to become a hopeless student, while Dumpling supports Tom's patient counting by expressing frustration at her 'brother's' feeble attempts to master even basic words. In the middle of this lesson Tom wistfully notes, 'I've had no-one to practice with'. Later he shares information about his schooling in Hong Kong, about his work there, and even a very convincing story about a recent visit where he met up with old friends. He is engaged and alive. Later we learn that Tom hasn't left the nursing facility for many years.

This vignette is based upon data collected within the pilot phase of a research project entitled *Playful Engagement* and offers insights into the play approach adopted across it. In particular, it highlights Tom's *Yum Cha moment* as a defining one for his developing relationship with Tiny and Dumpling. More importantly in the context of this paper, it provides a useful example of how moments of connection and engagement can be generated for people living with dementia through the reflexive and spontaneous application of play vocabularies.

In this paper, these and other aspects of the play approach adopted within the *Playful Engagement* project will be examined. Developed to identify the impact of playfulness on the quality of life (QOL) of people living with mid- to advanced-stage dementia, the project employs an approach best described as relational clowning. Funded by an Australian Research Council grant in partnership with Wesley Mission Brisbane, a large not-for-profit Australian aged-care provider, it will adopt a mixed-methods approach and operate across four long-term care facilities. At each facility, approximately 15 participants will be visited weekly across a six-week period. Visits will vary in duration, but will generally extend for up to 20 minutes per participant.

Across the pilot phase, conducted at an additional site, a similar model of delivery was adopted, with individual visits being conducted in the residents' rooms. During these visits, two members of the research team accompanied the applied theatre artists to record detailed observation notes and video. Introduced by Tiny and Dumpling as their cousins, the research team members occasionally got drawn into the action to become co-players.

In developing this pilot, the team had several purposes. We wanted to trial key video technologies to ensure that they could be applied in a sensitive but effective manner; our two applied theatre artists, new to working as a team, were looking for opportunities to develop their clown relationship within authentic contexts; and finally, the multidisciplinary research team needed to achieve a shared understanding of the nature of and possibilities for play and playfulness in dementia contexts. Of course, we were also keen to ensure that the participants involved in the visits would have playful and engaging experiences.

With these purposes in mind, data collection was mainly focused on the play form itself, with the data set including more than 20 hours of video recordings, written observation notes of each session, and audio recordings of reflective conversations between research team members and the two artists, created immediately following each set of visits. The important quantitative measures to be used within the main study, including those that will provide health and well-being data about each individual participant and those that will identify changes in QOL, were not collected. In addition, key qualitative methods, including staff and family interviews, were not conducted.

In light of this reduced data set, this paper will not offer any claims about the impact of the work in relation to improvements in the participants' QOL. Instead, it will focus only on what we learned about the vocabularies of play practice that were applied and the key factors that influenced their spontaneous and reflexive application. To support this discussion, background details relating to the *Playful Engagement Project* and its approach are provided, while engagement stories based on visits with Tom, Valerie, Gwen, and Edgar (pseudonyms) are offered later in the paper.

Background and approach

In Australia, the number of people suffering from dementia is predicted to be 731,000 by the year 2050 – an increase of 327% from its 2008 levels (Access Economics, 2006, 2009a). Predictions also suggest that by 2020 dementia will have overtaken cardiovascular disease to become one of the major chronic diseases in Australia (Access Economics, 2009a). The high financial and personal costs of dementia have also been highlighted in recent reports commissioned by Alzheimer's Australia (Access Economics, 2006, 2007, 2009a, 2009b), with health and long-term care expenditure on dementia projected to increase by 225% between 2003 and 2030, far outstripping that of any other health condition and accounting for approximately 1% of Australian gross domestic product (Access Economics, 2009a, 2009b; Australian Institute of Health and Welfare, 2007).

In the absence of a cure for this illness, there is an increasing recognition of the need to develop approaches that address its key impacts of social isolation, depressed mood, and QOL. Recent research (Moyle, Kellett, Ballantyne, & Gracia, 2011) emphasizes the importance of meaningful relationships between people with dementia, family, and staff and their significance in improving QOL, reducing depression and feelings of loneliness, and social isolation in this population. The research literature confirms that depressed feelings and apathy occur in up to 90% of people living with dementia (Zuidema, de Jonghe, Verhey, & Koopmans, 2007), and such conditions can affect QOL, not only for the person with dementia, but for their family and carers as well.

In recognition of this situation, the *Playful Engagement* project was developed, built upon an approach designed to create opportunities for playful interaction between individuals living in residential aged-care facilities and two applied theatre artists using a relational clowning approach. This approach, described by Killick (2013, p. 24) as being much more 'friendly, playful, gentle and empathic' than approaches to clowning typically used in circus performances, is built on pioneering Elderflowers work developed in the Dementia Research Centre at the University of Stirling. This approach, underpinned by a relationship-centred philosophy (Nolan, Davies, Brown, Keady, & Nolan, 2004), recognizes and values mutual recognition between people and the opportunities this recognition offers. For this reason, the play is not built around pre-scripted monologues or performances designed to entertain. Rather, whenever possible, the approach is highly dialogical, with these dialogues (including those that are mainly non-verbal) being spontaneously generated in action and honed to the perceived needs of each individual participant. Of course, during the visits the artists may also interact playfully with others they encounter, including visiting family members, carers, and staff, but the focus is on maximizing the engagement of residents one person at a time.

The applied theatre artists involved in *Playful Engagement*, Clark Crystal (Tiny) and Anna Yen (Dumpling), have backgrounds in performance training with artist/teachers Phillipe Gaulier and Monika Pagneaux, with Clark previously applying this training within the Elderflowers project (Killick & Allan, 2001). As part of the permission for play, red noses and costumes are worn by Tiny and Dumpling, providing important signals of a changed frame (Goffman, 1974), but the costumes are not gaudy and no face paint is applied. Instead, the approach is understated and respectful.

Arts-based responses within health contexts represent a growing trend, with researchers and artists alike believing that there is significant scope for its application. Nicholson (2011), in describing her work in an aged-care context, encapsulates this view when she suggests:

By moving beyond the idea that the arts are an activity that help older adults pass the time in their care home, this research attends to the relational aesthetic inherent in the performance of everyday life as participants move between material and imagined worlds, between attention and inattention, between memories of the past and their creative responses to living in the here-and-now. (p. 50)

As part of this attempt to extend opportunities and review notions of the value of the arts in aged care, specific approaches involving playfulness and humour have been growing steadily in recent years. For example, within the Netherlands there are more than 150 certified miMakker elderclowns who, according to Hendriks (2012, p. 463), establish contact in a quiet, nontheatrical way, with the clown approaching the other person 'respectfully and enquiringly, to pick up the weakest signals and to process them in a creative fashion'. Within this approach, individual clowns use a range of strategies including body language, movement, facial expression, singing or speaking, and music. Bernie Warren's work in this area is also well known and documented (Warren, 2008a, 2008b; Warren & Spitzer, 2011).

Within the Australian context, a large-scale, funded research project entitled SMILE was recently completed by the Humour Foundation (Spitzer, 2011), with findings emerging from this project suggesting that the approach used in that work had a positive impact, especially in terms of reducing anxiety and agitation of people living with dementia. However, while sharing an overall goal of improving QOL, the SMILE project differs from *Playful Engagement* in some key ways including our focus on connection and relationship building through individual visits supported by biographical details, and the distinction that the SMILE work includes a specific training dimension where staff from within long-term care facilities are trained to become laughter bosses.

The specific approach used within *Playful Engagement* initially grew out of innovative work that had been running at Wesley Mission Brisbane's Hadden Place Day Respite Centre. There the participants were non-residential and mainly experiencing early- to mid-stage dementia. Based on the responses generated, Wesley staff members and the applied theatre artists involved in that work were keen to apply this approach within more complex care settings and thoroughly investigate its effectiveness. To this end, a multi-disciplinary team made up of researchers from both health and applied theatre, two artists and Wesley Mission Brisbane staff came together to seek funding for the large-scale project.

In the following section, an analysis of the play practices applied across the six-week pilot study is offered. This analysis is based on two distinct and contrasting frameworks – Lieberman's five dimensions of playfulness (1977) and the elements of drama (see for example Haseman & O'Toole, 1986). It was achieved through close examination of the data set, with the video data being of most significance. Recorded in two formats and offering two different perspectives on each interaction, the first video format provided an overview of the work, with those recordings being captured by a hand-held camera positioned in the doorway of each participant's room. The second format, recorded using a *Go Pro* micro video camera mounted on Tiny's chest, offered an entirely different view of the play (Figure 1). With its close proximity to the interactions and its focus mainly directed at recording participant facial responses, the *Go Pro* recordings offered the additional benefit of better-quality sound recordings of verbal responses.

Framework one – analysing the vocabularies of play

Vandenberg (1986, p. 18) believes that part of the problem of defining play stems from the fact that play 'has as much to do with the way something is done, as it does with what is done; it is more like an adverb than a noun'. This notion is highly relevant here, for some of the interactions between Tiny, Dumpling, and the project participants were not overtly playful. For example,

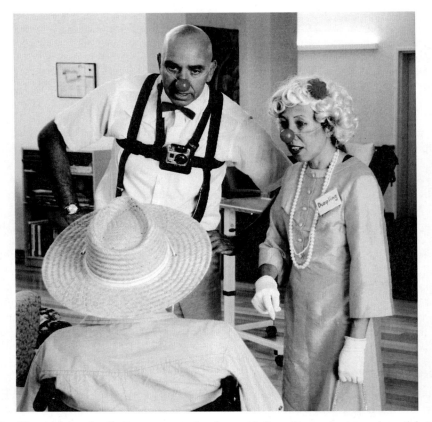

Figure 1. Tiny wearing the Go Pro camera as he plays with Dumpling and a research participant.

activities like singing, knitting, selecting hats, playing a ukulele, or discussing the height of a typical horse are not generally considered as being play activities, but by approaching these everyday actions in a way that Sutton-Smith describes as being 'disruptive of settled expectations' (1997, p. 148), Tiny and Dumpling were able to transform them into play. For this reason, playfulness in this project seems to be more apparent in the how rather than the what of the play, so that as Csikszentmihalyi (1981) notes, it is not so much defined by its form or content, but instead by the experience of the players.

To explore this concept further and to better understand how the play vocabularies operated in this project, Lieberman's (1977, p. 21) five dimensions of playfulness were used as an interpretive framework. Including physical spontaneity, cognitive spontaneity, social spontaneity, manifest joy, and a sense of humour, analysis of the play sessions according to these dimensions revealed that within almost every visit a combination of these was present. Of particular relevance was the notion of spontaneity, with this aspect of the work, particularly between the two artists, being a key feature. Driven, at least in part, by a shared performance philosophy that positions pleasure, presence, complicity, and the rules of the game (constraints) as being central (Yen, 2012, p. 6), analysis reveals that Tiny and Dumpling drew upon the five dimensions of playfulness in different ways within each visit, combining them with sensitively attuned reflexivity in response to the unique and highly individual needs and personalities of each participant.

According to this shared performance philosophy, pleasure refers to the joy experienced through play, while presence encompasses sensitivity and requires that the artist is fully present in any engagement. Here, a key skill is the ability to follow an embodied impulse in the moment. Complicity, however, relates to all participants in a play event, and is aimed at ensuring that everyone involved is 'in on the joke', playing as a team. Finally, in the context of their work, a shared understanding by the two artists of the 'rules of the game' ensures that status, focus, eye contact, and moments of dynamic stillness known as fixed points are spontaneously and effectively managed.

Physical spontaneity

Built on their shared philosophy and play vocabularies, the approach to physical spontaneity adopted by Tiny and Dumpling within each visit and indeed across visits was highly varied, ranging from whole-body, slapstick-style physical movements to highly sensitive, physical encounters involving close-up, focused, and very slow movements. Shifting from high-energy games of make-believe lawn bowls with powder puffs to an almost still rhythmic engagement involving continuous physical contact between two human hands, physical interactions were adapted to suit the needs of individuals. In some cases, the physical spontaneity generated by the applied theatre artists was reciprocated by the resident, with all three participants becoming involved in the essentially physical work, but at other times, the action was more one-sided, with the applied theatre artists creating spaces for response and recognition so that when ready, the resident could re-engage.

Physical spontaneity was also supported by the use of props, with the suitcases carried by Tiny and Dumpling offering a rich array of materials to stimulate and extend the physical responses of residents. These props, including wigs, newspapers, lengths of material, dolls, odd hats, and musical instruments, each offered different opportunities to generate engagement, with one key benefit of applying these within the play being a reduced reliance on linguistic engagement. In addition, as the visits progressed, and the biographies of individuals expanded, props specific to each individual's life experience were added, with the goal being to create interactions offering additional layers of meaning and relevance. In this way, we hoped to personalize the visits so that the artists were not focused on using the play vocabularies just to get a laugh (although of course this was important), but also to connect and build relationships.

Cognitive spontaneity

Cognitive spontaneity was another dimension of playfulness apparent in the interactions. Here language was a key feature, with questions, playful conversations, and problem posing being used, often in partnership with physical spontaneity. Within this dimension, sibling rivalry was used to strong effect, including good-natured arguments about Dumpling irresponsibly spending money set aside for paying the gas bill or Tiny not being able to find a wife because of his inability to make a decent cup of tea. Here, the philosophy of the clown came keenly into play, for a clown is always dreaming of a perfect world where all things are possible, but in reality, each of them always falls short. This inflection informed the play and depending on individual responses, histories, and previous engagements, it was explored in different ways.

Songs and music could also be considered to be an aspect of cognitive spontaneity, although of course there is a strong physical component to music as well. Used quite regularly, music emerged quite spontaneously at times, often in response to a specific idea arising within an interaction. Alternatively, songs likely to promote engagement were also planned and rehearsed in advance. Within these sung moments, the status of at least one of the characters (Tiny or

Dumpling) was lowered, with the singing being far from pitch perfect, while words were intentionally muddled or confused. In spite of this, however, songs used within individual visits often become a contagion, so that visitors, staff, and even members of the research team joined in.

Social spontaneity

Engagement within this project also emerged in response to or as part of the social interaction between all three participants – not simply between the two artists. In early visits, *some* established scenarios were used, however, based on information gleaned as the weeks progressed or from biographical information offered by staff and family, opportunities for personalized social interactions grew. For example, information gathered might have revealed that an individual had a background in a particular business area, with this information then being built upon through rich social spontaneity. Photographs or other personal artefacts found within each resident's room were a further stimulus for social play. Here, for example, a photograph of a horse framed and displayed in a prominent position within the resident's bedroom might be used to stimulate an exchange where the resident's background knowledge of horses is used to create physical play, discussions about where to buy a good horse or even sibling rivalry between Tiny and Dumpling as they described the other's ineptness as a rider. From this banter, questions about horses might also emerge, with the aged-care resident being positioned as an expert in all matters relating to horses and horse purchasing.

Manifest joy and a sense of humour

While these final dimensions are the ones most commonly associated with playfulness, they were not always overt or explicit within every interaction. However, in most cases, the absence of one or both of these was due to either the general extent of an individual's dementia or to their well-being on a particular day. On these occasions, the play vocabularies available to Tiny and Dumpling were more limited, with close human contact involving slow rhythmic work or the simple singing of a gentle song being the default approaches when other vocabularies appeared to be unworkable. However, in almost all of these cases, in spite of the absence of explicit humour, the engagement emerging from the interactions could still be described as playful, for as Killick (2013, p. 27) notes, 'playfulness and humour are not the same thing: the former encompasses the latter'.

Of course, there were also plenty of occasions, where manifest joy and humour were both present in spades, growing out of the physical, cognitive, and social spontaneity of the artists and the contributions of their co-player residents. Here, responses ranged from riotous laughter through to engagement expressed through less-explicit means such as extended and enlivened eye contact or a firmly held handgrip. This differentiation in response was at times due to physical incapacities, but at others, additional or alternate features were in play such as the level of trust already existing, the number of visits to date, the relationship that had already emerged between the artists and the person living with dementia, or the individual's natural inclination to play and playfulness.

Framework two – the elements of drama

An additional and equally useful means of understanding the play approach used within this pilot study is to consider how key elements of drama were managed within the interactions. Including role, tension, and contrast, analysis according to these elements offers complementary insights. For example, an exploration of role highlights the importance of Clarke and Anna's decision to present themselves as identical twins. A clearly preposterous proposition given that Clarke is male, Caucasian, bald headed, and extremely tall, while Anna is female, petite, and of Asian descent, this overt 'disruption of settled expectations' clearly signalled from the first introductions that 'this was play'.

The use of role also opened up possibilities for shifts in status to occur, with one or both of the 'twins' regularly dropping their status in order to seek help or advice from the person living with dementia. Drawing upon biographical information to support this process, the applied theatre artists created moments of genuine and often highly playful engagement as they pretended to struggle with small physical problems such as knitting, or asked for information about topics ranging from romantic relationships through to the purchase of cosmetics. Given that individuals living with dementia are rarely in a position of heightened status, genuine delight was created by these shifts. Of course, depending on an individual's stage of dementia or well-being on any given day, attempts at playing with status were not always successful, but when they were, they seemed to achieve some of the keenest moments of engagement.

As we have seen by exploring the dimensions of playfulness above, the role selections made by Clarke and Anna also offered opportunities for the enactment of sibling rivalry, which can be understood in relation to the elements of drama as the use of dramatic tension. Drawing mainly on the tension of relationships, their decision to work as siblings was critical in stimulating engagement. Significantly, this pairing also offered the participants choice over how involved they wanted to be during any particular visit, with some participants occasionally opting to sit back and enjoy the playful tensions between Tiny and Dumpling, without the pressure of feeling that they must be playful in response.

Finally, the dramatic element of contrast was also critical, with the artists continuously aiming to effectively manage the contrast between sound and silence and between movement and stillness so that spaces could be opened up for the person living with dementia to take the lead. Managing the contrast between sound and silence was the most challenging of these, especially given the spontaneous nature of the work and the variations in each individual's ability to respond. The *Yum Cha moment* described in the vignette is a good example of the importance of silence as a means of opening up opportunities for individuals to have a voice.

In order to explore these elements of drama and dimensions of playfulness further, four engagement stories are now shared.

Engagement stories

The concept of engagement is a complex and multi-layered one, dependent upon context and, to a degree, the purpose of that engagement. For example, within a school environment, engagement is generally seen as a necessary condition for learning, with Kress (2009, p. 38) proposing that engagement is 'the meaning-maker's interested, energetic and sustained involvement with a framed segment of the world, which is at issue in an interaction'. Like Kress, Bundy (2003), who works within the field of applied theatre, also emphasizes meaning-making in her attempts to define engagement – in her case, aesthetic engagement. She argues that the 'value of engaging in a drama experience is that it affords the possibility of an aesthetic response; a particular way of perceiving and knowing the world and our relationship to it' (p. 171). She proposes that aesthetic engagement is characterized by three basic qualities: connection, animation, and heightened awareness, with heightened awareness being 'a product of the simultaneous experience of animation and connection' (p. 180). Bundy goes on to suggest that connection occurs when participants in drama work experience a 'connection to an idea stimulated by the work but not necessarily contained in it' (p. 177).

Bundy's ideas are, therefore, quite similar to those offered by Kress, for both writers place an emphasis on the outcomes of engagement, such as heightened awareness and meaning-making. In this way, they also echo earlier work by Abbs (1987), Brook (1989), and Marcuse (1979) who have all focused on engagement as being connected to heightened experience. For example, Marcuse (1979, p. 27) believes that aesthetic experiences open up our perception and understanding, transcending the given context, to create an experience that may be 'more real than reality itself', while Brook (1989, p. 21) claims that through any aesthetic experience 'our everyday perception of reality, confined within invisible limits, is momentarily opened up'. Finally, Abbs (1987, p. 53) suggests that, 'through aesthetic activity we half apprehend and half create a world of understanding, of heightened perception, of heightened meaning'. Common to all of these definitions then are notions of meaning, connection, and heightened awareness, with transcendence of the given context being a key additional feature of some.

Within the *Playful Engagement* project, these meaning-focused definitions of engagement encouraged us to look not just for the physical indicators of engagement, but also to search the data for moments when individuals appeared to make connections to the ideas offered both *within* interactions and *outside* them. Once again, reflexivity and responsiveness were key to achieving these points of connection, with selection of the most appropriate play grammars being a critical part of this process.

Engaging with Tom

Tom's journey towards playful engagement began slowly, with Tiny and Dumpling initially drawing upon a very limited vocabulary of practice in order to establish a connection. Tom seemed disinterested in verbal interaction and indeed, following our first visit, researcher field notes ask the question, 'How can we engage with Tom without language?' Given how the interactions between Tiny, Dumpling, and Tom eventually unfolded, with the approach being focused on opportunities for Tom to recall and practice his Cantonese, this question would prove to be quite ironic. However, within the initial visit, interactions were largely non-verbal, with Tom setting a slow pace that focused on limited levels of physical spontaneity.

With the benefit of the biographical information routinely collected by staff about Tom's earlier life in Hong Kong, the second visit saw a shift in approach, with Tiny and Dumpling using this information to slowly open up new avenues for spontaneous play. Here the intentional and highly effective use of the pause – known as point fix – was critical, leaving extended silences for Tom to fill. These points within the play allowed for significant moments to be highlighted and reflected upon before the focus was changed or redirected and, indeed, it was during one of these pauses that Tom's first Cantonese words, in the form of 'Yum Cha', emerged. In that moment, he revealed something of himself to Tiny and Dumpling, with this revelation shifting both the relationship between them and the play vocabularies applied across the remaining sessions.

By our last visit, field notes reveal that upon entering his room, Tom is immediately alert and eager to talk. With his newfound status as Tiny's language teacher in place, Tom surprises the whole team with the marked shift in his ability to engage, with the language lessons apparently generating rich connections to a childhood language long forgotten and unused. Significantly, this heightened status and sense of connection was only made possible through Tiny's and Dumpling's patience, playful use of status, reflexivity in terms of selection of play vocabularies, and perhaps most importantly, understanding of the importance of letting Tom set the pace.

Engaging with Valerie

In contrast to visits with Tom, multiple dimensions of playfulness characterized visits with Valerie, with her laughter infecting all around her including passing staff and the research team members. From the outset, Valerie appeared to be comfortable with the disruptive nature of play, using it to provide herself with opportunities to be socially spontaneous. Tiny and Dumpling visited Valerie five times over the six-week period of the pilot, with these visits ranging from shorter visits of around 10 minutes to others stretching closer to 20. She always recognized them when she saw them in the hallway or communal living rooms, and all members of the research team were drawn to her bubbly character. She seemed to be always ready to play.

The first visit, in the absence of accessing biographical information, began with a default scenario, Tiny's inability to find a girlfriend. With Dumpling playfully seeking Valerie's advice about the approaches that might serve to help Tiny find his one true love, we started to learn things about Valerie herself, about how she met her husband and about their marriage. During one particular exchange, she offered surprisingly detailed information about a tennis match where she recalled getting whacked in the backside by a ball hit by her future husband. Here it seemed that Tiny's struggle to find a partner had connected with her and that her animated responses involved some kind of reflective engagement.

As the visits progressed, sibling rivalry between Tiny and Dumpling grew and was used effectively to lift Valerie's status to the extent that we began to wonder if her dementia was not as advanced as we had been led to believe. Notes from one visit reflect our response to her playfulness: 'Valerie is feeling playful today ... she has come to really enjoy us' (Field notes 17.10.12). With her giggles and active involvement in the play, it took us until the fifth visit to fully comprehend how advanced her dementia actually was. On this occasion, when asked to pretend to be a lady bus driver, the object of Tiny's affections, Valerie struggled and became confused, unable to respond spontaneously and unclear about how to handle this complex shift in frame. Her inability to engage in this activity appeared to make her feel like she had been caught out, and she began to respond with phrases like, 'You've got me there'. Of course, true to her nature, she was still giggling and involved, but our team had learned a valuable lesson about the limits of play with people with dementia and the need to focus on strategies less likely to cause anxiety.

Nevertheless, Valerie seemed to revel in the energy and special attention the visits from Tiny and Dumpling generated, especially when not too much was asked of her, and where she could create connections between the play and her own life experiences.

Engaging with Gwen

Tiny and Dumpling met with Gwen three times over the six-week period of the pilot and like Valerie Gwen enjoyed a good laugh. However, unlike Valerie, Gwen was also capable of engaging in cognitive and social spontaneity, rather than simply responding to it.

During our initial visit Gwen's daughter was present, but nevertheless she seemed interested and curious about how the visit from Tiny and Dumpling might play out. Right from the start she assumed a type of empowered position, able to initiate humour and happy to share her thoughts when asked. Later, this polite and somewhat guarded approach shifted and Gwen interacted on a different more relaxed and casual level until during the final visit she really took the reigns.

During one playful exchange with Gwen, Tiny declares that he will make a grand entrance, suggesting that, 'When I walk in – I want you tell me how I look. Tell me if you think I can get a girlfriend with this wig'. With a reddish punk style wig on his head, Tiny enters the room in an exaggerated and highly physical manner and Gwen is visibly appalled. She gasps, and says, 'Oh My God! I don't like to swear, but it looks bloody awful ... . You'll lose a girlfriend with that thing on ... ' Tiny responds by asking, 'So, is that a strong no Gwen?' Immediately she reacts, 'A very strong no'!! (Field notes 17.10.12). Later she offers Tiny further good advice, suggesting that if he does find a girlfriend he should keep his hands in his pockets, be a gentleman, hire a car to take her out, buy her chocolates, etc. Her ideas are highly spontaneous and she is animated and alert, laughing heartily and leading the play.

Given these confident and playful responses, the relationship between Gwen and Tiny, in particular, had shifted markedly and although the play vocabularies used with Gwen were similar to those used with Valerie, the outcomes were very different.

Engaging with Edgar

The final story of engagement is brief but significant. It began with a session characterized by the slow and careful manipulation of a puppet. With Edgar appearing to be incapable of responding through any other medium, his face was a fixed mask, apart from eye movement strongly focused on Dumpling. The session was brief but intense. Two visits later, and the contrasts were stark. Morning tea arrived on a tray and Dumpling asked Edgar if he wanted the team to leave so he could enjoy his tea. Edgar clearly announced, 'No' and his face broke into a broad smile that was sustained as he seemed to revel in rejecting the routine in favour of more play. Soon he was sharing with Dumpling and Tiny an extended set of ideas that although difficult to understand seemed to represent a real desire to communicate, including extended eye contact. Eventually the game became the wearing of silly hats, with Edgar indicating with his eyes who should wear particular hats. He even, very playfully, indicated once again with his eyes and a broad smile that a research team member should join in. There was laughter all round and Edgar appeared to be keenly engaged.

Suddenly, in the midst of the excitement, Edgar speaks clearly, saying, 'It was my fault, you know, I had a seizure'. There is silence in the room as the idea offered is allowed the space it deserves. Dumpling is the first to respond, offering the comment that these things happen and that they are no one's fault. Again, silence follows. Then with great skillfulness, Dumpling points to her brother Tiny and playfully announces that she cannot help it if she is beautiful and her brother isn't! It is not her fault! Edgar smiles broadly and shakes her hand. 'Thank you', he says as Tiny grabs his suitcase and Dumpling suggests that they will miss the bus again, and that this will once again be her big brother's fault.

Conclusion

As these four engagement stories show, each visit had its own rhythms, with Tiny and Dumpling needing to reflexively apply different vocabularies of practice depending upon the needs of each individual during any given visit. While some of these practices were overtly comedic, rich in physical, cognitive, and social spontaneity, others were more serious and intense, with the outcomes being more focused on creating connections than creating play. Nevertheless, all were highly spontaneous, and in spite of their occasionally outward appearance of seriousness, almost all were, to some extent, joyous.

Within initial sessions, before relationships were established, playfulness of a generic kind dominated most interactions. At these times, the play approaches were, in a way, diagnostic – giving the artists time to build trust and establish a foundation for further interactions. However, as the highly skilled artists involved in the project became more adept at reading the temperature within each room, building on each individual's play preferences and personality and indeed the relationships this knowledge supported, more space was created. In these spaces, relationships were slowly built, with opportunities for the person living with dementia to gradually take more control. For this reason, one of the challenges of playfulness in contexts such as this appears to be that of transitions, with the artist being required to quickly recalibrate their vocabulary as they transition from one individual to the next. At times, these transitions did not always run smoothly, with room entrances being too loud or too energetic leading to moments of confusion or anxiety for individuals. In addition, as we have already seen, pace within the session also needed to be managed, with long pauses sometimes being required to open opportunities for individuals to respond and take some control, while at other times and for other individuals, long pauses were a negative, leading to a reduction in interest and engagement. However, in spite of the risks of disengagement, the creation of space was necessary for the person to emerge, for them to become active and present in each encounter. In addition, as relationships developed and the team gained a richer understanding of the needs of individuals, their biographies, and their play preferences, play vocabularies also shifted to meet these needs.

Together, the analysis process and these engagement stories suggest that applied theatre artists working in dementia settings need to be responsive to a range of factors as they prepare, but even more importantly as they engage in the 'moment'. They need to consider:

- The well-being of each individual participant – both generally and more specifically during any particular visit.
- Knowledge about the individual and their life experiences.
- Their existing relationship with the person living with dementia based on their shared experiences to date.
- The personal play preferences of each participant, including their highly individual attitudes towards playfulness.

More importantly perhaps, analysis of the data collected across this pilot suggests that by adopting a responsive approach that takes account of these factors, positive shifts in relationships seem to emerge, with these relationship shifts generating new options for play. Together, these discoveries remind us of the highly individual nature of play and serve to support our initial decision to work with individuals rather than groups. They also suggest that our desire to adopt a relationship-centred approach appears to have been appropriate, with the vocabulary of practices used within the pilot study being mostly successful in achieving engagement 'in the moment' (Killick & Allan, 2001).

As we commence the main study, we hope that the understandings gained through this pilot will support the play practices to be reflexively applied in the wider study, ensuring that those important *Yum Cha moments* – moments of genuine engagement and connection – are generated with all our participants, influencing in a positive manner their QOL.

Acknowledgements

The authors would like to acknowledge the contribution and support of our funding partner, Wesley Mission Brisbane. In particular we would like to thank the residents, their families, and the staff of the Wesley Mission long-term care facility where this pilot study was conducted. The research was also supported by an Australian Research Council Linkage Grant.

References

Abbs, P. (1987). *Living powers*. London: The Falmer Press.

Access Economics. (2006). *Dementia in the Asia Pacific region: The epidemic is here*. Report for ADI, September. Canberra: Author.

Access Economics. (2007). *Dementia estimates and projections: Queensland and its regions*. Report for Alzheimer's Association. Canberra: Author.

Access Economics. (2009a). *Keeping dementia front of mind: Incidence and prevalence 2009–2050*. Report for Alzheimer's Association. Canberra: Author.

Access Economics. (2009b). *Making choices. Future dementia care: Projects, problems and preferences*. Report for Alzheimer's Association. Canberra: Author.

Australian Institute of Health and Welfare. (2007). *Older Australians in hospital*. Cat. No. AUS 92. Canberra.

Brook, P. (1989). The culture of links. In P. Abbs (Ed.), *The symbolic order* (pp. 19–25). London: The Falmer Press.

Bundy, P. (2003). Aesthetic engagement in the drama process. *Research in Drama Education, 8*(2), 171–181.

Csikszentmihalyi, M. (1981). Some paradoxes in the definition of play. In A. T. Cheska (Ed.), *Play as context* (pp. 14–26). New York, NY: Leisure Press.

Goffman, E. (1974). *Frame analysis – an essay on the organization of experience*. New York, NY: Harper and Row.

Haseman, B., & O'Toole, J. (1986). *Dramawise*. Melbourne: Heinemann.

Hendriks, R. (2012). Tackling indifference—clowning, dementia, and the articulation of a sensitive body. *Medical Anthropology: Cross-Cultural Studies in Health and Illness, 31*(6), 459–476.

Killick, J. (2013). *Playfulness and dementia: A practice guide*. London: Jessica Kingsley.

Killick, J., & Allan, K. (2001). *Communication and the care of people with dementia*. Buckingham: Open University Press.

Kress, G. (2009). Assessment in the perspective of a social semiotic theory of multimodal teaching and learning. In C. Wyatt-Smith & J. Cummings (Eds.), *Educational assessment in the 21st century: Connecting theory and practice* (pp. 19–41). Dordrecht: Springer.

Lieberman, J. (1977). *Playfulness: Its relationship to imagination and creativity*. New York, NY: Academic Press.

Marcuse, H. (1979). *The aesthetic dimension*. London: Macmillan.

Moyle, W., Kellett, U., Ballantyne, A., & Gracia, N. (2011). Dementia and loneliness: An Australian perspective. *Journal of Clinical Nursing, 20*(9–10), 1445–1453.

Nicholson, H. (2011). Making home work: Theatre-making with older adults in residential care. *NJ: The Journal of Drama Australia, 35*, 47–62.

Nolan, M. R., Davies, S., Brown, J., Keady, J., & Nolan, J. (2004). Beyond 'person-centred' care: A new vision for gerontological nursing. *International Journal of Older People Nursing, 13*(3a), 45–53.

Spitzer, P. (2011). The laughter boss. In H. Lee & T. Adams (Eds.), *Creative approaches in dementia care* (pp. 32–53). New York, NY: Palgrave Macmillan.

Sutton-Smith, B. (1997). *The ambiguity of play*. Cambridge, MA: Harvard University Press.

Vandenberg, B. (1986). Play theory. In G. Fein & M. Rivkin (Eds.), *The young child at play – reviews of research* (pp. 16–28). Washington, DC: National Association for the Education of Young Children.

Warren, B. (2008a). The fools are come hither. *Research in Drama Education, 13*(3), 365–369.

Warren, B. (2008b). Healing laughter: The role and benefits of clown-doctors working in hospitals and healthcare. In B. Warren (Ed.), *Using the creative arts in therapy and healthcare* (pp. 213–228). London: Routledge.

Warren, B., & Spitzer, P. (2011). Laughing to longevity—the work of elder clowns. *The Lancet, 378*(9791), 562–563.

Yen, A. (2012). Monika Pagneux. *The Feldenkrais Journal, 25*, 4–10.

Zuidema, S., de Jonghe, J., Verhey, F., & Koopmans, R. (2007). Neuropsychiatric symptoms in nursing home patients: Factor structure invariance of the Dutch nursing home version of the neuropsychiatric inventory in different stages of dementia. *Dementia & Geriatric Cognitive Disorders, 24*(3), 169–176.

From playground to patient: reflections on a traditional games project in a pædiatric hospital

Judy McKinty

Independent Children's Play Researcher and Consultant, Glen Iris, Australia

> This article describes an innovative, but little-known Australian project, which took place in 1990. *Tops, Tales and Granny's False Teeth* was an initiative to introduce children's own play culture into the Royal Children's Hospital, Melbourne, in the form of an interactive exhibition of children's traditional playground games. While play was valued in the hospital for its therapeutic role, children's own play culture, with its child-initiated rituals and rules, was somewhat different. Throughout the project, the exhibition staff witnessed connections being made between children and their own play culture and the unexpected benefits this had for the patients' well-being. The day-to-day happenings in the exhibition were documented, and this detailed documentation reveals, so many years later, the effect of this pioneering project on those involved and prompts reflection on its relevance to children in hospital today. Is there a place for children's own play culture in today's paediatric hospitals?

The role of play in children's hospitals

A Few of 'Our Boys'

I confess I am drawn to the rowdy, boisterous natures that would convert the ward into a football-ground did not authority prevail upon them to modify their transports. 'Nurse, you always have the rowdiest ward,' says the doctor, after encouraging them by a spirited round of playing catches, during which the balls fly around the beds amid a chorus of boy voices that never seem to belong to sick children …

The big ward on the upper flat has been well chosen for the lads; it has more sunshine than any other, and looks out with all its windows on to two public schools … so the sick boys can look out upon their old playfellows … It is no uncommon thing to see boys in the street below gesticulating to the children in the ward, or even holding conversations with them through the open windows. (Jennings Carmichael, 1891/1991, pp. 31, 32)

This description of lively play in a children's hospital was written by Sister Grace Jennings Carmichael, one of Melbourne's earliest formally trained children's nurses, who worked in the Melbourne Hospital for Sick Children, now the Royal Children's Hospital, during 1888–1890. Her descriptions of everyday life in the hospital were based on notes written during her days and nights in the wards, caring for children from Melbourne's slum areas who were suffering from diseases such as diphtheria, tuberculosis of the hip or the dreaded typhoid. The extracts reveal a tolerant, and even playful, attitude to the children playing games on the ward and their unorthodox way of keeping in touch with their friends, and an acceptance that this is part of their normal lives, even when ill or suffering.

Children's hospitals, and the facilities they provide for their young patients, have changed profoundly since Sister Jennings Carmichael wrote so fondly of the children in her care, and there has long been an acceptance of the need to adopt a 'whole-child' approach to the treatment of children in hospital:

> For the last 20 years, due mainly to an increased knowledge of child development and psychology, there has been a shift in focus from disease-oriented to patient-oriented paediatric care. The realisation that, in order to reduce the possible traumatic effects of hospitalisation, the child's emotional, developmental and social needs should be met, has brought about extended visiting hours, possibilities for parent participation, and a general humanising of the hospital environment.

> One of the most vital needs of the child is the need to play. It is through play that the child grows, develops his physical and mental skills, and learns to cope with the physical world and with his own feelings. (Langley, 1976, p. iii)

Acceptance of play as a normal activity, and a right, for children in hospital now underpins the work of play therapists worldwide and influences the planning of hospital policy and practice (Association for the Wellbeing of Children in Healthcare [AWCH], 2002; Ure, 1993). One of Australia's leading advocacy organisations, the Association for the Wellbeing of Children in Healthcare, has produced policy papers on the care of children in hospital, in which play has an important therapeutic role: 'Play for children in hospital introduces some normality into the child's day within the unfamiliar hospital environment. It can provide an opportunity for peer interaction and reduce the degree of developmental regression that some children may experience during hospitalisation' (AWCH, 2002, p. 3).

Play is also seen as having a functional role in the treatment of paediatric patients. In addition to aiding normality, play can reduce stress and anxiety, speed recovery and rehabilitation, facilitate communication, act as an outlet for the expression of feelings, help children regain their confidence and self-esteem, aid in assessment and diagnosis and help to prepare children for hospitalisation or surgery (Gillis, 1989; National Association of Health Play Specialists, 2013; Save the Children, 1989, pp. 11–13).

These concepts of play have grown out of many long years of research and professional practice in the area of paediatric health care. They have been formulated to promote the well-being of children in hospital and assist the adults who are responsible for their care – it is an admirable and practical view of children's play from a professional adult perspective.

Children's own play culture, on the other hand, with its child-initiated rituals, adaptations, irreverence and rules, is somewhat different – it is a rich subculture which has been passed down from child to child over countless generations, largely by oral transmission, to the children of today. The games, rhymes, riddles and jokes adults remember from their own school days are all part of the dynamic culture of children's play. Is there a place for this kind of lively, unruly play in a modern paediatric hospital, and how would it affect existing therapeutic play programmes, medical processes and, most importantly, the patients themselves? Surprisingly, some insight may be gained by looking back at a little-known Australian project from 1990.

Tops, Tales and Granny's False Teeth

A century after Sister Jennings Carmichael sat writing her notes in the darkened wards, an innovative project to bring children's own play culture to the patients in the Royal Children's Hospital (RCH), Melbourne, began. It took the form of an interactive exhibition of children's traditional games. Called *Tops, Tales and Granny's False Teeth,*[1] the exhibition was based at the hospital for one month during April 1990. As it was a highly unusual, if not unique, approach to children's well-being, the day-to-day happenings in the exhibition were recorded in both written and visual form. That documentation brings to life this imaginative project so many years later, and offers a chance to reflect on its relevance to the well-being of children in hospitals today.

Tops, Tales and Granny's False Teeth began as a relatively modest idea to have a display of toys from different countries, and became instead a remarkable project to introduce children's own culture into one of Australia's leading paediatric hospitals. The project was planned and carried out by an innovative group of people led by Australian writer, folklorist and childhood consultant Dr. June Factor, with the support of a number of organisations, including RCH Foundation, the Australian Centre at the University of Melbourne and Melbourne's first Children's Museum. The aim of the exhibition was to 'act as a bridge between the lives of children inside and outside the hospital, and also between children, their parents and hospital staff – all of whom share in common the play practices and traditional lore of childhood' (Factor, 1989). It would also provide a much-needed distraction from the clinical environment of the wards and an interesting and unusual experience for patients, visitors and staff at the hospital, at a time when two of the most popular places to visit were the shop and the canteen.

Elements of the project

The exhibition

There were four separate but related elements to the project. The first was the interactive exhibition space – the heart of the project. In 1990, the RCH was still occupying its old building,[2] and had a disused lecture room in an area undergoing extensive renovation (Figure 1). This was the site for the installation. Mary Featherston, one of Australia's foremost interactive exhibition designers, was presented with the challenge of transforming a bare, ugly, concrete space with no ceiling – merely an open metal grid with visible wires, cables and ducts – into a pleasant, welcoming, comfortable space suitable for children, some of whom were very ill or with impaired movement.

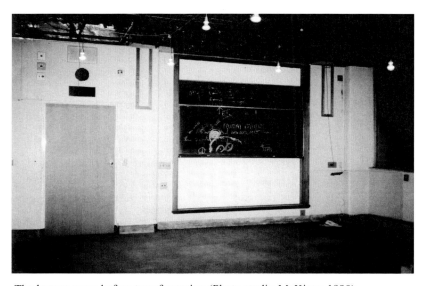

Figure 1.   The lecture room before transformation (Photo credit: McKinty, 1990).

Plain calico panels were hung around the walls and giant red and yellow balloons covered the ceiling, softening the sounds in the room in contrast to the noisy hospital corridors (Figure 2). The seating was large, square cushions which could be stacked, placed together or moved apart when children in wheelchairs came to visit.

The room contained a number of traditional games common to children in many parts of the world – Marbles, Jacks,[3] string games (also known as Cat's Cradle), spinning tops, cup and ball, paper and pencil games and a 'making' table. There was also a reading and storytelling corner with a supply of books donated by publishers, and a listening post with a selection of audiotapes, where children could sit and become completely absorbed in listening to stories or songs through headphones.

A large colourful display of traditional playthings from the Australian Children's Folklore Collection (ACFC),[4] with some additional toys donated by the embassies of several countries, was set up along one wall (Figure 3). These precious items were protected behind acrylic sheets – a 'looking-at' display which eventually proved to be as popular among some of the hospital staff as the 'playing-with' games were with the children. In a sense, the exhibition was an extension of the playrooms found in children's hospitals, and it had many of the attributes that were recommended at the time:

> The environment needs to be made as welcoming as possible, with toys, books, music and equipment available which reflect different cultures ... (Hogg, 1990, p. 15)

The environment was flexible and easily adapted to accommodate visitors with different physical capabilities. Initially, it was thought that the exhibition space would be mostly used by fully ambulant patients, their families and visitors to the hospital. The number of children who visited in wheelchairs, trolleys or attached to drip machines, drawn by the promise of a new but culturally familiar experience, far surpassed our expectations:

> A group of children from 3 W (Orthopaedic Ward) visited the exhibition. We had 5 wheelchairs, 1 trolley and 1 ambulant patient in the space – had to move some cushions to allow for free movement. (*Tops, Tales & Granny's False Teeth* (*TTGFT*) Diary,[5] Monday, 2 April 1990)

Figure 2. An area of the exhibition space. (Photo credit: Featherston, 1990)

Figure 3. The display of traditional playthings. (Photo credit: McKinty, 1990)

Almost everything was moveable – tables or trolleys with a lip around the edge allowed children in wheelchairs to play with spinning tops, jacks and marbles at a raised level, and the cushions could be quickly spread out for the audience when a puppet show was beginning. This was a neutral, non-threatening space where people could forget, for a while, the reasons why they were in the hospital. Patients and their families could play games, read books, listen to stories or just relax away from the clinical environment of the wards.

The combination of fabric, soft furnishings, carpet and cushions had a softening effect on the space, and people liked to sit and play games on the floor. In this soft space full of interesting things to explore, a two-year-old boy crawled for the first time since the accident which sent him to hospital and interrupted his motor skills development:

> Great excitement because L, a two-year-old who was hit by a car, crawled for the first time since the accident. Mum was delighted by the soft carpet and soft furnishings, which were so appropriate to encourage her son to crawl and walk ...

> Today I learned again how very important it is to let children do things for themselves – especially in a hospital. In L's case, the aim was to encourage him to crawl instead of shuffling along on his bottom, so we let him go and get the things he wanted (which was everything!) and throw them around. He covered quite a lot of ground with great results! (*TTGFT* Diary, Tuesday, 17 April 1990)

L and his mother returned to the exhibition several times, and his movement and use of his limbs continued to improve to such an extent that a video of his achievements, made as part of the documentation of the project, was borrowed by the hospital's Physiotherapy Department to show to the staff (*TTGFT* Diary, Tuesday, 24 April 1990).

While it is usual for children to be sent home from hospital as soon as possible, we found there was a great need among the longer-term patients and their families to have somewhere away from the wards where they could relax, to talk and think about the ordinary things of life. The exhibition, full of lively, positive, active play was welcomed by everyone as 'a safe environment where the children could move around freely' (*Tops, Tales & Granny's False Teeth* Evaluation, 1990). Also, for a child in hospital things seem to be always changing – staff rosters, tests and treatment, patients being admitted, others leaving – so the exhibition became something in the children's lives that was constant and continuing – albeit for only a month. One boy had a chapter of a serial read to him each day, and we also had 'regular' children who visited often, picking up where they had left off the day before.

Play baskets

The second component of the project was developed in collaboration with the hospital's Play Specialists, with the aim of including children who were restricted to the wards. A number of 'play baskets', one for each ward, were filled with games and playthings similar to those in the exhibition space (Figure 4). In this way the children who were confined to bed upstairs on the wards, or otherwise unable to visit the exhibition, could share the play experiences being enjoyed by the children below. The play baskets were managed by the Play Specialists, who documented their use on the wards:

> The baskets were a brilliant idea – the jacks and O-Tedama[6] being the most-used items – closely followed by the string. Parents used the jacks <u>a lot</u>, sometimes very grudgingly giving them to their children to play with!! The string was mainly used by girls (from 8–13 years approx.) and they taught me several new tricks. This also became a great 'ice-breaker' with several of the more reserved girls on

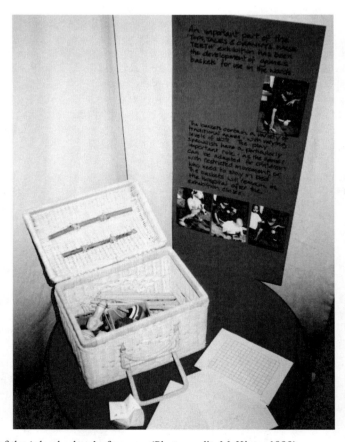

Figure 4. One of the 'play baskets' of games. (Photo credit: McKinty, 1990)

the ward. Parents would also use the string a lot, prompting many 'I remember when ... ' stories. (*TTGFT* Evaluation, 1990)

Collaboration with the Play Specialists was critical to the success of the project, as they regularly brought children down to the exhibition as well as sharing the games in the play baskets with parents and children on the wards.

Reading and storytelling

Children's books donated by publishers provided the third element to the project – reading was considered very important for the children. In a hospital ward, where there is a lot happening and very little privacy, reading books allows children to engage deeply with the story and suspend reality for a while, whenever they need to. Books and stories were also a good way to involve younger children and those not able to play the games. The children's books were read eagerly by all ages and used every day by the volunteer storytellers.

The books were particularly welcome to a family of seven children from country Victoria, who were discovered waiting patiently in a small room. The children had been spending long hours at the hospital, just waiting around while their parents were with their baby brother in Intensive Care: 'We waited for five hours on Monday. We got so bored that we rearranged the furniture' (McKinty, *TTGFT* Notes for Report, April 1990). These children were sharing the family's anxiety and needed to relieve the tension and boredom of waiting. They visited the exhibition at every opportunity, and spent many hours playing games or lying on the soft cushions, reading book after book. We developed a kind of library service for them, where they borrowed books overnight to take back to their temporary accommodation. By the time they went home they seemed like old friends.

Storytelling was a popular activity in the exhibition and on the wards, and there were numerous requests from the Play Specialists or Charge Nurses for someone to visit a particular patient who needed company or special attention. The volunteers read stories to children in bed, in intensive care and, in one case, to a girl in a coma.

Puppets were also used in storytelling. They allowed the volunteers to engage with the patients in a completely different way, and finger puppets enabled a hospital play worker to reach a girl who was previously quite withdrawn and uncommunicative (*TTGFT* Diary, Friday 20 April 1990). *The Very Hungry Caterpillar* was a special favourite, particularly when coordinator Dorothy Rickards[7] brought her specially made transforming puppet into the exhibition and presented the story, with educator June Epstein[8] reading, to an enthralled audience of patients, family members and visitors (Figure 5). The caterpillar puppet was a great favourite among the volunteer storytellers. Children also made simple puppets from materials available in the exhibition space to take back to their wards.

The day-to-day running of the exhibition was shared by two co-ordinators. Volunteers from the Storytelling Guild of Victoria, the Country Women's Association and tertiary colleges, plus a few interested individuals, were rostered over the month to read stories and play games in the exhibition and up on the wards. Children's writers came in to read their books to enthralled listeners and Amy Saunders,[9] an Aboriginal 'explainer', who was particularly skilled in sharing string games, visited children on the wards. The total number of volunteer helpers who played games, told stories, cuddled babies, sang songs, talked with parents and presented puppet shows was 140 – truly a 'goodwill' project.

Collecting

The fourth element of the project was a 'collecting' component. During the month-long project games, rhymes, riddles and jokes were collected from patients, parents, medical staff and visitors

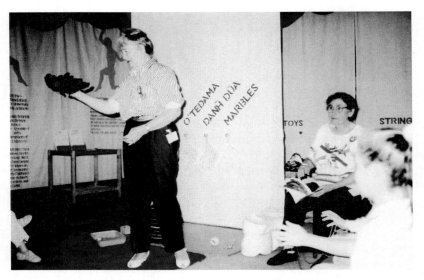

Figure 5. Storytelling with puppets. (Photo credit: McKinty, 1990)

and written down on collection sheets, to be added to existing material in ACFC. Among the verbal lore collected were skipping rhymes, counting-out rhymes, 'Doctor, Doctor' jokes and riddles:

> Doctor, Doctor, I feel like a pair of curtains.
> Pull yourself together man!
>
> Doctor, Doctor, I've only got 59 seconds to live.
> Hang on. I'll be with you in a minute!
>
> Q. What's the difference between snot and brussels sprouts?
> A. You can't get children to eat brussels sprouts.
> (*Rhymes and games*, 1990)

Adolescent slang terms, like 'skinners',[10] 'Marios'[11] and 'skegs',[12] and their meanings, were documented, together with games descriptions, including different versions of Marbles, a Jacks game from Uruguay and a game called 'Thornimat', after the boys who made it up. 'Thornimat' was created in the exhibition by three patients and adapted for playing upstairs on the ward. Based on ice hockey, it was played with coloured plastic discs and 'frog cups', the small round plastic containers with lids used by Cystic Fibrosis patients for collecting sputum.

'Frog cups' is one example of the hospital slang collected from adolescent patients by folklorist Heather Russell[13] during the project. In her report, *The Subculture of a Children's Hospital*, she wrote:

> During the *Tops, Tales and Granny's False Teeth* exhibition, some time was spent investigating whether children create a subculture of their own within the hospital context. Stuck in a formal institution like a hospital, children are denied their familiar friends and peer group with whom they muck around, joke and play. But children's need to play and establish a common bond with other children is enormous, so it is highly likely that even in such restricted and often traumatic circumstances like a hospital, children will still play and joke with each other...

The subculture that existed on these wards was expressed mainly in the form of slang. Children made up their own words, phrases and abbreviations for drugs, treatments or equipment and passed them on to other patients ... [Some of the nurses] agreed that a common language or slang runs between patients and nursing staff. The nurses pick up slang terms from the children, and the children pick up and modify technical and medical terms used by the nurses. Some slang is made up by the nurses specifically to help children understand and agree to undergo certain treatments ...

Grasping the language of their illness and turning it into slang helps kids gain some control over their situation. Many children, some from a very early age, develop an extraordinary understanding of the treatments, drugs, routines and protocol of the hospital. Some of them then use this to exert some influence over their lives.
(Russell, 1990b, pp. 1, 2)

Russell then went on to described the 'three tries' rule, where a child will let a doctor have three tries at getting an intravenous drip into his arm, and after the third (failed) try say, 'That's your third, you're out!' The children called the treatment room the 'torture room' – sometimes, perhaps, with good reason (Russell, 1990b, p. 2).

The use of jokes and other humour is one of the ways children cope with the clinical processes and procedures of a hospital:

Humor plays a major role in positively affecting the dispositions of children who are ill. Those who work with children in health care facilities value the power of humor to offset arduous medical treatment and the uncertainty that accompanies illness. Humor provides opportunities for hospitalized children to experience normalcy through joy and laughter ... (Klein, 2003, p. 5)

Russell also collected copies of *The Incredible Times*, a newsletter produced by patients in the Adolescent Ward. The pages contain rhymes, jokes, limericks, cartoons, puzzles and a page for hospital autographs. Among the puzzles is a Word Search, with the title 'Cystic Fibrosis' and fifty-eight related words, like 'court needle', 'nebulise', 'pipercillin' and 'friends' to find among the letters in the grid. One contributor wrote a report on his visit to the first National Transplant Games, and with the clear eye of adolescence he describes a memorable moment: 'Afterwards we all went to St. Kevin's College, where we were meant to have a barbecue, but we had cold meats and salads instead. The food was awful and no-one enjoyed it at all!' (*Jokes, Limericks and Cartoons*, 1990).

Children's traditional games in a hospital

Games like Marbles, Jacks, top spinning and string games are part of the play traditions of the schoolyard. School playgrounds are among the few remaining places where children's own culture and traditional play can thrive, given the right conditions – it is here that friendships are made and lost. Children in hospital are remote from their familiar play environments, some for a long time and others for regular, shorter periods, so they miss out on the day-to-day happenings among their peers – the latest craze or 'in' joke, the games, lively banter and shared secrets that are part of the culture of childhood. The boys described by Sister Grace Jennings Carmichael at the beginning of this article were fortunate, in a non-medical sense, because their ward overlooked their school playgrounds and they still had daily contact with their friends, albeit conversations carried on by shouting through the open windows.

The gaining of new skills and play knowledge is an important consideration for children in hospital, particularly long-term patients who are in danger of returning to school with their play repertoire seriously depleted due to their long absence from the playground. The games, tricks and skills that the children learned through *Tops, Tales and Granny's False Teeth* were

PLAY AND WELLBEING

valuable resources to have when they rejoined their friends. Instead of returning to school feeling out of touch with the culture of the playground, they were able to bring something new from hospital to share – a string figure, a rhyme, riddle or joke or the knowledge of how to make a friendship bracelet from coloured threads.

The games, rhymes, riddles, jokes and other activities that form the richness and diversity of children's traditional play are a fundamental part of childhood and remain in the memory for a long time. Several adult visitors to the exhibition were pleased that they still remembered some of their childhood games: 'I'm surprised I still know how to do it – it's been 30 years!'[14] To child: 'Bet you didn't know I could do that, did you!' (McKinty, *TTGFT* Notes, April 1990). This reaction and interaction make these types of games particularly suitable in situations where parents and children are forced to spend an extended period of time together in an unfamiliar environment. Boredom is often an unexpected and unwelcome consequence of illness or injury:

> Parents who accompany their children throughout their period of hospitalisation often find it very difficult when it comes to devoting all their time exclusively to one child without the interruptions normally provided by the daily chores. (Save the Children, 1989, p. 5)

If the child also has some knowledge of the game there is an immediate, and sometimes unexpected, connection between parent and child – sometimes the parent is surprised that the child knows the game, sometimes the look of amazement will be on the face of the child. Either way, these games allow parents and children to relate in new ways and establish mutual experiences that can open the door to a deeper level of communication. At the very least, they provide a moment of fun and pleasure in a sometimes long drawn-out day.

Medical staff and students, as well as other people who were in the hospital to work, not play, were drawn to the exhibition and the opportunities for fun and challenges it provided. Sometimes there was an unlikely combination of players, as noted in the diary on the fourth day of the exhibition:

> OUR FIRST MARBLES TOURNAMENT! Five fifth year medical students called in to look, and started a marbles game. Then two workmen and two painters [who were doing renovation work in the hospital] came in to look and joined in. Then they moved on to the diabolo.[15] They stayed for about an hour and a half. Much laughing. (*TTGFT* Diary, 4 April 1990)

After this first visit, one of the painters became a regular visitor to the exhibition – he arrived rather sheepishly each day to use the diabolo. He was determined to master it!

The traditional games of childhood are played in similar ways throughout the world, although elements of a game may vary depending on where it is played. Members of the hospital staff and other visitors of different cultural backgrounds were delighted to find activities and objects they recognised among the games and toys on display. Some shared their own versions of the games and brought in toys to add to the shelves. Upstairs, on one of the wards, a Play Specialist watched a parent demonstrate how she played a jacks game with chopsticks and a ball, using play materials from the 'play baskets':

> The baskets were very useful and children found some activities that they already knew so they could teach them to other children. There were some different games which they enjoyed learning. One day a large group of children and staff sat in the hall with the basket and played the games. A Vietnamese mother taught the children to do the chopsticks game'. (*TTGFT* Evaluation, 1990)

The games and playthings were easily adapted to different ages and abilities (Figure 6). Children too young to play the actual games enjoyed simply playing with the materials, which were

Figure 6. Playing marbles on the mat. (Photo credit: Russell, 1990)

unusual, tactile and had interesting shapes and sounds. Older patients often learned how to play a new game, make a string figure or gain some kind of new skill, which helped to raise their confidence and self-esteem, in some cases quite markedly. The following diary extract concerns a group of children from the Psychiatric Ward who were visiting the exhibition:

> When they first entered the exhibition they just stood there – only a couple of children started to look around the different activities (the younger ones). The rest seemed reluctant to do anything and there were no smiling faces. We talked to them and told them about the games, and one girl, about 15, asked what the little bean-bags were for. I showed her, and we started a game of O-Tedama. She soon relaxed as she moved through the stages of the game and it got harder. She was smiling and talking as we played, and when I looked around almost everyone was involved with the activities. [One girl] had picked up the knucklebones (real, not plastic) and was smiling as she threw them up and caught them on the back of her hand. She played by herself and was absorbed in the game – didn't ask anyone else to play, just kept going. There were quite a number of people with her on the red carpet, all playing different games. (*TTGFT* Diary, Thursday, 26 April 1990)

The play activities also allowed children to exercise control, freedom of choice and self-expression in an environment where these are often taken away from them. A good example is the making of the beautifully rebellious paper 'fortune tellers' or 'chatterboxes'. This is a game where children fold a paper shape with numbered flaps, which are chosen at random by another player. Under the flaps there are often rude messages for unsuspecting medical staff or parents who are asked, quite innocently, 'Do you want to play?' This game enables the reversal of the power relationship that exists between a child and the adults in the hospital:

> Play programs provide one of the few opportunities for a hospitalised child to make choices, to say 'no' and control part of his environment. (Hicks & Groves, 1982, p. 4)

The playthings in the exhibition were carefully chosen for the possibilities they offered to children who were physically incapacitated. One of the most successful toys, and the one that delighted all who used it, was a large pump-action spinning top on a stand. It produced a musical 'hum' when it rotated fast enough, and the challenge for most people – adults and children alike – was to 'make it sing':

> The pump-action top has been very popular. It's very colourful and spins on cue for even very young children, and has been particularly pleasing and rewarding for patients who have limited mobility [or strength] in their hands or arms – just one push of the plunger sets the top spinning. If someone makes the top spin fast enough to produce the three musical notes, they're usually asked to do it again and again. (*TTGFT* Diary, Thursday, 26 April 1990)

One of the most insightful reflections on the value of children's own play culture in a hospital came from one of the Play Specialists. When asked, on the last day of the exhibition, what our visit had meant to her, she said that it had broadened the scope of activities she would be using with patients, but, more than that, it had made her realise that these games mean something special to children:

> They come from *within* the child. They're not just games, but something basic that children understand. They're simple, and it's this simplicity that makes them so important. In the hospital we try to keep up with the latest toys so the children won't feel as if they're missing out, but the traditional games seem to *connect* with the children in a way that the others don't. (*TTGFT* Diary, Friday, 27 April 1990)

After the exhibition, Heather Russell wrote a brief list of her observations and thoughts on the experience. In addition to comments on traditional play, Russell had this to say about the connections made through this type of play:

> The games in *Tops, Tales and Granny's False Teeth* are perfect bedside games. The materials are cheap to buy, easy to store. The games can be played alone as the child learns the skills involved and practises them to perfection, e.g. mastering a string figure or practising throwing up and catching a jack. But best of all, they draw in other playmates – parent, child, nurse, aunts, uncles, cleaners, domestic staff, even doctors can't resist a quick go at Marbles. These games are universally known across generations, across cultures and across the hierarchy of the hospital. They can reduce what is probably the most hierarchical institution to a common level of understanding. (Russell, 1990a. p. 2)

Summary

Tops, Tales and Granny's False Teeth was an intensive, month-long project which showed that it is possible to positively affect the well-being of children in hospital by introducing their own play culture, games and storytelling into their daily lives. The anecdotal evidence is found in the comments, observations and descriptions by hospital staff, parents, patients, exhibition staff and volunteers, recorded in detail in the daily exhibition diary, evaluation reports and notes written as part of the documentation of the project.

> Apart from the joy of shared play experiences, *Tops, Tales and Granny's False Teeth* provided a link between patients, their families, hospital staff at all levels, visitors and the exhibition staff. It was a bridge between the lives of the patients inside and outside the hospital and helped to provide a focus for the children and their families to relieve the tension of the long hours spent waiting. Having opportunities to make choices, follow their own interests, learn new skills, interact with other people and engage in their own culture positively affected the patients' wellbeing and their experience of being in hospital.

The exhibition space was informal, non-clinical, child-friendly and child-sized … the soft space was shown to encourage movement and exercise, and the playing of traditional games provided enjoyment, introduced new skills and raised self-esteem among the patients. Using the tactile games materials stimulated actions beneficial to the patients and exercised muscles, hand-eye coordination, concentration and memory. The materials were suitable for most ages and physical capabilities, and were also suitable for use on the wards. (McKinty, 2010, p. 8)

In 1990, children in hospital had very little, if any, access to the everyday play opportunities enjoyed by other children. In 2013, as the new RCH, Melbourne offers children and their families a two-storey aquarium, a 'bean bag cinema', interactive science and technology displays and award-winning outdoor spaces (The Royal Children's Hospital Melbourne [RCH], 2013), we face the well-documented problem of declining opportunities for children to spontaneously play the games enjoyed by previous generations (for example Davey, 2012; Gill, 2008; Gray, 2011; Hall, 2010). The reasons why hospitalised children need to be able to connect with their own play culture remain as compelling in 2013 as in 1990.

Tops, Tales and Granny's False Teeth was an indirect approach to treating the child, which dealt with the *whole* child and the family, and as such, the experiences it provided could be considered to have real therapeutic value and ongoing benefits for the well-being of children in hospital. The project had a remarkable effect on the hospital for a relatively short time, although its influence on some of the individuals involved was permanent. Perhaps this might be a good time to reflect on the experience of this project from the past and what it might offer for the well-being of children in hospital today.

Notes

1. 'Tops' refers to spinning tops, 'Tales' refers to storytelling and 'Granny's False Teeth' is one of the steps in playing Jacks with knucklebones. When the bones are picked up they are placed between the fingers of the other hand, where they look like 'granny's false teeth'.
2. RCH is now a new, $1 billion facility, built next-door to the old hospital. The new RCH was officially opened by Her Majesty the Queen in late October 2011.
3. Several kinds of jacks from different countries were available: knucklebones, metal 'star' jacks, chopsticks and bean-bags.
4. ACFC was co-founded in 1979 by June Factor and Gwenda Davey, and has grown to be one of the largest and most significant collections of children's folklore in the world. At the time of *Tops, Tales & Granny's False Teeth* it was housed in the University of Melbourne Archive. In 1999 June Factor donated the ACFC to Museum Victoria and in 2004 the collection was placed on the prestigious UNESCO Australian *Memory of the World* Register.
5. During the *Tops, Tales & Granny's False Teeth* exhibition a daily diary was kept with observations, personal thoughts, information and notes about interactions contributed by exhibition staff and volunteers. Most of the entries were written by the exhibition co-ordinators, Judy McKinty and Dorothy Rickards.
6. O-Tedama is the name of a traditional Japanese version of Jacks, played with six small fabric bean-bags.
7. Dorothy Rickards was an author and lecturer in drama and puppetry at the Melbourne College of Advanced Education, Institute of Early Childhood Development. She wrote several books and plays for children and was a co-editor of the *Big Dipper* series with June Epstein, June Factor and Gwendda McKay.
8. June Epstein was a musician, author, teacher and academic. She was senior lecturer of music at the Melbourne College of Advanced Education, Institute of Early Childhood Development, and had a long association as a musician and writer with the Australian Broadcasting Commission.
9. Amy Saunders was an 'explainer' in the Children's Museum's 'You're IT!' exhibition of traditional children's play and a member of the singing group Tiddas.
10. 'Skinners' – like punks – people who do not have pubic hair.

PLAY AND WELLBEING

11. 'Marios' – people who wear their hair with lots of gel.
12. 'Skegs' – surfies; surfing devotees.
13. At the time of *Tops, Tales & Granny's False Teeth* Heather Russell was a folklorist conducting research into children's play. In 1986 her ethnographic study of children's relationships in a Melbourne primary school playground, titled *Play and Friendships in a Multi-Cultural Playground*, was published by Australian Children's Folklore Publications.
14. This remark was made by a mother who was playing Jacks with sheep's knucklebones.
15. A diabolo is a spinning toy shaped like two cones joined together. It is balanced on a string held between two sticks, and is sometimes used by jugglers and street performers.

References

Association for the Wellbeing of Children in Healthcare (AWCH). (2002). *Policy relating to the provision of play for children in hospital*. Gladesville: Author.

Davey, G. (2012). What is the state of play? *International Journal of Play, 1*(2), 115–116.

Factor, J. (1989). *Proposal for a 'Hands-on' exhibition of children's play traditions, Children's Hospital, Melbourne*. Unpublished. Australian Children's Folklore Collection (ACFC), reg. no. HT 8476.1, 12/1/4, Museum Victoria.

Gill, T. (2008). *No fear: Growing up in a risk averse society*. London: Calouste Gulbenkian Foundation.

Gillis, A. (1989). The effect of play on immobilized children in hospital. *International Journal of Nursing Studies, 26*(3), 261–269.

Gray, P. (2011). The decline of play and the rise of psychopathology in children and adolescents. *American Journal of Play, 3*(4), 443–463.

Hall, T. (2010). *The life and death of the Australian backyard*. Collingwood: CSIRO Publishing.

Hicks, J., & Groves, C. (1982). *Play in hospital*. Watson: Australian Early Childhood Association.

Hogg, C. (1990). *Quality management for children: Play in hospital*. London: Play in Hospital Liaison Committee.

Jennings Carmichael, G. (1991) [1891]. *Hospital children: Sketches of life and character in the Children's Hospital, Melbourne*. Main Ridge: Loch Haven Books. Originally published by George Robertson & Company.

Jokes, Limericks and Cartoons from The Incredible Times 3East (Adolescent Unit). (1990). Unpublished. ACFC, reg. no. HT 8476.1, 12/1/4, Museum Victoria.

Klein, A. J. (Ed.). (2003). *Humor in children's lives: A guidebook for practitioners*. Westport, CT: Praeger.

Langley, E. M. (1976). *Play and the hospitalized child: A selected bibliography 1960–1975*. Sydney: The Association for the Welfare of Children in Hospital.

McKinty, J. (1990, April). *TTGFT Notes for report*. Unpublished. Copy in possession of author.

McKinty, J. (2010). Tops, Tales and Granny's False Teeth: 20 years on. *Play and Folklore, 53*, 4–8.

National Association of Health Play Specialists. (2013). *Play in hospital*. Retrieved April 10, 2013, from http://nahps.org.uk/index.php?page=resources

Rhymes and games collected from visitors to Tops, Tales and Granny's False Teeth. (1990). Unpublished. ACFC, reg. no. HT 8476.1, 12/1/4, Museum Victoria.

Russell, H. (1990a). *Some observations and thoughts arising from Tops, Tales and Granny's False Teeth*. Unpublished. ACFC, reg. no. HT 8476.1, 12/1/4, Museum Victoria.

Russell, H. (1990b). *The subculture of a children's hospital*. Unpublished. ACFC, reg. no. HT 8476.1, 12/1/4, Museum Victoria.

Save the Children. (1989). *Hospital: A deprived environment for children? The case for hospital playschemes*. London: Author.

The Royal Children's Hospital Melbourne. (2013). *A-Z guide*. Retrieved September 4, 2013, from http://www.rch.org.au/info/#tabs-All

Tops, Tales & Granny's False Teeth Diary. (1990). Unpublished. ACFC, reg. no. HT 8476.1, 12/1/1, Museum Victoria.

Tops, Tales & Granny's False Teeth Evaluation: Play specialists. (1990). Unpublished. ACFC, reg. no. HT 8476.1, 2/1/4, Museum Victoria.

Ure, C. (1993). The rights of children in the hospital environment: Play and the importance of the adult's role. *UN Convention on the Rights of the Child: Implications for policy and practice in Australian paediatric health care.* Proceedings of the AWCH National Conference, University of Western Sydney, NSW, 7–8 October. Westmead: Association for the Welfare of Child Health, pp. 25–31.

Living in a broken world: how young children's well-being is supported through playing out their earthquake experiences

Amanda Bateman[a], Susan Danby[b] and Justine Howard[c]

[a]*Early Years Research Centre, Faculty of Education, University of Waikato, Hamilton, New Zealand;* [b]*Children and Youth Research Centre, School of Early Childhood, Faculty of Education, Queensland University of Technology, Australia;* [c]*Centre for Child Health and Well-being, College of Human and Health Sciences, Swansea University, Wales, UK*

> The therapeutic value of play can be shown in spontaneous play situations following children's experiences of traumatic events. Following the events of the Christchurch earthquakes in New Zealand in 2010 and 2011, an investigation was conducted of how children used the earthquake event as a catalyst in pretend play with peers and in discussions with teachers. Supporting children's well-being is a focus area in New Zealand early childhood education, as it is a strand of the national curriculum *Te Whāriki* [Ministry of Education. (1996). *Te Whāriki. He whāriki mātauranga mōngā mokopuna o Aotearoa: Early childhood curriculum.* Wellington: Learning Media]. In this article, children are observed engaging in pretend play episodes, and with personalized Learning Story books, to explore personal reflections of the earthquake, prompting the children to make reference to things being 'broken' and needing 'fixing'. Analysis shows how the content of the pretend play experiences helped the children to come to terms with their experiences. Affording children time and interactional opportunities to play out and discuss traumatic experiences contributes to the psychological well-being of participants following a traumatic event.

Well-being, children's play and traumatic events

Play is important for children's emotional health and well-being. Children learn in a variety of ways but they learn more effectively when they learn through play (McInnes, Howard, Miles, & Crowley, 2009). When children engage in play they demonstrate increased meta-cognition and self-regulation (Whitebread, 2010). They make sense of the world around them, trying out and trying on roles, identities, and experiences. The concept that play is 'not real' offers dramatic distance and, to a certain extent, frees participants from the consequences of their actions. Play protects children from the fear of failure and acts as a defense mechanism for self-efficacy and esteem. Play is also a means by which children can express worries and concerns, and communicate their understanding of the world (Haight, Black, Ostler, and Sheridan, 2006). In their play, children may feel more comfortable discussing thoughts and feelings and, as such, play is an effective resource for counselors and therapists to draw on to understand children's degrees of well-being. The inherent therapeutic potential of play, apart from therapy, manifests in spontaneous play situations also, particularly when children have experienced traumatic events (Webb, 2007).

Children may re-enact stressful events directly in their pretend play. Particular themes may permeate their activities as they try to come to terms with their experiences. When painful or difficult feelings are not talked about, they can manifest as problematic behaviours or neuroses (Sunderland, 2006). When children have opportunities to play and talk about challenging events, conflict and anxiety are less likely to be repressed and less likely to impact negatively on behaviour and development (Little, Little, & Gutierrez, 2009). With caution, adults can observe children at play to learn about their thoughts and feelings. In addition, as play partners, adults can help children come to terms with difficult situations and act as role models, providing emotional cues as to how stressful events might be managed. Haight et al. (2006) have described how sensitive adult–child interaction and calm communication during play enhances resiliency and the successful resolution of trauma. Talking and storying about traumatic experiences serves multiple purposes. These opportunities allow children to express how they have understood an unfamiliar or distressing situation and to explore their feelings about it. Sensitive interaction with adults through this process means that children can receive acknowledgement that an event was extraordinary and be assured that the event need not undermine their sense of trust and confidence in the world around them.

Play is an important mechanism for children faced with adverse situations such as war, poverty, or abandonment (Fearn & Howard, 2011). Play contributes to children's feelings of emotional well-being (Howard & McInnes, 2012). Talking about traumatic events facilitates clear and coherent remembering that, in turn, enables the process of forgetting to begin (McMahon, 2009).

The emphasis on well-being in the New Zealand early childhood curriculum, *Te Whāriki*

The New Zealand early childhood curriculum, *Te Whāriki*, is world renowned for its holistic approach to young children's development (Waller, 2005). The framework is structured by weaving together principles that encompass five strands: Well-being, Belonging, Contribution, Communication, and Exploration. Guidance under the Well-being strand states that children should 'experience an environment where: their health is promoted; their emotional well-being is nurtured; they are kept safe from harm' (Ministry of Education, 1996, p. 15). The curriculum document recognizes well-being as the child's right in order for them to develop secure relationships with people, places, and things.

The teachers' attention to supporting children's emotional well-being is evident in how they promote and support spontaneous play activities and record them in Learning Story books for children's later reflection. The materials and prompts used in play episodes can stimulate the recall of events and experiences, often to a greater extent than verbal questioning alone (Priestly, Roberts, & Pipe, 1999). These materials and prompts need not necessarily be directly associated with events and experiences and might be metaphoric (Cirillo & Cryder, 1995; Schaefer & Drewe, 2011). Of importance is that the dramatic distance created via pretense enables information to be processed and organized in a safe context where the sense of self is protected.

Although children use their talk to communicate during free play, they also engage in talk with teachers when discussing learning episodes, which teachers then record in the child's Learning Story book. Sharing in dialogue about play events provides children with an opportunity to experience agency through engaging in talk about their personal experiences (Carr & Lee, 2012). The promotion of children's agency is essential in the development of well-being in order to support their feelings of self-worth (Mashford-Scott & Church, 2011). Through recall and reflection, children's talk about their play experiences affords the process of meaning-making and understandings, about events to be shared with valued others such as friends and family members. Through narrative, whether *in* free play or during exchange with teachers *about* play, children's talking about their experiences is 'an achievement of social practice that lends stability to the child's social life' (Bruner, 1990, p. 68).

This article contributes to understanding how teachers promote children's well-being in everyday teaching practice following a natural disaster, as observed recently following the Christchurch earthquakes in New Zealand. At the same time, the teachers themselves were experiencing the same traumatic aftermath as the children in their classrooms. As shown here, children engaged in pretend play and talked about their experiences using Learning Story books as tools to support emotional well-being. Telling stories is a strategy often used by counselors and other professionals to support trauma recovery with children and young people (Ertl, Pfeiffer, Schauer, Elbert, & Neuner, 2012; Stokoe & Edwards, 2006). Within early-years settings, teachers are responsible for promoting young children's social and emotional health, particularly in times of traumatic events.

Much of the literature surrounding the value of play in relation to children's ability to cope with traumatic events is clinical, establishing the efficacy of a play-based approach to counseling or psychotherapy (Bratton & Ray, 2000; Bratton, Ray, Rhine, & Jones, 2005). Petriwskyj (2013) describes how re-enactment through play, along with talking and storying, were particularly powerful tools for increasing children's confidence and resiliency when recovering from trauma following natural disaster. In particular, with play as their tool for communication, children were able to reframe the traumatic event, rebuilding their confidence and security in an environment that had, through the disaster, become associated with instability and fear. Children can also re-enact specific traumatic events in their play so that they are able to gain control over any negative effects. Baggerly and Exum (2008) describe the play of a five-year-old boy with a toy dinosaur who had experienced Hurricane Katrina. During therapy sessions, the boy named the toy dinosaur 'the sea monster' and spun it in circles, repeatedly knocking down the doll family and furniture in the doll house. In a later session, he used the army men to kill the sea monster. This, they argue, demonstrates how the boy re-enacted his hurricane experience in order to gain mastery of the situation. Although focusing on effective clinical techniques for children following natural disaster, Baggerly and Exum (2008) not only describe the effectiveness of combining cognitive behavioural therapy, family therapy, and play therapy, they also highlight the importance of children's day to day play experiences with friends, family members, and non-clinical professionals. Howard and McInnes (2012) demonstrate that event within a day to day educational context, when children engage in activities they perceive as play, they show heightened signs of emotional well being such as contentment, confidence and perseverance. In addition, the same study demonstrated that during play, children tried out far more purposeful problem solving skills compared to the skills they used in less playful situations; in less playful contexts, they more often repeated actions they knew to be incorrect. Whilst this study was focused on problem solving from a cognitive perspective, the same is true when children are dealing with problems at an emotional level. When engaged in play, children develop ideas as to how a problem might be resolved and test these out at their own pace and in their own way. Through their play, children are able to discern adaptive coping mechanisms from those that are maladaptive (Felix, Bond, & Shelby, 2006).

The Christchurch earthquake

On 4 September 2010, the first of two significant earthquakes hit Christchurch, New Zealand. The first earthquake measured 7.1 in magnitude, occurring during the night with no deaths recorded. The second of the large earthquakes involved a 6.3 magnitude that struck on 22 February 2011

PLAY AND WELLBEING

during the daytime; the second earthquake resulted in the death of 185 people (police.gov, NZ Police 2012). As the February earthquake struck in the daytime, when it occurred many people were at work and their children at school or preschool, heightening anxiety amongst families as to the state and whereabouts of their loved ones. This was the case at the New Brighton Community Preschool and Nursery in Christchurch; its location was severely affected by the earthquake and many family members were working in the city centre at the time. All parents and children of the New Brighton Preschool were reunited at the end of the day. Following a structural inspection, the preschool reopened shortly after the earthquake event. Many post-earthquake events such as loss of water, aftershocks, and road closures had occurred and were still occurring during the study. The teachers made a conscious decision to support communication and play involving earthquakes, in order to support children to come to terms with their experiences. The teachers are not counselors or psychologists, and they did not engage in clinical therapeutic sessions with the children. They did, however, make themselves available to talk with the children, support them through their play experiences, and let them share their experiences of the traumatic events of the earthquakes.

The following story was written by the New Brighton Community Preschool and Nursery teachers and distributed to the families following the February earthquake; it offers insight into the events of the earthquake from the perspective of teachers who experienced it:

Our Earthquake story ...

On February 22nd lives were changed and will struggle to be the same again. Christchurch came to a stand still as the whole world watched in shock. Buildings were brought down, and searched by hand and machine ... the list [of victims] grew longer.

On this day the world became one, joining hands with us, bringing love and hope as we stick together to rebuild this city, our city, the city of Christchurch, Aotearoa ...

Just before 1pm on the day of the magnitude 6.3 earthquake the teachers and children at the centre were going about their daily routines and play. Preschool kai time [meal] had come to an end and many of the children were playing outside. The nursery was quiet and calm too; most of the children were sleeping in the sleep room.

We heard a long, low rumble and the building started to shake. It did not take us long to realize this was not just another aftershock but something bigger. The teachers in the preschool playground gathered the children onto the grassy area (many of the children were here already, playing a game, which made this task much easier!) Teachers worked together to form a safe circle around the group of children, calling it the 'Ring-a-ring-a-rosy hug'. Children in the preschool indoor environment were told to get under the tables. The teachers got under the tables too, around the outside with the children in the middle. The teachers in the nursery reached for the toddlers and stayed down on the floor where it was safe.

The shaking and rocking subsided. Those people inside were instructed to exit the building and meet the rest of the whanau on the grass. We quickly realized that the sleep room door had jammed. Thanks to some quick thinking and MacGyver-like actions, some teachers got the door open. Some children in the sleep room were crying but as soon as a teacher appeared and said, 'Hi everyone, I'm here,' the crying stopped and was replaced with broad smiles. We worked together to get these children outside to be reunited with their friends.

More quick thinking and action meant that in no time at all we had a collection of beanbags, pillows and blankets to make a lovely calm and comfortable outdoor lounge. Food and water was shared out and we had a make-shift picnic, complete with lots of singing and story telling! One-by-one our parents arrived to pick up their children ...

To the children present at preschool on that day, you did yourselves and your parents very proud. You were all so brave and trusting that we could make this situation work.

To the parents who walked through the gates wondering what on earth they would meet, we saw your pain and then your relief. We knew we had your greatest treasures in our care and worked to ensure your treasures were kept safe and sound.

To the teachers there on the day, you all made this work and ensured all with us were ok to say the least.

New Brighton Community Preschool and Nursery, long will you remain a key and important part of our community. This is due to the foundation the centre is built upon, that is the people, the people, the people.

Supporting children to talk about their experiences is a central concern of early childhood curricula (Ministry of Education, 1996). There are few documented examples, however, showing how teachers sensitively engage in conversations, after children have experienced traumatic events. As Bateman, Danby, and Howard (2013) discuss, communicating about ongoing everyday events following a disaster helps children come to terms with, and make sense of, their situations. Encouraging children to talk about their everyday experiences helps them to communicate their feelings and beliefs and to develop strategies for building relationships with others. When traumatic events are being talked about, these interactions place even greater emphasis on adults to support the children in sensitive ways. These communications support young children as members of their local communities, helping them realize that they are not alone in being affected by the disaster. This sense of belonging strengthens the children's sense of well-being, important for building positive identities as individuals and as members of society.

The method

Investigating everyday interactions

Investigating the interactions of children and teachers moment by moment in everyday early childhood settings builds understandings of how children and teachers attend to the daily activities of the setting, and the strategies they employ to make sense of what they are doing and how they engage with others around them. Using ethnomethodological (Garfinkel, 1967) and conversation analysis (Sacks, 1995) approaches, analysis can examine the joint interactions of participants as they produce social action and collaboratively construct together shared meanings of events. A particular analytic focus is on the sequential development of interactions (Sacks, Schegloff, & Jefferson, 1974), where attention is given to how participants orient to what the speaker has just said and then contribute further to the talk. Known as adjacency pairs, where the first utterance sets up the second utterance, these turns work to build intersubjectivity, as participants work to build and maintain shared meanings and shared social orders (Danby & Baker, 2000; Heritage, 1984). In this article, analysis shows how the children and teachers oriented themselves to talk about the earthquakes through their play and reflective talk, providing interactive spaces to build and share meanings of the event. For the sake of readers who are not linguists, the talk is shown without formal linguistic notation. The analysis shows how the teachers engaged in the strategy of using recipient design, listening for how the children wanted to be heard and designing their subsequent turns accordingly (Danby, Baker, & Emmison, 2005; Sacks, 1995).

The New Brighton Community Preschool and Nursery is physically located on the outskirts of Christchurch city centre on the East coast of the South Island of New Zealand. As with most early-childhood centres in New Zealand, the outdoor area is used as a play space, where a considerable amount of time is spent during everyday activity. The outside area has structured play equipment including a large fort, a bridge over a concrete slope, a large grassy area, a large sunken sandpit, and decking with a roofed conservatory room. This setting affords opportunities for free play as well as more structured play activity.

At the time of the project, there were an approximately equal number of girls and boys attending, ranging from birth to school age; the children attending were from a range of backgrounds including Māori and white New Zealanders.

Data collection

The study was initiated to investigate the ways in which teachers and children engaged in everyday teaching and learning following the Christchurch earthquake. Ethical consent was gained from the lead researcher's academic institution, as well as all teachers at the preschool, all families who had children attending the preschool and all children present at the preschool. Consent to participate in the project was secured from 8 teachers and 52 children. The preschool-aged children and toddlers took turns to wear a wireless Bluetooth microphone and to be video recorded during their everyday activities. Eight hours and twenty-one minutes of video footage was collected over the period of one week from Monday 14 November to Friday 18 November 2011. Talk about the earthquake and the associated continuing disruptions, as well as pretend play involving safety jackets and traffic cones, were evident throughout the data even though the footage was collected nine months after the fatal earthquake event.

Planning and organization of this research, following an unpredicted earthquake, necessitated the nine-month delay before data could be gathered. A team needed to be assembled; the lead researcher approached two co-researchers with relevant expertise. Cooperation of a preschool team, who were in a relevant location to be involved in the research, was sought. Ethical issues arose, given the goal of investigating post-disaster human behaviour. Ethical matters were complicated by the almost overwhelming presence of journalists and researchers who swarmed to post-disaster sites, often creating unintentional barriers due to the 'little consideration for the ethical boundaries surrounding highly sensitive post-disaster issues [resulting in] ongoing trauma and waning tolerance for outsiders' (Parkes, 2011, p. 31). Once an interested preschool was found, the process of achieving ethical consent for the project from the lead researcher's university ethics committee, the preschool teachers, families, and children was undertaken. All these issues contributed to the research being initiated some time following the earthquake; nevertheless, this process was essential for establishing a sound and ethical research design, where ethical considerations were paramount.

Earthquake talk in teacher–child discourse

In this section, we present two extracts that show two children, Cayden (Extract 1) and Baxter (Extract 2), talking about their earthquake experiences using their Learning Story books, part of the school's curricula, to support their telling. Both Cayden and Baxter were four-year-old white New Zealand children; they were almost ready for transition to primary school and had been friends for some time during their attendance at New Brighten Community Preschool and Nursery. In Extract 1, Cayden talks about his experiences of the earthquake and, towards the end of his story, enters into playful talk about the earthquake with Baxter. In Extract 2, Baxter talks about his experiences involving significant others, as documented in his Learning Story book. Both extracts show how children made sense of elements from the earthquake by recounting their shared experiences and normalizing aspects of what happened, through their descriptions and assessments of the effects of the earthquake. The children oriented to their environment as one that was broken and fixed, revealing the connection between their documented experiences here (Extracts 1 and 2) and their play activities in the play episodes that follow (Extracts 3–5).

PLAY AND WELLBEING

Extract 1: Cayden

Cayden approached the researcher and asked if he could show her his book. The researcher agreed and Cayden placed his book on the table and opened it on a page about the earthquake. Cayden held the clip-on microphone close to his mouth and began speaking into it whilst pointing, with his other hand, to the picture in his book.

01	Researcher	okay
02	Cayden:	thethe earthquake breaked the stuff so we
03		so we didn't go there (*pause*) coz
04		there was there was lots of holes (*pause*) and
05		and er(*turns 2 pages*)oopsy(*looks at*
06		*Baxter and turns 1 page back*) coz the
07		earthquake was strong (*pause*) and and
08	Baxter:	and it broke our fence(*laughs andleans towards*
09		*Cayden and makes eye contact*)
10	Cayden:	and it broked the preschools fence(*looks at*
11		*his book*)
12	Baxter:	and that was and they was say that was the
13		earthquake was a poopoo
14		(*long pause*)
15	Cayden:	(*smiles and looks at researcher, then to*
16		*Baxter and then at his book*) coz the
17		earthquakes strong but we don't know what
18		happened
19	Baxter:	say so so say now the earthquake was
20		a poopoo okay(*leaning across the table*
21		*towards Cayden*)
22	Cayden:	coz the earthquake (*pause*) is re:allytough
23		(*Baxter leans in, Cayden makes very brief*
24		*contact with him and looks down at his book*)
25	Baxter:	say that the earthquake is a poopoo
26	Cayden:	(*cough*) the earthqake is really strong
27	Baxter:	no the earthquake is a poopoo
28		(*long pause*)
29	Cayden:	I didn't write that in my book ((*leans*
30		*towards Baxter*))
31	Baxter:	okay say it (*pause*) and then it might get in
32		your book
33	Cayden:	the earthquake is a really reallyreally
34		tough
35	Baxter:	and the earthquake is a poo (*laughs*)
36	Cayden:	the earthquake is really stro:ng
37	Baxter:	and it's a
38		poopoo
39	Cayden:	don't go in don't go near the glass or uh
40		hurt you
41		(*Baxter leaves the table and talks to the*
42		*researcher. Cayden waits until Baxter leaves the*
43		*researcher and then continues with his story*)
44	Cayden:	and the earthquake (*pause*) iisis
45		not really nice (*pause*) but (*pause*) itis
46		really strong(*pause*) but it break
47		everythingof the preschool (*pause*) the some
48		of it is broken(*pause*) so we needed the
49		wor um eh a different world (*long pause*) and the
50		earthquake come all the preschools houses

51	(*pause*) and the earthquake was really strong
52	(pause) but (*pause*) you live somewhere else if
53	the earthquake happens (*pause*) that's it
54	((*looks at researcher and smiles*))

Cayden began talking about the events in his book by immediately referring to the earthquake and how it broke things (line 01) and how there were lots of holes (line 04). He continued to make further references to the earthquake breaking things throughout his entire telling. His reference to 'we didn't go there' (line 03) is made relevant later in the transcript (lines 49, 52–53) when reference is made to the many families, including Cayden's, having to move to another location, while their houses were assessed and possibly repaired following the earthquake damage. Cayden's introduction of the earthquake as a topic showed how these events are significant to him, despite happening nine months earlier. He chose to talk about this and not other topics (Enfield, 2013).

When Baxter joined in with Cayden's storytelling (line 08), Cayden initially accepted Baxter's contribution to the story as he reiterated what Baxter said about the preschool's fence (line 10). Baxter then instructed Cayden to say that the earthquake 'was a poo-poo' (line 13). As Danby and Baker (1998) show, young boys use scatological language such as 'poo-poo' to assert declarations of power over an event. Used here, Baxter's scatological language worked to counteract the effects of the earthquake. Cayden took some time to respond, perhaps aware the researcher was listening as he looked at her, and then smiled, indicating that Baxter's scatological formulation of the earthquake was received positively. However, Baxter continued quite insistently throughout the episode to refer to the earthquake as 'poo' or 'poo-poo'. This could also indicate that Baxter found the experience of talking seriously about the earthquake uncomfortable and attempted to manage this by interacting playfully in order to reframe the negative experience (Baggerly and Exum, 2008). Baxter's need to increase the playfulness in this episode could also have arisen because the story did not belong to him. As he was a listener and not in control of events he may have attempted to manage this by adding playfulness and humor, acting as a distraction from the traumatic event and/or restoring feelings of wellbeing (Berg, Parr, Bradley, & Berry, 2009). This position is supported when we consider Baxter's own factual recall of events with no inclusion of humor below (Extract 2).

Despite Baxter's persisting attempts to have Cayden say that the earthquake was a 'poopoo' (lines 20, 25, 27, 35, and 38), Cayden continued to reiterate that the earthquake was 'strong' (lines 17), 'really strong' (lines 26 and 36), 'tough' (line 22), and 'really really really tough' (lines 33–34), placing additional emphasis on these words (Walker, 2013). The more that Baxter insisted that Cayden call the earthquake a 'poopoo', the more Cayden's descriptions recognized the power and force of the earthquake. Cayden ignored Baxter's comments and followed his own agenda as he went on to give a justification for his action and explained that he 'didn't write that in my book' (line 29). His rationale oriented to a rule about Learning Story books: if something is not explicitly written in the book, then you cannot say that it is. On hearing this, Baxter aligned with this rule when he suggested that Cayden should 'say it' so that this idea legitimately could be written in his book (lines 31–32). The topic of how to describe the earthquake was brought to closure when Cayden introduced a new topic, a rule that people must avoid glass as it can be harmful (lines 39–40). Following this, Baxter left, and Cayden went on to tell more about the earthquake events that were documented in his book, making explicit reference to remembering the earthquake as being very destructive (lines 44–53).

Shown in this episode is the value of children being able to reflect upon, and talk about, their experiences, identifying the seriousness that children bring to authoring stories based on their

PLAY AND WELLBEING

experiences and events. Both boys' persistence to pursue their own descriptions of the earthquake shows that each made meaning of the event in their own way. Being able to share these meanings through the Learning Story books shows the value of such classroom resources, and how opportunities to talk with friends helps with the process of shared meaning-making. Providing contexts for such talk is a way that teachers can plan for opportunities for children to engage with other members to support emotional well-being (Ministry of Education, 1996).

Extract 2: Baxter

In this episode, Baxter showed the researcher his Learning Story book and started talking about events depicted within it. The researcher did not say anything as Baxter turned the pages of the book, selecting events to talk about.

```
01   BAX:   so these two truckshere(points to
02           page) they brokecoz coz w coz w coz thather
03           some of them got broken coz coz from the
04           earthquake s soum w we got some new trucks and
05           steelloaders and (pause) th we still gotthese
06           (pause) rollers (points topicture) andand
07           then we h went to (turns page) have a lookand
08           and we sawthis (points to picture and moves
09           fingerin a circular motion) big big digger and
10           (pause) then one day (turns page) fromthe
11           earthquake we we me and Corbin and mymum and my
12           friend Sandra and Pete and (pause) hisother friend
13           comed around andhad a look but we hada first
14           lookso we so we um we did itall in
15           here(points to picture) with (pause)u with my
16           friend Corbin with somvivasurvivaljackets from
17           my hou some fromfrom actuallySandra bought it
18           that day(turns page) sothen (pause) Corbin
19           didn't want it so I so he tookit off sothen um
20           they were maked a new fence(pause)(looks at
21           researcher and then out of thewindow and points
22           towards the window) ofoverthereand (pause) so
23           that's (pointsto picture)the same fence as that
24           one(points towards thewindow) and thenthis
25           fence (points to picture)brokedfr/ from the
26           earthquake s so then we hadgot this one and
27           that's the kia* teacherLeane andthere's me and my
28           friendMataioand my friend Kiro and my friend
29           Oliviaand my friend Lucy and my friend Lukeand
30           my friend u a amber and my friend Daniel so
31           and so then(continues talking about events
32           documented in his book)
*Kai is the Māori word for food
```

Baxter began telling about the events documented in his Learning Story book by referring to the pictures to prompt his talk and using photographs for 'setting up visual cues for remembering after the event' (Carr & Lee, 2012, p. 36). He pointed to specific photographs (e.g. lines 01, 06, 08–09) to direct the researcher's attention and chose to talk about only some photographs, making his reference as 'a matter of selection' (Enfield, 2013, p. 433). In introducing the topic, there were many instances of pauses as he broke off what he was saying (lines 1–6) and repeated words (e.g. 'coz' in lines 2–3); this feature of talk is found to be one of the conversational strategies used when telling difficult news (Silverman & Peräkylä, 1990). Within these initial turns of talk, Baxter placed emphasis on the words 'broke' (line 02) and 'earthquake' (line 04), which drew attention to the importance of these words for the teller (Walker, 2013). In introducing the topic, Baxter produced his agency through the choices he made in relation to what he talked about, and what he did not talk about, in his book.

As his telling continued (lines 11–12), Baxter used the word 'we' twice and self-repaired by naming who the people were (Corbin, his mum, and three friends). The use of the word 'we' ties together people as members of a specific group (Butler, 2008), where those members are affiliated through friendships (Bateman, 2012b). In this instance, Baxter demonstrated his preference for using names of people rather than using the collective 'we'. Naming participants can be explained as an interactional resource designed to inform the recipient (the researcher) who may not be aware of who the collective 'we' include (Pomerantz & Heritage, 2013). This strategy demonstrates Baxter's social competence in relaying information about an event to a less knowledgeable audience, the researcher. His recall of events through reference to himself and friends who were involved in the incident revealed the referenced people as members of a group who have experienced the earthquake events (Bateman, Danby, & Howard, 2013). Through identifying himself as a member of a group affected by the earthquake, Baxter asserted himself as having reciprocal relationships with people who have experienced the same event (Ministry of Education, 1996); recognition of not being alone in experiencing this event, but one of a group, actively develops a sense of well-being, where recollections of the event are shared. His recall of events showed the common themes of things being broken from the earthquake, and the presence of family and friends during that time. These entwined themes were ones that Baxter returned to many times during the course of the week the researcher spent with the children. What Baxter chose to continue to talk about remained important at the time of this telling, which was nine months after the event; the tellings involved him in continuing to share his experiences with his peers, teachers and others who listened, such as the visiting researcher.

Pretend play about broken things and fixing things

In Extracts 1 and 2, we observed how Cayden and Baxter talked about their earthquake experiences when looking through their Learning Story books, making explicit reference to things being broken and needing fixing. In this section, we discuss three episodes of children's play that show how the children made links to things being broken and needing fixing in their everyday pretend play. The children themselves oriented to the earthquake in their play, through the explicit reference to the words 'broken' and 'fixing', demonstrating that these were significant activities to them at this time, in this place, nine months after the earthquake. That such activities were continuing to take place so many months later shows the extent to which they were important for the children as a topic for building play activities.

Extract 3: Coz it's broken

This episode involved Ben, a three-year-old white New Zealand child, and four-year-old Cayden, introduced in Extract 1. The outdoor area afforded the opportunity for children of different ages to play together, encouraging a wide diversity of play partners for the attending children. The play began with Ben who ascended the climbing wall to approach Cayden who was playing on the upper level of the climbing frame.

PLAY AND WELLBEING

01	Ben:	stop (pause) come on lets go and see Cayden
02		(spoken in a robotic voice)
03	?:no	
04	Ben:	you look after mine while I see (pause) seeCayden
05		(approaches the climbing frame)
06		(long pause)
07	Cayden:	hey why wouldsomebody knocked this building
08		brick down
09		Teacher:alright (pause) Kapai
10	Ben:	(approaches the climbing frame and starts
11		climbing up the wall towards Cayden))
12	Cayden:	setting the building up now(pause)
13		get down (uses arms and legs to block the
14		entrance and then kicks his leg out towards Ben)
15	Ben:	(stays where he is)
16	Cayden:	((moves away from the entrance and brings back
17		traffic cones. Places one cone in front of Ben))
18	Ben:	((moves up the climbing wall slightly))
19	Cayden:	urgh((pushes Ben's shoulder))
20	Ben:	(stays where he is)
21	Cayden:	what you doinup here
22	Ben:	(undetermined utterance)
23		((Ben remains on the climbing wall whilst Cayden
24		fetches more cones and lines them up in front of
25		him))
26	Ben:	why are you tryinto not let me in
27	Cayden:	um coz it's broken(leans towards Ben with his
28		hands on is knees))
29		(long pause)
30	Ben:	well I'm a worker
31		(long pause)
32	Cayden:	alright(kicks the cones out of the entrance
33		and laughs)
34	Ben:	(laughs and enters the top level of the
35		climbing frame)

This episode started when Ben suggested that he and his friends see Cayden by using a collective word 'lets' (line 01) to establish a cohort (Butler, 2008). However, none of his friends wanted to join him so he went alone towards the climbing frame, where Cayden was standing at the top. Ben immediately began engaging in pretend play by referring to the climbing frame as a knocked down building (line 07). Here, Cayden's pretend play is done by reference to broken buildings, a common occurrence in his current post-earthquake environment, where there is much rebuilding and cordoning off of buildings with the use of traffic cones.

When Cayden saw Ben approaching, he indicated that he was not yet ready for Ben as he had not yet set up the building. Cayden explicitly told Ben to get down as he used his arms and legs to block the entry, maximizing a joint understanding (Bateman, 2012a). He then further blocked the entrance, this time by using traffic cones. However, as Ben continued to move forward slightly, Cayden pushed him and asked him what he was doing up there (lines 19–20). It is not possible to hear what Ben said next, but he remained on the climbing frame. The outcome was that Ben was excluded through the use of rules made up by Cayden (that the building is not ready for public access) and by the social rules evident in the children's everyday lives (Cromdal, 2001), and the use of traffic cones that blocked the disrupted and broken areas.

Cayden's use of the rules of his immediate cultural context worked to legitimately exclude Ben, which Ben recognized. When Ben asked Cayden why he was being excluded (line 26), Cayden reiterated his use of the cultural context to justify the exclusion by telling Ben that 'it's broken', offering a legitimate excuse for the exclusion, as a person cannot access a broken building. Following a significant pause (line 29) Ben aligned with the rules of the game in a way that legitimately allowed him access; in pretend play mode he told Cayden that he was a worker (line 30). Cayden accepted this as a genuine reason to be allowed in, and allowed access to the 'broken building'.

It is possible that this re-enactment of the event gave Cayden a sense of control over what was a chaotic experience (Petriwskyj 2013). Pretend play offers the opportunity for children to play out their traumatic experiences in a safe and consistent environment (Haight et al., 2006), where children have autonomy over their choice of play activity. This play enables Cayden and Ben to make sense of the events they have experienced, creating a narrative that enables understanding and acceptance (McMahon, 2009). References to broken buildings work to exclude children from activities and also as resources to gain play entry. Teachers' provision of opportunities for children to engage in pretend play is one way to support their agency and decision-making through social interactions, necessary elements for supporting children's wellbeing (Ministry of Education, 1996).

Extract 4: Look from the earthquake

This extract begins with a group of children, including Baxter and Cayden, who were sitting in the large sandpit area making volcanoes with the sand. A male teacher has approached Baxter to help him.

Extract 4

01	Teacher:	ok hang on I've justgotta help Baxter(pause)
02		phwor (pause) right you ready
03	Baxter:	Yep
04		(long pause)
05	Teacher:	now it's not gonna work properly so it's gonna
06		turn out like that again okay
07		(long pause)
08	Teacher:	but if
09	Baxter:	how did you know
10		(pause)
11	Teacher:	coz the sand's too soft(*turns bucket upside*
12		*down and then lifts it up, revealing the*
13		*sandcastle*)ah no
14		(pause)
15	Baxter:	there we are, my first volcano
16		(*teacher stands and walks towards other children*)
17	Cayden:	but it's not the same as mine eh
18		(*Baxter fills his bucket with sand again*)
19	Baxter:	I'll make you a decent one for you okay(*talks*
20		*to Cayden*)
21	Cayden:	Polly was trying to smash it
22		(pause)
23	Baxter:	look from the earthquake(*points to a*
24		*crack in his sandcastle*) it's got a crack in it
25		(*knocks it down with his spade and laughs and then*
26		*starts to walk away*)
27		(long pause)
28	Teacher:	what happened to your volcano Baxter
29		(*approaches Baxter*)
30	Baxter:	Broken
31	Teacher:	how did you break it
32	Baxter:	(*quickly walks away*)

PLAY AND WELLBEING

The teacher's entry was marked by his warning to Baxter as he explained that the sandcastle may not turn out properly as the sand was too soft (lines 1–11). By preempting a possibly unsatisfactory situation, in which Baxter might be disappointed by the outcome (which happened previously as indicated by the teacher's talk in lines 5–6), the teacher treats the situation cautiously and as a matter of delicacy. This 'expressive caution' (Silverman, 1997, p. 66) was questioned by Baxter (line 9), suggesting opposition to the teacher's stance, and he is proved right as the sandcastle building does work (lines 11–15).

Baxter then initiated contact with his friend Cayden, saying that he was going to make a sandcastle for him (line 19). However, when making it, a crack appeared in his own sandcastle. Baxter initially drew his friend's attention to the event when he shouted 'look from the earthquake' (line 23) and pointed to the break whilst telling everyone that it had a crack (line 24). Baxter reacted to the situation physically by knocking the sandcastle down with his spade and he then walked away (line 25). The teacher asked Baxter 'what happened', a question found to be asked of children in order to draw attention to a problem and mobilize a discussion about that problem (Bateman, Danby, & Howard, 2013; Kidwell, 2011), and Baxter responded that the volcano was 'broken' (line 30). The teacher's next question suggested that Baxter had broken the sandcastle (line 31) and, rather than explain that he had not broken it, Baxter walked away, quickly disaffiliating himself from the interaction. Even without intent, Baxter's play naturally evolved to include elements of trauma-related material, demonstrating the potentially therapeutic value of spontaneous play as a form of communication and understanding (Webb, 2007). Cracks in a sandcastle spontaneously led to talk about the earthquake, also demonstrating that pretend play need not directly model the traumatic experience (Schaefer & Drewe, 2011).

In this episode, Baxter used his past experiences of the earthquake and related it to the everyday play activity of building a sandcastle. Although the teacher did treat the situation cautiously at the outset (Silverman, 1997), his use of the direct question about the immediate situation could have been interpreted as confrontational (Hutchby, 2007). The teacher's strategy of seeking an opportunity for further talk about breaking things, and initiating a possible 'active listening' sequence (Antaki, 2008; Hutchby, 2007), in this instance was not successful. Potentially, teachers can work to support emotional healing through play (McMahon, 2009), by taking a role of offering support for children 'in expressing, articulating, and resolving a range of emotions' (Ministry of Education, 1996, p. 49). However, in this episode, Baxter chose to disaffiliate himself from the interaction by walking away, indicating that he perhaps was not ready to discuss this further, an action accepted by the teacher.

Extract 5: The earthquake waked me up

Two three-year-old girls, Zoe and Narelle, were playing together with a group of four girls on large pieces of soft PVC covered foam in the preschool garden. Zoe and Narelle are both white New Zealand born girls who often played together, especially engaging in pretend play involving family members that included 'a baby' as Zoe has recently had a new baby sister. The episode began when Zoe laid down on a piece of foam and pretended to cry while Narelle talked to another girl on a mat nearby.

01	Zoe:	*mummymummy help mummy(pause)*	
02		*mummy mummymummymummymummymummy*	
03		*mummy(looks around and then at Narelle)*	
04	Narelle:	*cock-a-dock-a-doo*	*(approaches Zoe)*
05	Zoe:	*mummymummymummy*	
06	Narelle:	*what*	
07		*(long pause)*	

08	Zoe:	*um erthe earthquake waked me up*
09	Narelle:	*I will fix it*
10		*(long pause)*
11	Zoe:	*will you fix da earthquake*
12		*(long pause)*
13	Narelle:	*go to sleep baby*
14	Zoe:	*okay(lays back down)*

In a pretend play sequence that began by mapping the family role of mother (Butler & Weatherall, 2006), Zoe called out to her friend. She called for help (line 01), indicating that the game involved Zoe being rescued. Zoe mapped Narelle in the role of 'Mummy' through calling to her and making eye contact (line 03) to maximize the possibility of Narelle understanding that it is her being addressed (Filipi, 2009). Zoe's initial repeat of calling for her 'mother' along with the word 'help' had a matter of urgency about it in that a number of the reference terms were spoken quickly and linked together (line 02).

Narelle responded to Zoe's initiation of pretend play by approaching Zoe and making the sound of a cockerel (line 04), which indicated that she was orienting to Zoe lying down and possibly sleeping. Zoe called Narelle in her role of Mummy again, steering the play back to the roles of family members. Narelle's reply was a question that gave Zoe the floor to speak and to reveal the reason for the call. After a brief pause Zoe responded with the conversation fillers 'um' and 'er', which worked to hold the floor for her (Schegloff, Jefferson, & Sacks, 1977) before answering with 'the earthquake waked me up' (line 08). Narelle promptly replied in her role as the Mummy by telling Zoe that she would fix the earthquake, which proffered an immediate solution to Zoe's problem.

The girls' talk demonstrates their fluidity and comfort with producing and enacting family roles, including a call for help from a 'baby' (Zoe) answered by the mother (Narelle). The next turns of conversation (lines 9-14), however, indicate possible interactional trouble (Schegloff, 1968). When Narelle suggested that she could fix the earthquake, there was initially a pause followed by Zoe explicitly questioning whether Mummy (Narelle) would fix the earthquake (line 11). Followed by another longer pause (line 12), marking that a possible difficult reply will follow, Narelle (Mummy) did not answer Zoe's question but instead told Zoe (the baby) to go to sleep. This short sequence of pretend play conversation marks what the children faced in their real everyday lives, that is, it is not really possible to 'fix da earthquake'. The difficulty for the players was the pretend-real nexus, as shown by the pauses (Sacks et al., 1974; Schegloff, 2007a) following the questioning of the mother's ability to 'fix' the earthquake and her avoidance of an answer. This is an excellent example of children using their play as means of testing out ways that a problem might be resolved at their own pace and in their own way (Felix et al., 2006; Howard & McInnes, 2012).

Playing at family relationships is a common activity in young children's play; acting out these roles can contribute to supporting children's well-being as problems can be fixed in pretense that may not be fixable in real life. At the same time, this extract shows that pretend play is a means whereby difficult events can be raised and where socio-emotional issues can be explored in an affective sense. This play interaction afforded Zoe and Narelle the opportunity to play out the very real distress of the earthquake in a safe environment, whereby the earthquake in a pretend frame might be easily fixed by an attentive mother. It also demonstrated the children's anxieties tied to her being unable to 'fix' a problem; the baby's question of whether a parent can bring back an earlier order by fixing it closes down the play as the mother tells the questioning baby to go to sleep. Through engaging in pretend play, the children communicated their worries to each other (Haight et al., 2006). Pretend family play became a socio-emotional resource to 'do' supportive relationships and care for each other in traumatic times. In this way, play is one way to promote a sense of well-being, where 'children develop trust that their needs will be responded to' (Ministry of Education, 1996, p. 46).

Discussion and conclusion

The children used a number of classroom experiences to prompt and explore personal reflections about the earthquake, by which they made reference to things being 'broken' and needing 'fixing'. Analysis shows how the content of the pretend play experiences, and the content of discussions about the Learning Stories books, helped them come to terms with the meaning of their experiences. Analysis revealed how the children oriented to people, places, and things in relation to their earthquake experiences. Through direct references, the children made links between their earthquake experiences as they came to terms with the experience nine months after the disaster.

Sharing important experiences is encouraged in the early childhood curriculum *Te Whāriki* where it states that children should be given 'the opportunity to share and discuss their experiences in a comfortable setting' (Ministry of Education, 1996, p. 47). Pretend play offered opportunities to talk about the earthquakes, and children used their documented stories about the disaster as an interactional resource to discuss their accounts of events. For teachers, their role was to make relevant such links for the children, in line with the well-being strand of the New Zealand early childhood curriculum.

Pretend play was a means to relive and try to better understand traumatic events, in ways that were meaningful to children. Through discussing and acting out their experiences in these ways, the children communicated their interpretation and understanding of the earthquake, as well as the anxieties and worries surrounding these traumatic events (Haight et al., 2006). As shown in the examples, and most notably in the final episode (Extract 5), pretend play is a valuable resource for opening up possibilities to explore painful events, and to grapple emotionally with difficult issues.

Learning Story books, as a curricular feature, encompassed a wide variety of experiences in which each child had been involved over a course of time; the children's selective use showed that they oriented to the earthquake events in the books. The approach of listening to children's stories about traumatic events has been encouraged to promote recovery and support emotional well-being (Ertl et al., 2012; Stokoe & Edwards, 2006). Through documenting children's experiences in such a way, the children were able to return to their stories when they wanted to, reaffirming their agency and supporting the iterative process of coming to terms with a traumatic event (McMahon, 2009).

While specific to the New Zealand early childhood context, the observations and findings of this paper are relevant for understanding how children use play and teacher assistance in the aftermath of disaster. In the study, the children were observed engaging in play that reflected their local situation, demonstrating the value and importance of time and space for the children to follow their own interests, so as to come to terms with their experiences of the natural disaster. Despite not having psychology or counseling qualifications, the teachers made themselves available to talk and support the children through their play experiences, and shared their experiences of the traumatic events of the earthquakes. In this natural setting the activities formed a relevant part of everyday activities, and were not made 'remarkable' as something to be talked about and distinct from preschool play and talk.

References

Antaki, C. (2008). Formulations in psychotherapy. In A. Peräkylä, C. Antaki, S. Vehviläinen & I. Leudar (Eds.), *Conversation analysis and psychotherapy* (pp. 26–42). Cambridge: Cambridge University Press.

Baggerly, J., & Exum, H. (2008). Counseling children after natural disasters. Guidance for family therapists. *The American Journal of Family Therapy, 36*, 79–93.

Bateman, A. (2012a). When verbal disputes get physical. In S. Danby & M. Theobald (Eds.), *Disputes in everyday life: Social and moral orders of children and young people* (pp. 267–296). Emerald.

Bateman, A. (2012b). Forging friendships: The use of collective pro-terms by pre-school children. *Discourse Studies, 14*(1), 165–180.

Bateman, A., Danby, S., & Howard, J. (2013). Everyday preschool talk about Christchurch earthquakes. *Australia Journal of Communication, 40*(1), 103–123.

Berg, R. G., Parr, G., Bradley, L., & Berry, J. J. (2009). Humor: A therapeutic intervention for child-counseling. *Journal of Creativity in Mental Health, 3*(4), 225–236.

Bratton, S., & Ray, D. (2000). What the research shows about play therapy. *International Journal of Play Therapy, 9*(1), 47–88.

Bratton, S. Ray, D., Rhine, T., & Jones, L. (2005). The efficacy of play therapy with children: A meta-analytic review of treatment outcomes professional psychology. *Research and Practice, 36*(4), 376–390.

Brown, R. (2012). Principles guiding practice and responses to recent community disasters in New Zealand. *New Zealand Journal of Psychology, 40*(4), 86–89.

Bruner, J. (1990). *Acts of meaning*. Cambridge, MA: Harvard University Press.

Butler, C. W. (2008). *Talk and social interaction in the playground*. Hampshire: Ashgate.

Butler, C. W., & Weatherall, A. (2006). "No we're not playing families": Membership categorization in children's play. *Research on Language and Social Interaction, 39*(4), 441–470.

Carr, M., & Lee, M. (2012). *Learning stories: Constructing learner identities in early education*. London: Sage.

Cirillo, L., & Cryder, C. (1995). Distinctive therapeutic uses of metaphor. *Psychotherapy, 32*(4), 511–519.

Cromdal, J. (2001). Can I be with?: Negotiating play entry in a bilingual school. *Journal of Pragmatics, 33*, 515–543.

Danby, S., & Baker, C. D. (1998). How to be masculine in the block area. *Childhood: A Global Journal of Child Research, 5*(2), 151–175.

Danby, S., & Baker, C. (2000). Unravelling the fabric of social order in block area. In S. Hester & D. Francis (Eds.), *Local educational order: Ethnomethodological studies of knowledge in action* (pp. 91–140). Amsterdam: John Benjamins.

PLAY AND WELLBEING

Danby, S., Baker, C., & Emmison, M. (2005). Four observations on opening calls to *Kids Help Line*. In C. D. Baker, M. Emmison & A. Firth (Eds.), *Calling for help: Language and social interaction in telephone helplines* (pp. 133–151). Amsterdam: John Benjamins.

Dean, S. (2012). Long term support in schools and early childhood services after February 2011. *New Zealand Journal of Psychology*, *40*(4), 95–97.

Enfield, N. J. (2013). Reference in conversation. In J. Sidnell & T. Stivers (Eds.), *The handbook of conversation analysis*. Oxford: Blackwell Publishers.

Ertl, V., Pfeiffer, A., Schauer, E., Elbert, T., & Neuner, F. (2012). Community-implemented trauma therapy for former child soldiers in Northern Uganda: A randomized controlled trial. *Journal of the American Medical Association*, *306*(5), 503–512.

Fearn, M., & Howard, J. (2011). Play as a resource for children facing adversity. *Children and Society*, Online first. doi:10.1111/j.1099-0860.2011.00357.x

Felix, E., Bond, D., & Shelby, J. (2006). Coping with disaster: Psychosocial interventions for children in international disaster relief. In C. Schaefer & H. Kaduson (Eds.), *Contemporary play therapy: Theory, research, and practice* (pp. 307–329). New York, NY: The Guilford Press.

Filipi, A. (2009). *Toddler and parent interaction: The organisation of gaze.*

Garfinkel, H. (1967). *Studies in ethnomethodology.* Englewood Cliffs, NJ: Prentice-Hall.

Haight, W., Black, J., Ostler, T., & Sheridan, K. (2006). Pretend play and emotional learning in traumatized mothers and children. In D. G. Singer, R. M. Golinkoff, & K. Hirsh-Pasek (Eds.), *Play = learning: How play motivates and enhances children's cognitive and social-emotional growth.* Oxford: Oxford University Press.

Heritage, J. (1984). *Garfinkel and ethnomethodology.* Oxford: Polity Press.

Howard, J., & McInnes, K. (2012). *The essence of play: A practice companion for professionals working with children and young people.* London: Routledge.

Hutchby, I. (2007). *The discourse of child counseling.* Amsterdam: John Benjamins.

Kidwell, M. (2011). Epistemics and embodiment in the interactions of very young children. In T. Stivers, L. Mondada & J. Steensig (Eds.), *The morality of knowledge in conversation* (pp. 257–284). Cambridge: Cambridge University Press.

Little, S., Little, A., & Gutierrez, G. (2009). Children and traumatic events: Therapeutic techniques for psychologists working in the schools. *Psychology in Schools*, *46*(3), 199–205.

Mashford-Scott, A., & Church, A. (2011). Promoting children's agency in early childhood education. *Research on Youth and Language*, *5*(1), 15–38.

McInnes, K., Howard, J., Miles, G. E., & Crowley, K. (2009). Behavioural differences exhibited by children when practising a task under formal and playful conditions. *Educational & Child Psychology*, *26*(2), 31–39.

McMahon, L. (2009). *The handbook of play therapy and therapeutic play.* London: Routledge.

Ministry of Education. (1996). *Te Whāriki. He whāriki mātauranga mōngā mokopuna o Aotearoa: Early childhood curriculum.* Wellington: Learning Media.

NZ Police. (2012). http://www.police.govt.nz/list-deceased

Parkes, E. (2011). 'Wait! I'm Not a Journalist': Conducting qualitative field research in post-disaster situations. *Graduate Journal of Asia-Pacific Studies*, *7*(2), 30–45.

Petriwskyj, A. (2013). Reflections on talk about natural disasters by early childhood educators and directors. *Australian Journal of Communication*, *40*(1), 87–102.

Pomerantz, A., & Heritage, J. (2013). Preference. In J. Sidnell & T. Stivers (Eds.), *The handbook of conversation analysis*. Oxford: Blackwell Publishers.

Priestly, G., Roberts, S., & Pipe, M. (1999). Returning to the scene: Reminders and context reinstatement.

Sacks, H. (1995). *Lectures on conversation* (Vols I & 11). Oxford: Blackwell.

Sacks, H., Schegloff, E. A., & Jefferson, G. (1974). A simplest systematics for the organization of turn-taking for conversation. *Language*, *50*, 696–735.

Schaefer, C., & Drewe, A. (2011). The therapeutic powers of play and play therapy. In C. Schaefer (Ed.), *Foundations of play therapy.* John Wiley.

Schegloff, E. A. (1968). Sequencing in conversational openings. *American Anthropologist* [oNew Series], *70*(6), 1075–1095.

Schegloff, E. A. (2007a). *Sequence organisation in interaction: A primer in conversational analysis* (Vol. 1). Cambridge: Cambridge University Press.

Schegloff, E. A., Jefferson, G., & Sacks, H. (1977). The preference for self-correction in the organization of repair in conversation. *Language*, *53*(2), 361–382.

Silverman, D. (1997). *Discourses of counselling: HIV counselling as social interaction.* London: Sage.

Silverman, D., & Peräkylä, A. (1990). AIDS counselling: The interactional organisation of talk about 'delicate' issues. *Sociology of Health and Illness*, *12*(3), 293–318.

Stokoe, E., & Edwards, D. (2006). Story formulations in talk-in-interaction. *Narrative Inquiry*, *16*(1), 56–65.

Sunderland, M. (2006). *Using storytelling as a therapeutic tool with children*. London: Speechmark Publishing.

Walker, G. (2013). Phonetics and prosody in conversation. In J. Sidnell & T. Stivers (Eds.), *The handbook of conversation analysis*. Oxford: Blackwell Publishers.

Waller, T. (2005). International perspectives. In T. Waller (Ed.), *An introduction to early childhood: A multidisciplinary approach*. London: Sage.

Webb, N. B. (2007). *Play therapy with children in crisis: Individual, group, and family treatment* (3rd ed.). Guilford: The Guilford Press.

Whitebread, D. (2010). Play, metacognition & self-regulation. In P. Broadhead, J. Howard & E. Wood (Eds.), *Play and learning in early years settings: From research to practice*. London: Sage.

Physical activity play in local housing estates and child wellness in Ireland

Carol Barron

School of Nursing and Human Science, Dublin City University, Dublin, Ireland

Much of children's play involves physical activity, such as chasing games (Barron, 2011) and climbing (Smith, 2010). Despite this fact, physical activity play has to-date largely been ignored in relation to studies of physical activity in children in the prevention and treatment of childhood overweight and obesity. This paper focuses on the physical activity play of children in middle childhood (8–13 years) in Ireland within local housing estates. The study sought first to identify both the preferred forms of physical activity play as well as the physical spaces in which this play occurs, and second to provide insight for national policy in relation to child wellness and obesity prevention or intervention in childhood.

Introduction

Much of children's and young people's play involves physical activity, such as chasing games (Barron, 2011) and climbing (Smith, 2010). Nevertheless, physical activity play has to-date largely been ignored in studies of physical activity in children relevant to the prevention and treatment of childhood overweight and obesity. Existing Irish national research (Woods et al., 2010), as well as international research (Summerbell et al., 2005) on physical activity in young people, recommends increased time in physical activity sessions such as physical education in school settings and/or sports inside and outside of schools. However, not all children engage in organized sports. The research to date has ignored the role of physical activity play, which all children **do** engage in to varying degrees. As Meire (2007) points out, play does not occur in a vacuum, it happens 'somewhere' in a physical, social and cultural context. This paper focuses on children's play places and physical play activities, which occur in the outdoor play spaces of the housing estate.

Physical activity play

Physical activity play in children has been termed the 'neglected aspect of play' (Smith, 2010). Pellegrini and Smith (1998) offer the following well-known definition:

Physical activity play, specifically, may involve symbolic activity or games with rules; the activity may be social or solitary, but the distinguishing behavioural features are a playful context, combined with … moderate to vigorous physical activity, such that metabolic activity is well above resting metabolic rate. (Pellegrini & Smith, 1998, p. 577)

Smith (2010) and Pellegrini and Smith (1998) have repeatedly criticized the neglect of physical activity play across scholarly disciplines; however, this oversight seems to be changing within health-care fields. The World Health Organization (2009) as part of their Global Strategy on Diet, Physical Activity and Health offer the following interpretation of physical activity when applied to children:

> Physical activity includes play, games, sports, transportation, recreation, physical education or planned exercise, in the context of family, school, and community activities. (p. 7)

Play, games and recreation are now being included within the scope of physical activities in childhood. Arguably, this new interest in physically active forms of play is stimulated by global concerns about childhood obesity. Nevertheless, it offers an opportunity for investigating our knowledge base within this specific area of children's play.

Childhood obesity, wellness and physical activity

Childhood obesity is a result of increased energy content in the diet, decreased levels of physical activity and increasingly sedentary lifestyles (Brownell & Rodin, 1994; Prentice & Jebb, 1995). One only has to examine the flood of literature that has emerged over the last two decades on the 'epidemic' that is childhood obesity to see the link between organizations such as the World Health Organization and play, specifically physical activity play:

> The child epidemic of child obesity demands serious action, and around the world many people have looked at ways of helping children exercise more. (Summerbell et al., 2005, p. 3)

The 'epidemic' of childhood obesity has also resulted in a significant policy response from health organizations such as The International Obesity Task Force and governments around the globe, in relation to the promotion of physical activity in children (Lobstein & Jackson-Leach, 2006). Existing Irish data tell us that the overall rate of overweight and obesity in nine-year-olds is 26% (Growing Up in Ireland Study, 2011) and, in children aged between 4 and 13 years, 24.6% (Barron, Comiskey, & Saris, 2009). A positive and significant correlation was observed between age and BMI (body mass index), indicating that as age increased so too did BMI ($R = 0.35$, $p < 0.001$). A staggering 80% of Irish children are viewed as insufficiently active (Layte & McCrory, 2013). Physical inactivity is now identified as the fourth leading risk factor for global mortality (6% globally) with overweight and obesity being responsible for 5% of global mortality (World Health Organization, 2009). Increasing physical activity levels in children, and decreasing physical inactivity, are now seen as 'solutions' to the childhood obesity problem, in terms of both its prevention and treatment. Children's physical activity play, therefore, now has health-relevant functions: to decrease the incidence of childhood obesity and risk factors for global mortality, and to improve child wellness globally. This functionality afforded to physical activity play, however, fails to take into account the intrinsic value of physical activity play to and for children themselves.

Child wellness promotion

Miller, Gilman, and Martens (2008) argue that wellness promotion addresses the decreasing of disorders and disease, as well as the enhancement of mental and physical health. Present-day models of health and wellness promotion go beyond the medical model of the physical body, to focus on inter-related social, psychological, behavioural (Peterson, Park, & Seligman, 2006)

PLAY AND WELLBEING

and environmental factors on health and well-being. I suggest that all play, but specifically for this discussion, physical activity play, has a part to play in maintaining and increasing children's wellness. Systematic reviews of the child well-being literature conducted by Amerijckx and Humblet (2013) and Pollock and Lee (2003) both found that there is no agreement on a definition of child well-being. Moreover, Cheevers and O' Connell (2012) explain that this issue is compounded by a lack of consensus on what key indicators and domains should be included in measuring child well-being. Despite the lack of consensus, consistent themes have begun to emerge encompassing five distinct domains of well-being: physical, social, psychological, cognitive and economic. Cheevers and O' Connell (2012) suggest that these appear to be the key areas contributing to a child's overall well-being and development.

Prilleltensky, Nelson, and Peirson (2001) suggest that child wellness is determined by the level of parental-familial, communal and social wellness. This view of child wellness may initially appear to place the child in a passive role, whereby their wellness needs are provided for them by others. Yet Prilleltensky and collaborators do acknowledge that children are not passive recipients of 'wellness'; rather after the early years of childhood, they gradually develop the ability to reciprocate and contribute to their own as well as the family's well-being. I suggest that opportunities for children to exercise personal control (Prilleltensky et al., 2001), empowerment and self-determination (Ryan & Deci, 2000) in their play activities contributes to their general health, as well as mental health and wellness.

Bradshaw, Hoelscher, and Richardson (2007) published an index of child well-being in the 25 nation-states of the European Union. The index was developed from national sample surveys and indicators collected routinely by international organizations. They analysed children's well-being in eight differing clusters (material situation, housing, health, subjective well-being, education, children's relationships, civic participation, risk and safety), covering 23 domains and 51 indicators. Whilst they state that the clusters include topics that matter to children from their own point of view, surprisingly and disappointingly, play is neither included as an indicator nor as a domain within any of the clusters or within their examination of child well-being. This lack resonates with the views of anthropologist Schwartzman (1978, 2001) that Western society has viewed play as non-productive, non-serious and not work. Play and work are still predominantly, though inaccurately, viewed as binary oppositions; work is valued as a necessity for economic survival; play in comparison is often seen as frivolous and lacking the serious purpose of work, thus not worthy of inclusion in child wellness indicators. Cheevers and O'Connell (2012) report the development of a specific Irish index of child well-being using data from the first wave of the Child Cohort in the Growing Up in Ireland longitudinal study, which consists of three domains constructed using fourteen indicators of children's physical, socio-emotional and educational development. Again, play and physical activity play are not specifically identified as an indicator of child well-being.

Fieldwork site and methodology

This paper reports the findings from an ethnographic study examining the physical activity play and play places of Irish children in middle childhood (7–13 years). Rathvarna (pseudonym) is the town in which the fieldwork took place. Rathvarna has grown extensively in the last three decades as it is within the 'commuter belt' to Dublin. In 2011 the town had a population of 19,537 of which 4,979 are children aged 0–14 years (Central Statistics Office, 2011). The overwhelming majority of children in this study live in housing estates within the town, the majority of which were built between 1992 and 2006 to accommodate the town's growing population. Within Ireland, houses are the common form of family dwellings, with apartment complexes predominantly being situated in the main cities. Moore and Young (1978) discuss the importance of housing estate design and residential location in restricting children's play opportunities. The same authors highlight how each estate or area creates opportunities for play, irrespective of the architectural design. All of the housing estates within the town have a communal green area with trees, bushes and flower beds at differing stages of maturity, dependent on when the estate was established. None of the estates have any communal seating areas or fixed play equipment. The housing estates typically have one access road into the estate, just like the human lungs, with small side roads or bronchioles leading into the small composition of houses, usually in a circle or semi circle formation, normally ending in cul-de-sacs similar to the alveoli at the end junction of the bronchioles. Thus all children, families and visitors to the estates must pass up and down these physical spaces, just as oxygen flows in and out of the lungs. As with the human lungs, the housing estates are separate from each other, yet lie in very close proximity to each other. The function of the bronchus and alveoli in the human body is the exchange of gases to sustain life, just as the housing estates provide space, place and opportunity for children to play, along with protection, warmth, a home, as well as social and peer support for its residents, things necessary for societies to survive.

Child-centred anthropology views children as the best informants about their own lives and worlds (Montgomery, 2009). Given that ethnography attempts to center on young participants' own perspectives (Hammersley & Atkinson, 2007), ethnography is eminently suited to examine the lived experiences of children in relation to their physical activity play and play spaces. Participant observation was the dominant method of data generation in this study, throughout a year-long fieldwork in two single-sex school settings in Rathvarna and in the local housing estates where the children lived. Children are active agents in their own lives, a fact reflected in the participatory methodologies employed. I endeavoured to enable as much data as possible to be generated *by* rather than *about* the children, thus enabling insight into each child's perspective and lived experiences. Photography, with subsequent photo elicitation focus group interviews, draw and write technique, and mapping exercises were also employed. The findings from participant observation in the local housing estates, an analysis of the children's photographs of their play and play spaces, in combination with the photo elicitation focus group discussions, are the central focus of this paper.

The aim of the photography generated by children was to identify their play activities and play spaces. This phase of the research was explained to the children in the individual classrooms in both schools and was supported with written information sheets and age-appropriate assent forms. Separate information sheets and consent forms were also supplied for the parents. In total, 60 children gave their written assent along with their parents' consent to take part. Disposable cameras were distributed for a week's duration in the winter and summer months, to allow for observing seasonal variation in their play and play spaces. In total, 32 girls (21 in the winter and 11 in the summer) and 28 boys (14 in the winter and 14 in the summer) took part. Girls ranged in age from 9 years 3 months to 13 years ($M = 10.99$). The boys ranged in age from 9 years 10 months to 12 years 9 months ($M = 10.99$). Both the children and their parents reviewed the photographs once they were developed and had the opportunity to remove any of the images from the study.

This was followed by 11 photo elicitation, focus group interviews. Photo elicitation is a data-gathering technique where the researcher introduces the children's photographs as part of the interview. The aim is to explore the significance or meaning of the images (Prosser, 1998) with the children. Each focus group consisted of children of the same gender and age group, as suggested by Morgan (2002). The literature provides varying advice about the ideal group size for focus groups (Morgan, Gibbs, Maxwell, & Britten, 2002). In this study, the focus groups ranged in size from five to seven child participants. The interviews lasted between 40 and 60 min. All 11 focus group interviews were tape-recorded, transcribed verbatim and analysed using content analysis.

PLAY AND WELLBEING

Table 1. Boys and girls outdoor play spaces in the housing estate.

	Boys				Girls					
	Winter	Summer	Subtotal	%	Winter	Summer	Sub total	%	Total	Overall %
Back garden	18	30	48	28	20	41	61	53	109	38
Road in H. Est.	0	42	42	25	20	6	26	22	68	24
Front garden	6	23	29	17	8	14	22	19	51	18
Green area in H. Est.	2	40	42	25	2	2	4	3	46	16
Cul-de-sac in H. Est.	0	3	3	2	0	3	3	3	6	2
Front driveway	0	5	5	3	0	0	0	0	5	2
Total	26	143	169	100	50	66	166	100	285	100

In total, 960 photographs were included in this phase of the study. The photographs were analysed using visual content analysis, known as an 'empirical and objective procedure for quantitatively recording visual representations using reliable and explicitly defined categories' (Bell, 2001, p. 14). Coding categories were adapted from the categories developed by Sharples et al. (2003) and Cherney and London (2006). Boys recorded 258 and girls recorded 203 outdoor images, respectively. Outdoor images made up slightly under half of all the images recorded over the year. Unsurprisingly, more of the outdoor images were recorded in the summer for both genders (boys 69%: girls 73%). The outdoor images depicted by both the boys and girls fell into two main categories. The first category is the Housing Estate, which includes the private space of the back garden, the semi-private space of the front garden, paths, roads, cul-de-sacs and communal green spaces. The second outdoor category is of the local amenities such as sports fields, clubs and locations in the local town. Although both boys and girls play in the same physical places, there are differences in how frequently they photographed individual play spaces, specifically in relation to the back garden and the communal green area in the housing estate. See Table 1 for an overview of boys' and girls' housing estate play spaces and places.

Back garden

Parts of the home have a duality of roles, as is true of the back garden. Rasmussen (2004), in her work on children's places, argues that until the age of 11 or 12 children regard the back garden as part of the home and thus an indoor space. After this age, she suggests they regard just the home as the indoor space. In this study, children consistently referred to and defined the back garden as an 'outside' space; for the purposes of this research, the back garden was defined as the children described it – a private outdoor space. In Ireland, back gardens are mainly enclosed by walls or fences; since the space is clearly demarcated, it is a private space. Many of the back gardens contained fixed play equipment such as swings, slides and trampolines. I would argue that the back garden is the new private, personalized playground for children. Playgrounds have been adapted by both parents and children and have been moved from shared 'public space' of the neighbourhood to the 'private space' of the back garden (Figure 1); this is reflected by the huge number of images of the back gardens which contain fixed play equipment.

Figure 1. Back garden as physical playground.

This transformation of the back garden to a private children's playground, I suggest, affects children's mobility. By providing for their children's play needs that historically have been met by the public playground, there is less opportunity or need for children to travel outside of the immediate home environment and neighbourhood. Thus, parents with good intentions may be depriving their children of opportunities to mobilize beyond their immediate environment. In addition to fixed playground equipment, children portrayed the back garden as a space in which they could perform and practice sporting skills such as dribbling a football, skipping, swinging golf clubs, activities which clearly involve physical activity. These were normally portrayed as solitary activities, particularly in the winter period. The back garden was also portrayed by both boys and girls as a place to socialize, especially with their siblings (in the winter) and their friends (in the summer).

Overall boys depicted 28% of their outdoor images taken in the back gardens, whereas girls depicted almost double this, 53%, in the back gardens. Thus, girls remain more hidden and protected from the outside world compared to boys, as the back garden is a private space that is not open to the public gaze. Girls spend more of their play time 'back stage' than front of stage. Both boys and girls recorded more images in the back garden in the summer period than in the winter period. It is significant that both boys and girls depicted themselves in the back garden more than any other outdoor space. Because the back garden is situated immediately beside and behind the physical building of the home, adults can monitor and survey their children's activities and behaviours from the comfort of the inside.

Front gardens

Many of the front gardens face towards the public space of the housing estate and have a driveway, lawn, shrubs and flower beds. However, many of the front gardens are treated similarly to the back gardens, in that they are enclosed by smaller walls and fences to demarcate the boundaries of the front garden. Domestic front gardens have been presented as a place designed for the benefit of others (Grampp, 1992) or alternately, as a sanctuary from public life (Kaplan & Kaplan, 1989) carried out in a semi-public space. Ravetz and Turkington (1995) view the front garden as a 'buffer zone' between the public street and private sphere of the home. In the summer, boys recorded 17% of their outdoor images in the front garden; the girls were only slightly higher with 19% of their outdoor images there (Figure 2). Again both boys and girls recorded images of their front gardens as a play space disproportionately in the summer (rather than the winter). Several of the front gardens also contained movable play equipment, specifically goal posts and toy objects. Again, this served to keep children physically close to the family home, where children are under direct supervision of parents. Of all the outdoor images including homes and the local neighbourhood, the back and front garden represented a significant play space for both boys and girls in both winter and summer. Over 50% of all images portraying the housing estate, recorded by boys and girls in either season, were in the back or front garden, with the majority being recorded in the summer.

Play in the housing estate

With the exception of research in children's geographies, research on 'street play' is surprisingly absent from the literature on children's play. There is not much information on how or what children play in their neighbourhoods, or how or why they move from one place to another while playing together. A quiet road with parked cars may not initially appear as a 'safe' or 'appropriate' play space for children, yet 25% of the boys' and 22% of the girls' outdoor housing estate images are of the roads and paths in their immediate housing estate – demonstrating the importance children place on these spaces for a multitude of play activities. Seemingly innocuous objects like lampposts and trees are vitally important as a den or 'home' in games of chasing, tag and tip the can; they are also changed into goal posts for games of soccer. These objects are transformed

Figure 2. Front gardens as a physical play space.

by children from functional or decorative objects for adults, into a part of their play space. See how Tony (nine years) demonstrated his transformation of a conveniently situated lamppost and tree, into two goal posts for soccer and other team ball games (Figure 3). Tony recorded these two images in sequence; the initial image shows us a tree and a lamppost, positioned in a line, several feet apart – a natural goal post. In the image, Tony places himself in the frame, between the tree and lamppost with his foot on a football. During the group discussions about the pictures, Tony also verbally reinforced the point that these images showed 'our goal posts for soccer and stuff'.

The roads and paths as a stage for performance

The demonstration of physical/sporting skills within the physical space of the paths and roads of the housing estate was particularly important to the boys, as was clearly evident in the pictures they produced. Boys who were not on the school teams for football, soccer, hurling and so forth portrayed themselves playing the game(s) with their peers, demonstrating their skill level. For example, boys recorded images of themselves catching balls, heading balls, performing back kicks, dribbling the ball and so on. Unsurprisingly, soccer was also popular with the boys on the roads. In such pictures, boys always situated themselves within the image; they wanted to portray their abilities and skills in physical activities. The boys 'performed' these activities in the public sphere or 'front of stage'. Other activities included their skateboarding, gymnastics (Figure 4) and rollerblading skills. Boys portrayed themselves as physically active and skilled on roller blades, skateboards and wheelies, performing skilled 'tricks' on the roads and indeed the paths within the estates. Girls depicted themselves as playing chasing, walking the dog with friends, cycling their bikes, 'hanging around' or standing beside objects of importance such as a lamppost that was transformed into a 'den' in chasing games. Similar to the boys, many of the activities that the girls portrayed themselves in, within the roads in their estates, involved the companionship of their friends. One of the attractions of outdoor play is the possibilities it offers for children to appropriate public space normally taken for granted as an adult space (Skelton & Valentine, 1998) for themselves, including the roads within the housing estate.

Figure 3. Transformation of objects for physical play activities.

Figure 4. Using kerbs and roads for physical activity play.

Communal green areas

The most obvious front of stage play space depicted by the children was the communal green area within a housing estate, normally overlooked by a semicircle of houses within the estate. These areas were called 'the green' or 'the big green' by the children. The girls were noticeable by their absence from this space, with only 3% of their summer images depicting the green area as a play space. This finding contrasts with girls' spoken discourse that indicated girls liked and used the green as a play space with their friends. As Colleen described:

> Well me and my friend, I always call for her after we've finished our homework, we text each other, and then we go outside and there's a really big green and while we're not doing gymnastics we practice, doing the exercise, you kind of run and that sometimes. [Colleen, 10 years]

Within this communal green space, girls portrayed images of themselves located on the margins of the physical space, standing or walking generally in the company of their friends (Figure 5). Some girls did use the whole physical space of the green; however they were in the minority. The overwhelming majority of the girls pictured themselves on the margins of 'the green', echoing the longstanding and repeated evidence within anthropology, folklore, educational studies and sociology that girls in mixed-sex school playgrounds occupy the peripheries of the playground (Blatchford & Sharp, 1994; Pellegrini, 2004; Thorne, 1993). A significantly higher percentage of the boys' images (boys 25% *vs.* girls 3%) depicted the green. Boys, in comparison to girls, showed themselves as occupying all the physical space on the green and being very physically active in this space: playing soccer, gymnastics, chasing, rough and tumble and so forth. Boys had effective ownership of the green areas, which was reflected in their use of it. A lot of their images in this space were of team sports, or showing team sport players socializing. To the degree that other research shows that boys consistently interrupt girls' games, much more so than girls do with boys' games (Thorne, 1993), it is reasonable the girls occupied the peripheries so as to prevent the boys disrupting their games. While a safe play area or green space in local neighbourhoods in Ireland increases children's ability to engage in unstructured activities (McCoy, Quail, & Smyth, 2012) such as physical activity play, this study suggests there is a gender-related difference for its use in middle childhood.

Chasing games in the housing estate

There are several large group chasing and play fighting games which are played regularly, in which both boys and girls of differing ages play together and will occupy all of 'the green' as well as the roads, paths and front gardens in the housing estate; large group games are very,

Figure 5. Girls on the margins of the play space.

very popular in the housing estate spaces. One of the most popular of these games is called 'Manhunt' and it is a commonly enacted game. Manhunt involves groups of players: while generally the lowest number of children involved was 6, 10–12 players would normally take part. The groupings can consist of mixed-gender or single-gender groups. Gender composition and age range of the players vary. This I suggest is because there are not always enough children of the same age group or gender living within the same housing estate and in these instances it is acceptable to allow a variety of ages to play the game to make up the two teams. Cathal and Matthew describe the game.

Researcher: What is 'Manhunt'?

Cathal (Age 9): You pick, just say there's 6 people playing, one team are the hunters and the other team run away [i.e. three on each team]. The people who are trying to run away make up the 3 letter word, just say SKY [each child has one letter of the word each] and then you can run. The people that are not hunters run away and then if the hunters find them they beat you up until the others say the letters.

Matthew (Age 8): Yeah they beat them up.

This is a form of chasing game with two teams of equal size. The objective is for the members of one team known as the hunters to chase the other team and individually 'beat' a letter of a word out of each child on the opposite team, letters or words which they have collectively agreed upon before they start. The hunters then put all the letters together to make up the word. When the hunters have all the letters and say the correct word the game is complete and usually starts up again with the hunters in the prior game now being chased. While many adults may wrongly identify elements of these games as 'fighting', the children did not. Clear rules were in force

PLAY AND WELLBEING

which differentiated Manhunt play from fighting. For example, Sam echoed what many of the children, both boys and girls, said when I asked them the difference between Manhunt playing and fighting:

> Well Manhunt is always playing, well nearly always; you would never hit your friends on the face to get their letter. That's not playing that's fighting; everyone knows that, you only beat the hell out of them. [Sam, 11 years]

Both boys and girls have a shared, working knowledge and understanding of the rules of the game and could quickly and accurately differentiate episodes of Manhunt play fighting from fighting. I observed and participated as a player in Manhunt. Manhunt was a group game that spread out throughout the gardens, roads and greens in the housing estate. Manhunt and other chasing games are play contexts that break down the social barriers of ownership of physical space. The groups of children playing these games held a collective belief that playing Manhunt gave them the right to travel across, through and hide in 'others' gardens, behind their cars and so forth.

The overwhelming majority of outdoor play activities depicted in the photographs and observed throughout the fieldwork – from demonstrations of physical skills with soccer balls and skate boards, to small group games of soccer, to chasing games such as 'Manhunt' – can be classified as physical activity play. All of these activities clearly demonstrate that children are physically active outside of the school environment. The physical spaces in which children live everyday hold direct impact, I suggest, on their ability (or lack thereof) to take part in physical activity play forms, thus decreasing sedentary lifestyles and aiding in the prevention or management of childhood obesity. National and local policies related to planning and urban and rural development can and do directly impact on children's physical activity play (and thus childhood obesity).

Tether length: geographical movement of children related to gender and age

Anthropological literature is inundated with ethnographic examples of girls and boys being subject to differing 'tether lengths' (Lancy, 2008). In other words, spatial limits of movement for boys and girls differ. The anthropological evidence in traditional societies consistently shows that boys travel further from the homestead than girls (Morton, 1996; Rossie, 2005; Wenger, 1989). Regardless of gender, though, the overwhelming majority of images recorded by these Irish children were taken in their own housing estate, as Harry and Terence explain:

> Harry (Age 11): I'm not allowed outside my estate. I will be soon, so that's where I play [in the estate], there's lots of trees in my estate.
>
> Researcher: What do you mean you will be allowed outside the estate soon?
>
> Harry: My mam just says I'm old enough now but she has to see that she can get my trust. She says that she knows that I'm old enough; she just wants to make sure that I'm responsible enough to actually go out and watch [for] the cars on the road and stuff.
>
> Researcher: What about yourself Terence?
>
> Terence (Age 10): No, I'm not allowed out of my estate but I'm allowed to go around it.

Boys' ability to move geographically outside of their immediate housing estate depended on multiple factors: their chronological age, the location of their home, proximity to a busy road or narrow

PLAY AND WELLBEING

footpath, 'stranger danger' fears, parents' beliefs about an individual child's competence with traffic, and so forth. Girls were constrained in their movements, due to perceived fears of violence/assault upon isolated or empty roads, as Lilly and Megan recount:

Lilly (Age 9): I'd love a path going across from Rathvarna Manor to Abbey Road because my mam said if there was one I'd be able to walk to school but that road is so dangerous, there's no houses, it's just like abandoned and if something happens down there ...

Researcher: You'd like a path so you could walk to school?

Megan (Age 10): Yeah so I could just walk across and there are loads of houses.

Lilly: Not dangerous.

This evidence does not support the anthropological view (from traditional cultures) that 'tether lengths' or spatial limits of movement for boys are longer than that of girls, at least within modern Irish society.

Past studies have suggested that as children progress chronologically through middle childhood, the amount of time they spend outdoors increases. In a well-known study of a New England town, Hart (1978) identified a significant leap in children's, especially boys', spatial ranges at the age of 10. A decade later, Matthews' (1987) research in England found that parental restrictions on children living in a suburban housing estate became more relaxed at the slightly earlier age of eight to nine years old. My contemporary findings differ from both prior studies. Due to societal changes in the last three decades, children's 'tether length' has shrunk (through such factors as increased traffic, so called 'stranger danger,' as well as barriers introduced to the built environment) (Green, Mitchell, & Bunton, 2000; Valentine & McKendrick, 1997).

These restrictions on children's physical mobility do affect their ability to take part in unstructured physical play activities outside of the immediacy of their home and housing estate. Of the 940 images included in this study, 239 depicted a space outside of the home and immediate housing estate (25%), a finding that was fairly consistent across gender. Regardless of gender, the majority of these images were places for physical activity, though there were some differences in the type of locations depicted. Boys predominantly depicted sports clubs such as the tennis club, rugby club, Gaelic Athletic Club club and fields. Girls depicted their locations outside the housing estate as involved in their hobbies, such as horse riding, gymnastic clubs or sports.

Natural elements in the built environment

The space and place of children's play is, and always has been, a rich cultural landscape, infused with meanings that children make for themselves out of the materials and sites that occupy them. (Burke, 2008, p. 24)

The extent of the importance of nature to the children was surprising. Fully 60% of all the girls' outdoor images included aspects of nature (trees, shrubs, grass, canals, parks, fields). Boys were even higher with 76% of their outdoor images portraying nature. Images of trees were highly popular with boys and girls (Figure 6). Many boys showed themselves climbing trees or leaning over them. Note how Orlaigh [aged 12] in the bottom right picture in Figure 6 lay on the grass looking up at the tree to capture the branches as well as the trunk of the tree to show her 'favourite tree to climb'. Trees serve multiple functions; they can be climbed, used as a goal post, hidden behind or sat down against. Trees are transformed and retransformed by particular children in differing ways. Many children took images of tree-lined roads within their housing

Figure 6. The importance of trees.

estates; the trees were deliberately included in the images, thus supporting the importance children place on elements of the natural environment. Children never explicitly mentioned the role of trees in physical activity play and obesity; rather they described the fun and enjoyment derived from trees as objects of play or as enjoyable places to play.

Conclusion

Physical activity play has a role to play in the reduction and prevention of childhood obesity, a pronounced problem currently within health-related fields. Prior research on physical activities has focused on children in school settings. The research reported here underscores that the day to day world of the child outside of the school setting needs to be taken into fuller account, to give a fuller and more accurate evidence base on which to base anti-obesity policies and interventions at the local and national level.

Children in middle childhood devote the majority of their physical play activities to places within the sphere of their housing estate. Time and again research tells us that children like to play close to their homes (Meire, 2007), as these ethnographic findings also support. This research suggests that physical activity within housing estates encompasses a very significant amount of physical activity play. Further, children are intrinsically motivated to take part in such physical activity play. Where neighbourhood play within local estates incorporated into anti-obesity interventions, there would likely be a higher possibility of success than is the case for adult-devised and adult-ruled activities.

A huge amount of street play is evident from the children's photographed images and their discussions during the photo elicitation interviews. Play in public spaces such as streets and housing estates is much more important to children than adults realize. A quarter of all the children's images in the housing estate were recorded in the streets and cul-de-sacs in their housing estates, demonstrating the significance of these spaces for physical activity play. The roads and paths serve as important places in which to meet, socialize and 'hang out' with friends. Equally, everyday objects like lampposts and trees become transformed and re-transformed by children, to suit differing physical play activities. An appealing facet, if not the very attraction, of outdoor play is the possibilities it offers for children to appropriate public space, such as the road outside their front doors, normally taken for granted as an adult space (Skelton & Valentine, 1998).

At the same time, it must be acknowledged that societies are not static. Increased parental fears about traffic, so called 'stranger danger', and barriers from the built environment (Green et al., 2000; Valentine & McKendrick, 1997) directly influence parental restrictions on children's independent mobility. If such trends are not addressed at local and national levels, policy and interventions will be less effective than they could be. As a case in point, the recent change in children's 'tether length' discussed in this paper, which is also mirrored in European childhood mobility studies (Cordovil, Lopes, & Neto, 2012), is a concerning outcome that may stem from recent societal changes and parents' increased fears for children's safety.

Many of the back gardens contained fixed play equipment, such that the back garden has become the new private playground for children. This transformation of the back garden serves to further remove children from public spaces within society, keeping them 'back stage' as opposed to 'front stage'. It also likely restricts children's mobility, as they no longer need to visit public playgrounds; in turn, their decreased mobility negatively impacts children's physical activity levels, and in turn childhood obesity.

In Ireland, most back and front gardens are enclosed by walls, fencing or shrubbery, for the purposes of setting off a private or semi-private space for the family and their domestic life. Such a pattern of housing design, which by no means is universal across cultures, merits critical consideration. More research needs to be undertaken, to identify the influence enclosed gardens have on children's physical activity play, and subsequently, childhood obesity.

The open space of the 'green' is a multi-functional space, home to gymnastic displays, demonstrations of tricks, a place to climb trees, build dens and 'hang out with your friends'. Group games such as chasing games like 'Manhunt', Soccer and the Irish games of camogie, football and hurling are played daily on the green in fine weather; notably, all of these activities involve physical activity play. The 'green' is transformed and re-transformed continuously by children of differing ages and genders. It serves various functions for a changing cast of children over time. A distinction to be noted, on the communal green, is the gendered use of space. For decades, numerous authors have reported that girls are marginalized on the edges of school playgrounds, when boys monopolize the centre area for their play (Thorne, 1993); girls play on the margins in mixed-sex school playgrounds (Smith, 2010). The 'green' within Irish housing estates is a versatile play space for children, where boys in middle childhood engage in numerous forms of physical activity play. While this amenity is highly effective as an intervention in the prevention and treatment of childhood obesity for boys, it may be less effective for girls, as they inhabit only the margins of the space.

There has been an emerging recognition that most built environments are created to reflect adult values and usages (Thomson & Philo, 2004). Children utilize all sorts of spaces, nevertheless, in non-adult ways in their play (Skelton & Valentine, 1998; Thomson & Philo, 2004). Play in informal and natural settings remains significant to children, as recent studies by children's geographers and others have shown; children's preferred play spaces are open spaces (Valentine, 2004) or local neighbourhood spaces that lend themselves to being appropriated by the children (Barron, 2011; Meire 2007). It cannot be overemphasized that this knowledge of children's use of space needs to be incorporated and reflected in local and national planning and policies. Otherwise, a form of physical activity play, that all children take part in to varying degrees, will be missed as a factor in both the treatment and prevention of childhood obesity.

Physical activity is known, of course, to be an important determinant of body weight (Department of Health and Children, 2005). Still, even though physical activity play has an important role to play in the prevention and treatment of childhood obesity, children do not engage in physical activity play for functionalist health reasons; they do not seek to increase their physical activity levels, so as to decrease their sedentary lifestyle, nor to reduce their weight. Rather children engage in physical activity play because of intrinsic motivation: they enjoy it and find it fun. In light of the stubborn persistence of obesity as a health problem, it may be time to take account in policy and interventions the ordinary, the mundane, and the day to day lived worlds and experiences of children, including self-motivated, child-powered physical activity play.

References

Barron, C. (2011). *Fun is a serious business: 'Sameness' and 'difference' in the play spaces, play activities and toys of Irish children in middle childhood* (Unpublished PhD thesis). National University of Ireland, Maynooth.

Barron, C., Comiskey, C., & Saris, J. (2009). Prevalence rates and comparisons of obesity levels in Ireland. *British Journal of Nursing, 18*(13), 799–803.

Bell, P. (2001). Content analysis of visual images. In T. van Leeuwen, & C. Jewitt (Eds.), *Handbook of visual analysis* (pp. 10–34). London: Sage Publications.

Blatchford, P., & Sharp, S. (1994). *Breaktime and the school: Understanding and changing playground behaviour.* London: Routledge.

Bradshaw, J., Hoelscher, P., & Richardson, D. (2007). An index of child well-being in the European Union. *Social Indicators Research, 80*(1), 133–177.

Brownell, K., & Rodin, J. (1994). The dieting maelstrom. Is it possible and advisable to lose weight? *American Psychologist, 49*(9), 781–791.

Cheevers, C., & O'Connell, M. (2012). Developing an index of well-being for nine-year-old Irish children. *Child Indicators Research, 6*, 213–236. doi: 10.1007/s12187-012-9171-5

Cherney, I. D., & London, K. (2006). Gender-linked differences in the toys, television shows, computer games, and outdoor activities of 5- to 13-year-old children. *Sex Roles, 54*(9), 717–726.

Cordovil, R., Lopes, F., & Neto, C. (2012, June 18–19). *Childrens independent mobility in Portugal: A shift from walking to driving.* Paper presented at The 26th ICCP World Play Conference, Tallinn, Estonia.

Department of Health and Children (2005). *Obesity: The policy challenges* (Report of the National Taskforce on Obesity). Dublin: Author.

Grampp, C. (1992). Social meanings of residentail gardens. In M. Francis, & R. T. Hester (Eds.), *The meaning of gardens* (pp. 178–183). Cambridge, MA: The MIT Press.

Green, E., Mitchell, W., & Bunton, R. (2000). Contextualizing risk and danger: An analysis of young people's perceptions of risk. *Journal of Youth Studies, 3*(2), 109–126.

Growing Up in Ireland Study. (2011). Key findings: 9 year olds. no 4. The health of 9 year olds. Retrieved September 2, 2013, from http://www.growingup.ie/fileadmin/user_upload/documents/Update_Key_Findings/Key_Findings_4.pdf

Hammersley, M., & Atkinson, P. (2007). *Ethnography, principles in practice* (3rd ed.). London: Routledge.

Hart, R. (1978). *Children's experience of place.* New York, NY: Irvington.

Kaplan, R., & Kaplan, S. (1989). *The experience of nature: A psychological perspective.* New York, NY: Cambridge University Press.

Layte, R., & McCrory, C. (2013). Paediatric chronic illness and educational failure: The role of emotional and behavioural problems. *Social Psychiatry and Psychiatric Epidemiology*, *48*(8): 1307–16.

Lobstein, T., & Jackson-Leach, R. (2006). Estimated burden of paediatric obesity and co-morbidities in Europe. Part 2. Numbers of children with indicators of obesity-related disease. *International Journal of Pediatric Obesity*, *1*(1), 33–41.

Matthews, M. H. (1987). Gender, home range and environmental cognition. *Transactions of the Institute of British Geographers*, *12*, 43–56.

McCoy, S., Quail, A., & Smyth, E. (2012). *Influences on a 9 -year-olds learning; home, school and community. Growing up in Ireland national longitudinal study of children.* Dublin: Government Publications.

Miller, D. N., Gilman, R., & Martens, M. P. (2008). Wellness promotion in the schools: Enhancing students' mental and physical health. *Psychology in the Schools*, *45*(1), 5–15.

Montgomery, H. (2009). *An introduction to childhood: Anthropological perspectives on children's lives.* Oxford: Wiley- Blackwell.

Moore, R., & Young, D. (1978). Childhood outdoors: Toward a social ecology of the landscape. *Children and the Environment*, *3*, 83–130.

Morgan, D. L. (2002). Focus group interviewing. In J. F. Gubrium & J. A. Holstein (Eds.), *Handbook of interview research: Context and method* (pp. 141–160). Thousand Oaks, CA: Sage.

Morgan, M., Gibbs, S., Maxwell, K., & Britten, N. (2002). Hearing children's voices: Methodological issues in conducting focus groups with children aged 7–11 years. *Qualitative Research*, *2*(1), 5–20.

Morton, H. (1996). *Becoming Tongan: An ethnography of childhood.* Hawaii: University of Hawaii Press.

Pellegrini, A. D. (2004). Sexual segregation in childhood: A review of evidence for two hypotheses. *Animal Behaviour*, *68*(1), 435–443.

Pellegrini, A. D., & Smith, P. K. (1998). Physical activity play: The nature and function of a neglected aspect of play. *Child Development*, *69*(3), 577.

Peterson, C., Park, N., & Seligman, M. E. P. (2006). Greater strengths of character and recovery from illness. *Journal of Positive Psychology*, *1*(1), 17–26.

Pollard, E. L., & Lee, P. D. (2003). Child well-being: A systematic review of the literature. *Social Indicators Research*, *61*(1), 59–78.

Prentice, A., & Jebb, S. (1995). Obesity in Britain: Gluttony or sloth? *British Medical Journal*, *311*(7002), 437–439.

Prilleltensky, I., Nelson, G., & Peirson, L. (2001). The role of power and control in children's lives: An ecological analysis of pathways toward wellness, resilience and problems. *Journal of Community & Applied Social Psychology*, *11*(2), 143–158.

Prosser, J. (Ed.). (1998). *Image based research. A sourcebook for qualitative researchers.* London: Routledge Falmer.

Ravetz, A., & Turkington, R. (1995). *The place of home: English domestic environments, 1914–2000.* London: Taylor and Francis.

Rossie, J. P. (2005). Children's play and toys in changing Moroccan communities. In F. F. Mc Mahon, D. Lytle, & B. Sutton-Smith (Eds.), *Play: An interdisciplinary synthesis. Play and culture studies.* MD: University Press of America.

Ryan, R. M., & Deci, E. L. (2000). Self-determination theory and the facilitation of intrinsic motivation, social development, and well-being. *American Psychologist*, *55*(1), 68–78.

Schwartzman, H. B. (1978). *Transformations: The anthropology of children's play.* New York, NY: Plenum Press.

Schwartzman, H. (Ed.). (2001). *Children and anthropology. Perspectives for the 21st century.* Westport, CT: Bergin & Harvey.

Skelton, T., & Valentine, G. (1998). *Cool places: Geographies of youth cultures.* London: Routledge.

Smith, P. K. (2010). *Children and play.* Oxford: Wiley-Blackwell.

Summerbell, C., Waters, E., Edmunds, L., Kelly, S., Brown, T., & Campbell, K. (2005). Interventions for preventing obesity in children (review). *Cochrane Database of Systematic Reviews*, Art. No. CD001871. doi: 10.14651858.

Synthesis. *Play and culture studies.* MD: University Press of America.

Taylor, A. F., & Kuo, F. E. (2006). Is contact with nature important for healthy child development? State of the evidence. In C. Spencer & M. Blades (Eds.), *Children and their environments: learning, using and designing spaces* Cambridge MA: Cambridge University Press.

Thomson, J. L., & Philo, C. (2004). Playful spaces? A social geography of children's play in Livingston, Scotland. *Children's Geographies*, *2*(1), 111.

Thorne, B. (1993). *Gender play: Girls and boys in school*. USA: Rutgers University Press.

Valentine, G., & McKendrick, J. (1997). Children's outdoor play: Exploring parental concerns about children's safety and the changing nature of childhood. *Geoforum, 28*(2), 219–235.

Wenger, M. (1989). Work, play, and social relationships among children in a Giriama community. In D. Belle (Ed.), *Children's social networks and social supports*. New York, NY: John Wiley and Sons.

World Health Organization. (2009). *Global health risks: Mortality and burden of disease attributable to selected major risks*. Geneva: Author.

Playfulness of children at home and in the hospital

Katherine Ryan-Bloomer[a] and Catherine Candler[b]

[a]Department of Occupational Therapy, Rockhurst University, Kansas City, USA; [b]School of Occupational Therapy, Texas Woman's University, Dallas, USA

Play is an essential childhood occupation and important for children's health and well-being. The hospital can be a stressful environment for children and negatively impact their ability to adapt and play. This study examined whether playfulness, an expression of a child's adaptation, would be different among children 14 months through five years in home and hospital environments. Playfulness as measured by the *Test of Playfulness* (Skard, G., & Bundy, A. C. 2008. Test of Playfulness. In L. D. Parham & L. S. Fazio (Eds.), Play in occupational therapy for children (2nd ed., pp. 71–93). St Louis, MO: Mosby Elsevier) was evaluated in eight children at home before hospitalization, at hospital admission, and at discharge. No significant differences were found in playfulness between the home and hospital environments. Playfulness increased between admission and discharge. In addition, correlation analysis indicated that children who exhibited high playfulness at home continued to be more playful in the hospital. The findings suggest that playfulness may be more related to internal, personal, and individual characteristics than environmental differences and children adapt to the hospital environment over time.

Occupations are meaningful and purposeful activities that individuals perform which add structure and routine to their lives and occupy their time (American Occupational Therapy Association, 2008). Childhood occupations include self-care activities, feeding, academic participation, and social participation. Play is one of the most important childhood occupations. Unlike the other childhood occupations that are product-oriented, play is process-oriented (Bundy, 1993). There is a correct way to tie shoes, brush teeth, and complete homework, but play enables a child to participate in fun activities without a specific end goal or correct criteria to meet (Miller-Kuhanek, Sptizer, & Miller, 2010; Skard & Bundy, 2008). Play additionally facilitates cognitive development (Piaget, 1962), language (Bruner, 1972), social skills (Parten, 1932), and psychosocial development (Erikson, 1963; Freud, 1961). Play provides children a vehicle through which they adapt to occupational challenges and form a sense of competency that fosters continued adaptation to challenges throughout the life.

The term playfulness has been used to describe the quality of play or the level of playfulness (Lieberman, 1977). Playfulness has been defined as the lightheartedness that represents as the quality of young children's activities, and later on, as the combinatorial play essential to imagination and creativity (Lieberman, 1977, p. xi.) Playfulness has also been described as a child's disposition to play (Barnett, 1991). Bundy (1993) as well as Skard and Bundy (2008) assert that playfulness is a style an individual uses to approach problems or activities that are characterized by flexibility, creativity, and open-mindedness. Bundy (1993) proposed a model of playfulness that outlines four critical elements: intrinsic motivation, internal control, freedom to suspend reality, and framing that influences the level of playfulness a child exhibits. Intrinsic motivation is the child's internal desire to select and participate in an activity that is pleasing to him or her. This intrinsic motivation may arise from desire for social interaction, a sense of mastery and accomplishment, or for the sensory stimulation the activity provides. Internal control refers to the child's ability to 'be in charge' of himself or herself and the outcomes of the activity. Children may assert internal control by modifying or adapting rules (Bundy, 1993; Skard & Bundy, 2008). Freedom to suspend reality is the ability to adjust the norms or rules for the purposes of play. Children may pretend play different roles or impose a different function on an object that an object does not usually have. For instance, a child may pretend a telephone is a helicopter or pretend to be a doctor and use various objects to 'examine the patient'. Imaginary play relies heavily on the ability to suspend reality. Additionally, framing is another aspect that influences play. Framing is the giving and receiving of social cues that children establish during play (Bundy, 1993; Skard & Bundy, 2008).

Playfulness has been associated with adaptation and coping skills among children (Hess & Bundy, 2003; Saunders, Sayer, & Goodale, 1999). Adaptation is an important feature for human survival and well-being. An individual who is adaptive is able to combat problems and create solutions. The occupational adaptation model within occupational therapy suggests that adaptation arises when there is a press for mastery between the person and the environment (Schkade & Schultz, 1992). When a person is presented with an occupational challenge, the individual must draw from his personal reservoir of traits including cognitive, motor, and psychosocial attributes in order to approach the challenge. The environment, with its physical, social, and cultural features, places a demand on the individual. Each individual must develop an internal adaptation process to meet the challenges faced.

For children, we theorize that play offers an opportunity for children to approach these occupational challenges. Through play, children can experiment with new methods for overcoming challenges without the pressure of having to reach precise, correct solutions as other activities such as setting the table or playing an organized sports game might require. Children can utilize creativity and flexibility to construct novel solutions to meet the challenges posed. Through trial and error during play, the child learns that some solutions bring a sense of happiness and mastery, while other methods do not produce satisfaction to the child, others, or the environment. We hypothesize that this process of a child creatively, spontaneously, and joyfully adapting to challenges during play can be viewed as an expression of playfulness.

Childhood hospitalization creates a unique environment that provides exceptional challenges for children. Hospitalization can produce major stressors for children that may limit their capacity to adapt in this setting. Childhood hospitalization can create feelings of anxiety (Board, 2005; Clatworthy, 1999; Koller, 2008), homesickness (Thurber, Patterson, & Mount, 2007), pain (Board, 2005; Kortesluoma, Punamaki, & Nikkonen, 2008; Stefanatou, 2008; Thurber et al., 2007), fear (Abbot, 1990; Shannon, 1984), and guilt related to viewing hospitalization as a consequence of bad behavior (Abbot, 1990; Shannon, 1984; Wikstrom, 2005). Children primarily adapt and achieve mastery within their environments through play.

Research has identified that hospitalization is associated with negative effects on children's play behaviors. Pediatric hospitalization can limit opportunities for play due to numerous contextual factors including physical, social, and cultural attributes of the hospital environment. The physical environment of the pediatric hospital provides children with stark differences from other familiar environments such as home, school, or a neighborhood park. Rooms are often shared among patients and filled with foreign-looking medical equipment. The hospitals also provide a plethora of sensory experiences that differ from home such as fluorescent lighting, loud noises from alarms and monitors, and potent smells. Often due to infection control, toys that provide calming tactile information such as favorite stuffed animals or blankets from home are restricted. Fleming and Randle (2006) found that every type of toy selected in their investigation of common hospital toys in the pediatric intensive care unit carried some form of bacteria or fungi. They suggested limiting the number of toys that could not be properly sanitized. This recommendation reduces children's opportunities to play with familiar toys that may help them better cope with the multitude of stressors caused by the hospital environment.

The hospital environment frequently offers few designated areas for play to occur. In order for children to engage in play and exude playfulness, a space must be established that is recognized by children as a safe place where it is okay to play (Kielhofner, Barris, Bauer, Shoestock, & Walker, 1983; Skard & Bundy, 2008). Kielhofner et al. (1983) suggested that the play environment must provide an optimal arousal for the children to be enticed to play. An environment that is overly arousing for children may propagate further anxiety and withdrawal, whereas an environment that is under-arousing, may result in decreased interaction from the children with the toys or others due to boredom (Kielhofner et al., 1983). It is important for the child life therapist in collaboration with the occupational therapist to assess each child's temperament, previous history of play experiences, sensory processing skills and current medical condition, in order to gage the child's exposure to novel and over-stimulating features of the playroom (Kielhofner et al., 1983; Koller, 2008). For children who are subjected to prolonged hospitalization, there is a risk of children developing boredom or diversional activity deficit (Kielhofner et al., 1983; Kuntz et al., 1996). Kuntz et al. (1996) suggested that children may become disinterested in participating in typical childhood occupations due to pain, isolation restrictions, or depression. Children may become acclimated to the limited toys available and become less interested in imaginary or symbolic play (Kielhofner et al., 1983).

In order to promote optimal playful behaviors among chronically hospitalized children, it is vital to provide toys and games that are appropriate for the child's cognitive and development level (Kuntz et al., 1996). Making the toys accessible to children is crucial in order to increase the child's engagement and use of the toys (Kielhofner et al., 1983; Prellwitz & Skar, 2007). Toy selection is an important factor in creating a playroom that is enticing for children to initiate and sustain play. Gender specific and gender-neutral toys can stimulate symbolic and imaginary play among preschoolers (Stagnitti, 2004). Landreth (2002) suggests that playrooms contain a variety of toys that allow children many opportunities for emotional and creative expression. Toys should be representative from the following categories: real-life toys, medical toys, creative and artistic materials, and aggressive toys (Landreth, 2002).

The social aspects of the hospital may inhibit opportunities for developmentally appropriate play. The pediatric hospital environment exposes children to a different social environment than their typical childhood environment. Children are often separated from close family and friends they are familiar with and thrust into an environment where they must interact with other persons such as the staff, other patients and their family, and visitors. Children must read and interpret cues from others to know how they may interact with others and what their roles are within this new environment. One of the most important factors influencing a child's adjustment to the social environment of the hospital is the involvement or presence of the child's primary caretaker (Abbot, 1990; Shannon, 1984; Shields, 2001). When a child feels securely attached to caregivers and is assured that the caregiver will be near if needed, then children tend to express themselves and explore their environment more readily (Greenspan, 2002). Often, however, hospitals only permit one caregiver or parent to stay with the child overnight or limit the numbers of hours that a caregiver can visit. Parents and caregivers display increased levels of anxiety when they have less information about upcoming procedures and less opportunity to participate in decisions (Shields, 2001). Similarly, hospitalized children who are given few opportunities to actively make decisions about their care have less than optimal autonomy (Runeson, Hallstrom, Elander, & Hermeren, 2002).

Very few studies have evaluated how children socially interact with other children in the hospital. Pass and Bolig (1993) found that only 29% of hospitalized children participated in group play. Kielhofner et al. (1983) and Gariepy and Howe (2003) similarly found that group play was diminished amongst hospitalized children. Both studies revealed that hospitalized children exhibited decreased levels of group play compared to non-hospitalized children. Morgan (2010) evaluated perceptions of healthcare providers, children, and pediatric hospital administrators on single versus double occupancy rooms. Though recent trends in pediatric hospitalization redesign have promoted single occupancy room for infection control and privacy purposes, there is a belief that single occupancy rooms may cause increased isolation amongst hospitalized children.

Cultural aspects of the hospital environment can influence play. The cultural subsystem comprises the 'procedures, methods, rituals, values, and constraints of the work, play, leisure, and self-maintenance contexts' (Schkade & Schultz, 1992, p. 831). Within a pediatric hospital setting, numerous cultures collide. Not only does each child bring his own religious beliefs, values, morals, and rituals from his own culture, but also each child is exposed to different cultural beliefs and practices from the other children in the hospital environment. Additionally, the hospital setting produces its own culture. There are rules and regulations such as visiting hours for families and guests or designated quiet time for naps. Each child has a designated schedule for waking up, bathing, dressing, attending therapy, and having medical procedures performed. When in the hospital, the goal is for patients to get healthier, discharge from the hospital, and return to their lives. Since the ultimate goal is to promote health and reduce medical problems, more focus may be placed on the patients receiving necessary medical treatments, participating in therapy, and resting than offering opportunities for free time. Often children are not given the opportunity to be a part of the decision-making process regarding their health care despite their ability to do so (Lindeke, Nakal, & Johnson, 2006; Runeson et al., 2002).

Hospitalization can place heavy demands and produce negative effects on children's play. Children who are hospitalized have been found to display delayed play skills compared to typically developing children (Gariepy & Howe, 2003; Kielhofner et al., 1983), decreased levels of playfulness (Kielhofner et al., 1983), and decreased variation in their play routines (Gariepy & Howe, 2003; Kielhofner et al., 1983; Kuntz et al., 1996). Play is a vital childhood occupation and pediatric hospitalization can limit opportunities for children to engage play, yet there are very few studies that investigate how the same children play and exude playfulness at home and in the hospital.

Kielhofner et al. (1983) compared play between three children hospitalized and three age-matched non-hospitalized peers. The children were videotaped playing in three environments: (1) a natural play environment with caretaker participating, that is, a hospital play room for hospitalized group and a typical play space at home for non-hospitalized children; (2) a standardized play environment with the caretaker present, but not actively initiating play; and (3) in the standardized play environment with the caregiver participating in play. The children were videotaped for 30 min sessions in the natural environment and 20 min in the standardized environment. Quantitative tools included the *Preschool Play Scale* (Knox, 1974), which was used to evaluate play age, and *Lieberman's Playfulness Scale* (Lieberman, 1977), which was used to assess playfulness. Results indicated that children who are hospitalized displayed significantly lower playfulness and lower developmental levels of play. Compared to non-hospitalized children, children who were hospitalized exhibited statistically significant lower levels of playfulness and play age scores.

Gariepy and Howe (2003) investigated play amongst 11 children aged 3.1–5.5 with leukemia, who received weekly treatments in a hospital, and 11 typically developing age-matched and gender-matched peers. Observations were made of the children over six weeks using a multiple-baseline design. Both play settings were found to be comparable as measured by the *Childhood Environment Rating Scale-Revised*. Each child's anxiety level was measured by having children rate pictorial cards. Children's social and cognitive play levels were measured by the *Ruben Play Scale* (Rubin, Watson, & Jambor, 1978). Mood was evaluated using the *Self-Distress Measure* (McCabe & Weisz, reported in Weisz, McCabe, & Denning, 1994). Anxiety level was assessed using the *Stress Inventory* (Chandler, 1981). Medical and non-medical toys were introduced and withdrawn throughout the study. Play observations were made using time sampling. Play was evaluated for recurrence of themes, type of social or cognitive play, and type of play as related to stress levels. Similar to the findings of Kielhofner et al. (1983), children who had experienced hospitalization showed significantly fewer play behaviors than typically developing children. Children who were hospitalized were found to display significantly less variation in play activities as compared to typically developing children, supporting the hypothesis that children who had been hospitalized would demonstrate repetitive themes in their play.

Though Gariepy and Howe (2003) did not utilize a specific playfulness measure, the results suggested that children who are hospitalized may display decreased levels of adaptiveness than typically developing children. When new toys were introduced, typically developing children displayed joyful interaction and reported being happy about the new toys. Children who were hospitalized tended to shy away from new toys in preference for familiar toys. Additionally they tended to exhibit similar play routines throughout the study, demonstrating very little variation to their play routine (Gariepy & Howe, 2003).

Pediatric hospitalization can create unique stressors for a child and for the child's family. Children who are hospitalized are at risk for increased levels of anxiety, self-blame, homesickness, and boredom. Depending on the child's developmental stage, the child may have difficulty understanding why he or she has been hospitalized and may attribute hospitalization as a punishment for something bad that he or she has done. Children who are hospitalized are removed from familiar environments and may have few opportunities to play. Since playfulness is an expression of a child's adaptiveness, a child who exhibits less playful behaviors in the hospital may be signaling difficulty coping with the stressors and adapting to the challenges of hospitalization.

Research indicates that children who are hospitalized display decreased variation to their play routines, decreased engagement in parallel or cooperative play with peers, and less exploration of the play environment when compared with typically developing children. In order to assess how playfulness differs at home compared to the hospital environment, it is important to assess differences across the same children. The purpose of this study was to evaluate the level of playfulness both at home and in the hospital to determine if playfulness varies across contexts. Since playfulness is thought to be an expression of a child's adaptiveness, it was hypothesized that children with high levels of playfulness at home would exude high levels of playfulness in the hospital. Additionally, it was expected that children's playfulness scores would increase from admission to discharge, indicating that as children adapted to the hospital environment, they would exhibit more playfulness.

Method

Design

This study employed a quantitative repeated measures design to assess playfulness at home prior to hospitalization, at admission during the first week of hospitalization, and during the last week before the child was discharged from the hospital. Participants in this study were children who were admitted into a hospital-based inpatient feeding program. Typical hospitalization for the inpatient feeding program lasted three to four weeks.

This study was designed to measure playfulness among children at home and at the hospital. Few studies within occupational therapy have evaluated playfulness among children in the hospital, and even fewer studies have investigated playfulness among the same children while at home and in the hospital (Gariepy & Howe, 2003; Kielhofner et al., 1983). Most hospitalizations are emergent, unplanned, and involve a change in medical or cognitive status. These factors have impeded studies on play to generate causal statements about how playfulness differs from the home environment compared to the hospital environment. The inpatient feeding program used in this study offered a unique opportunity in that each child had a pre-planned admission and discharge date that enabled the principal investigator to evaluate playfulness of children in their home environments prior to hospitalization and upon admission to and discharge from the hospital.

Participants

Twelve participants were recruited to the study. Three participants were discharged before the final discharge video was filmed. Pre-admission video was unreadable for one participant resulting in eight participants. The participants ranged in age from 14 months to 5 years ($M = 2.88$ years, $SD = 1.25$ years). Of the eight participants, six were male and two were female with varied diagnoses in addition to feeding issues. Inclusion criteria were that (1) the child be accepted to the inpatient feeding program and have a primary diagnosis of feeding disorder, (2) the child had an appropriate pre-admission evaluation, (3) the child's family was able to obtain and deliver pre-admission video footage of the child playing at home, and (4) the child's parents provided informed consent for the child to be a part of the study. Exclusion criteria were any child who was under the age of 1 year or above the age of 10 years or was under the custody of child protective services. Many of the children had other medical diagnoses in addition to a feeding disorder. More demographic information about the participants may be found in Table 1. Pseudonyms have been given in order to protect confidentiality of the participants.

Participants were selected using convenience sampling based from children selected to the inpatient feeding program. The inpatient feeding program is a specialized program that serves

Table 1. Demographic information.

Participant	Age	Gender	Race	Additional diagnoses
Aiden	2 years	Male	White	Coarcion of the aorta, pulmonary hypertension, developmental delay, apraxia
Janelle	2 years	Female	Black	Patent ductus arteriosus, congenital missing of a kidney, GERD, webbing of toes, missing of UE digits bilaterally
Mateo	5 years	Male	Hispanic	Type I diabetes, autism
Isaac	3 years	Male	Black	Global developmental developmental delays, s/p prematurity, short bowel syndrome
Sarah	14 months	Female	White	TAPVR (total anonymous pulmonary vein return)
David	3 years	Male	White	Hydronephrosis with renal insufficiency, hypertension, nerogenic bladder, anomalous left coronary artery, GERD
Joey	3 years	Male	White	Perinatal complications, Wolf-Hirsschorn syndrome, kidney reflux, asthma, seizure disorder, inguinal hernia, hypospadias, strabismus
Caleb	4 years	Male	White	No other diagnoses other than feeding disorder

children with a primary diagnosis of feeding disorder. Feeding disorder is a medical condition that results from a child not receiving adequate nutrition due to varying etiologies such as poor oral motor skills, sensory processing problems, or maladaptive behaviors during eating (American Speech-Language and Hearing Association [ASHA], 2007). This lack of nutrition, by definition, must last longer than one month and may not be attributed to a lack of exposure to food or other psychological problems (Kennedy Krieger Institute, 2011, retrieved October 7, 2011, from http://www.kennedykrieger.org/patient-care/diagnoses-disorders/feeding-disorders). The inpatient feeding program admitted three to four children for a four- week admission into an inpatient feeding unit at a pediatric rehabilitation hospital. The inpatient feeding team included a pediatric phychiatrist, a behavioral psychologist, nurses, speech language pathologists, occupational therapists, and physical therapists if applicable. During their stay in the inpatient feeding program, the children were provided five structured meals per day including breakfast, lunch, dinner, and two snacks in between meals. Children also attended speech therapy and occupational therapy five to six days a week and physical therapy as needed. Children were invited to participate in child life group sessions and were monitored by a child life specialist throughout their hospital stay. Children were allowed to engage in free play when they were not involved in an above-mentioned therapy session, meal, or snack. The children's parents were educated on behavioral modification and oral motor and sensory strategies to enhance their child's volume, variety, and acceptance of non-preferred foods to ultimately improve the children's nutritional status. Children were admitted to the inpatient feeding unit based on the level of nutritional need. Some children were admitted directly to the program following an outpatient feeding evaluation; other children were admitted from the outpatient feeding program if they were not making substantial enough gains in outpatient therapy to meet their nutritional needs. This inpatient feeding program had been able to reduce the need for gastrostomy tubes by 80% for inpatient feeding program participants at the time of the study.

None of the participants of this study were acutely ill. Some of the participants were receiving nutrition through a gastrostomy tube or naso-gastrostomy tube which supplemented the limited oral diet. The other children ate an oral diet that may have been supplemented by various calorie boosters. The other medical conditions that the children had were stabilized with the children's regimented medical intervention and did not require any surgical interventions. All children were ambulatory, none were connected to intravenous tubes or other medical tubes, so they were more mobile than children who were hospitalized for more acute medical conditions. The primary purpose for all of the participants' admissions was to increase the oral intake of the participants and reduce or eliminate the need for a gastrostomy tube.

Setting

The participants were videotaped indoors and outdoors at home, at admission, and at discharge. For the home visits, the parents or caregivers selected an area inside and outside of the home where the child most frequently played and recorded 15 min of video while the child was playing in each environment.

The majority of the children were filmed in living rooms, bedrooms, or play rooms of their homes for indoor home recordings. The play materials available for each child varied from participant to participant. Many children had manipulative toys available such as puzzles or blocks, cars, dolls, stuffed animals, push-cars, and figurines. Some of the children had pretend play structures such as a play kitchen or play tool bench. One child preferred letter magnets and flashcards while another child played on an iPad. Outdoor place spaces included the children's backyards or neighborhood parks. Some of the children's backyards featured swing sets or play structures. One child played in the front yard on a corner lot. The neighborhood playground structures included a variety of play spaces including slides, swings, rolling barrel apparatuses, spring-loaded bouncy toys, balance beams, climbing structures, and movable fixtures attached to walls such as wheels or latches. Some offered natural barriers and imposed barriers such as ponds, sidewalks, parking lots, or streets.

For the hospital video recording, the research assistant video-taped each participant in routine play areas of the hospital including the inpatient feeding wing play area, the child life playroom, and the outside playground. Figures 1–3 depict hospital play settings. The inpatient feeding wing play area (Figure 1) contained a couch, area rug, two bookshelves, a child-sized table, and bins filled with toys. The play area offered an array of toys designed for different developmental levels. Examples of toys housed in this room included musical and sensorimotor toys, pop-up or cause and effect toys, nesting cups, puzzles, push carts, figurines, magna-doodles, cars, and wagons. The children's rooms were adjacent to this feeding unit play area. The children had open access to this area throughout the day and spent majority of their free time in this area.

The child life playroom (Figure 2) was located across the hall through a set of double doors. The playroom was an open space with windows on one wall, cabinets filled with toys on another wall, a play kitchen along the third wall, and a hallway with hospital rooms attached serving as the fourth wall. Two large, adult-size tables and one small child horseshoe table were located in the middle of the room and a bookshelf with children's books served as a divider for the child life playroom and the hallway. There was an outdoor brick courtyard and small grassy area outside the wall of windows with French doors that were open occasionally during mild-climate months. The courtyard contained a plastic basketball goal, push car toys, and a sandbox. Due to the open nature of the playroom, children and families had access to the playroom during any free time throughout the day outside of child life hours. Child life sessions occurred once daily from 3:00 to 4:30 each weekday and 1:00–2:00 on Saturday, when child life specialists led children under 12 years of age in structured play activities. With the exception of child life times, the cabinets containing toys were kept locked. The play kitchen toys were accessible to the children during free time. There was a teen room available for older children, but was not used in this study since all participants used the younger child life playroom.

The outdoor playground (Figure 3) consisted of a fenced in area that opened up to the outpatient lobby and the inpatient hallway. The playground floor was constructed of recycled tires in a colorful blue and yellow pattern that provided a cushioned surface. There was a fort-like structure with a slide, bridge, and stairs that contained moveable parts on the side walls under the bridge. A few feet away there was a small train structure that children could climb in and out of through

Figure 1. Inpatient feeding unit play area.

Figure 2. Child life playroom.

Figure 3. Outdoor playground.

openings. There was a movable wheel that promoted pretend play to simulate driving. There were two bouncy, spring-loaded toys that children could ride along with a square spring-loaded platform close to the ground that children could climb on and bounce. Lastly a teeter-totter was available. All structures were permanent, fixed structures which primarily promoted gross motor play.

Instruments

Test of playfulness

The Test of Playfulness (ToP) (Skard & Bundy, 2008) is a 29-item standardized observational checklist to measure a child's level of playfulness based on Bundy's Model of Playfulness (Bundy, 1993). This instrument may be found in the appendix. According to the ToP protocol, the child is observed for a 15 min segment in both indoor and outdoor settings. This scale assesses the categories of perception of control, source of motivation, and suspension of reality. Each of the items is rated on a four-point ordinal scale for extent, intensity, or skill. The ToP has been administered to over 2000 children including typically developing children and children with various

PLAY AND WELLBEING

disabilities (Hamm, 2006; Harkness & Bundy, 2001; Hess & Bundy, 2003; Okimoto, Bundy, & Hanzlik, 2000; Reed, Dunbar, & Bundy, 2000). Each item was subjected to Rasch analysis to determine if the items met the assumptions that easy items are easier for everybody and that more playful children will have higher playfulness scores (Bundy, Waugh, & Brentnall, 2009). The ToP has demonstrated good test–retest reliability (Brentnall, 2005; O'Brien & Shirley, 2001; Scott, 2003). In order to administer the ToP, the examiner must be calibrated, which involves watching videos of children playing and submitting ToP scores to the authors. The authors assess the examiner's scoring for leniency and stringency using Rasch analysis. Once calibrated, the examiner may then administer the ToP for research purposes.

The ToP yields a raw score. This score is entered into the *Facets* Rasch analysis statistical program (Linacre, 2011) to produce a measure score and standard error. The measure score is an interval score that compares the child's mean level of playfulness amongst a normative sample of children. The mean ToP measure score for typically developing children is 0.33 and the mean ToP measure score of children with disabilities is −0.33 (A.C. Bundy, personal communication, 11 March 2011).

Data collection procedure

IRB approval was sought and obtained. The principal investigator engaged in the calibration process was approved for test administration for research purposes in all areas with the exception of the items 'mischief and clowning or teasing'. According to Dr Bundy, there were two items, extent of mischief and clowning or teasing, that fell out of acceptable range (>2 for MnSq). Dr Bundy stated that these items are commonly misinterpreted and will eventually be removed from the ToP. Dr Bundy consented to the principal investigator using the ToP for research purposes but requested that the mischief and clowning items listed above be removed from the ToP, when analyzing the data (A.C. Bundy, personal contact, 11 February 2011). Therefore, when the principal investigator evaluated videos of each play session, numeric scores were given for all items except for these items.

Video recording of play sessions was conducted by the parents in the home and by a research assistant in the hospital. The research assistant then constructed a system of organizing the hospital videos in a random sequence so that the principal investigator would be blinded to the order of the video clips. Because there was only one data collection point in the home environment, it was not possible to blind the principal investigator to the time frame of the video footage for the home environment. However, since video footage took place in the same indoor and outdoor settings within the hospital at admission and discharge, the principal investigator evaluated the video without knowing whether the video footage was of the child at admission or discharge. Once all of the videos had been scored, the principal investigator identified the admission versus discharge data in order to run statistical tests. The principal investigator completed a ToP score sheet for each data point.

Data analysis

Wilcoxon-signed rank tests were performed to examine the change in playfulness between each time period. Spearman rank correlations tested the hypothesis that participants with higher playfulness scores at admission would show higher playfulness in the hospital.

Results

The mean playfulness scores for the participants were 0.225 ($SD = 1.078$) at pre-admission, 0.069 ($SD = 0.763$) at admission, and 0.364 ($SD = 0.763$) at discharge. These scores indicate that the

PLAY AND WELLBEING

Table 2. Correlation of combined playfulness sores.

Measure	Pre-admission	Admission	Discharge
Pre-admission	–	0.857[a]	0.850[a]
Admission	0.857[a]	–	0.886[a]
Discharge	0.850[a]	0.886[a]	–

[a]Correlation at the $p < 0.01$ level.

participants as a group were not as playful as typically developing children who display an average playfulness of 0.43. However, the participants in this study were more playful at each time period than children with disabilities who display a mean playfulness score of −0.43; the comparison sample of children with disabilities included various medical diagnoses such as autism spectrum disorders, attention deficit disorder, cerebral palsy, and emotional disorders (Skard & Bundy, 2008).

In order to determine if there were any differences in playfulness between each of the time periods, three Wilcoxon-signed rank tests were performed for pair-wise comparisons. The results showed no significant differences in playfulness between pre-admission and admission ($Z = 0.338$, $p = 0.735$), or from pre-admission to discharge ($Z = 1.183$, $p = 0.238$). There was, however, a significant difference found between admission to discharge ($Z = 2.197$, $p = 0.028$). Figure 1 illustrates the change in playfulness scores for each participant across time periods. Spearman rank tests found strong significant correlations between all time periods. The correlations between combined ToP measure scores can be viewed in Table 2.

Discussion

In this study, playfulness among children at home and at the hospital was measured to examine for differences in playfulness across these environments. Both hypotheses, which stated '(1) children with high levels of playfulness at home will show high levels of playfulness in the hospital and (2) children's playfulness scores would be higher at discharge than at admission', were supported. The significant correlations of playfulness at pre-admission, admission, and discharge suggest that playfulness in participants may be attributed to individual differences in children rather than environmental differences between home and hospital settings.

For this group of children in the in patient feeding program, no difference in playfulness between settings was identified. The children were equally playful at home before admission and in the hospital. Playfulness within the hospital over time, however, did increase. The children were significantly more playful at the end of their hospitalization than they were at the beginning of their hospitalization. The increase in overall mean playfulness from admission to discharge may suggest that the children were able to adapt to the environment and become more playful as they became more familiar with the hospital.

The small sample size of the study may have decreased the ability to obtain statistically significant results. When examining the combined measure score of playfulness for each participant, the ToP measure scores were higher at discharge than at admission for all but two of the participants (Figure 4). One of the exceptions, Sarah, displayed the same level of playfulness at admission as she did at discharge.

The participants in this study were under the age of 6. Saunders et al. (1999) found that young children displayed higher coping and lower levels of playfulness than older children. Though no formalized coping inventory was taken for this study, the participants in this study seemed to have developed a sense of coping with the environment, as exhibited by their increased playfulness by

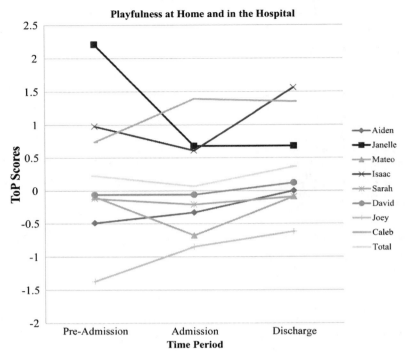

Figure 4. ToP scores.

the end of the hospitalization. Contrary to the findings of Shannon (1984) who found that preschool children were at greater risk for maladjustment to the hospitalization (due to not being able to cognitively understand why they were hospitalized) this study revealed that participants, all younger than 6, were able to be playful and presumably cope with the changes of environment between home and the hospital.

Playfulness is an expression of a child's individual adaptiveness, and play is a method of reaching mastery. The positive relationships found at each time period, across settings, support this possibility. The participants who were more playful at home were also more playful in the hospital. Likewise, children with lower playfulness scores at home were found to produce low playfulness scores in the hospital. More playful participants demonstrated the ability to exhibit intrinsic motivation, internal control, freedom to suspend reality, and appropriate framing. They had produced a playful experience in their familiar home environment. When more playful children were exposed to a new situation of hospitalization, they exhibited creativeness to approach the new environment with open-mindedness and joy. In short, the results indicated that this playful demeanor was comparably expressed in the hospital as at home.

Given the consistency of playfulness in individual children across environments, our findings suggest that children may exude differing levels of playfulness and retain these differences across a change in environment. These results, that playfulness remained relatively constant across time periods and settings, lend support to previous findings of O'Brien and Shirley (2001), who found playfulness scores to remain stable over several years. Bundy (1993) and Skard and Bundy (2008) suggest that playfulness consists of four factors that vary according to personal, individual attributes. Intrinsic motivation, internal control, freedom to suspend reality, and framing all require the child to utilize psychosocial, emotional, and cognitive functions. Unlike levels of physical skills, these characteristics may be more continuous in individuals over time. Schkade and Schultz (1992) similarly suggested that when individuals face an occupational challenge, there is a press for mastery between the personal factors and the environmental factors. Perhaps in this study, the personal attributes of the children were more influential to their playfulness than the environmental factors posed by a hospital feeding program.

Limitations

This study possessed limitations that may have impacted the results. The participants, recorded by a conspicuous video camera, may have been in some way reactive to the camera. The sample size of the study was small. Despite some ethnic diversity, with participants being of European American, African American, and Hispanic backgrounds, the sample was regionally limited and disproportionately representative of boys. Another limitation was that participants in this study were hospitalized, but not acutely ill or dependent on medical equipment, such as intravenous tubes or oxygen tubing, that otherwise may have impacted their mobility for play. The participants in this study were gaining nutritional support, through the feeding program intervention, which may have improved overall health and thus made the children more motivated to play. Since the participants in this sample did not endure changes in cognitive or physical status as do most children who enter the hospital for acute or emergent hospitalization, the results of this study must interpreted cautiously.

Though the principal investigator met calibration criteria to score the ToP and was given permission to utilize the ToP and score it independently from the test's authors, there was no other rater scoring the ToP aside from the principal investigator. However, the principal investigator submitted all scores to Dr Bundy, the developer of the ToP, to be analyzed using Rasch analysis. Dr Bundy was blinded to the study hypotheses as well as which time frame the participants' ToP scores were taken, which reduced investigator bias. Additional attempts to reduce investigator bias were taken. The principal investigator was blinded to the time each video was taken when watching and scoring the videos using the ToP. The principal investigator was also blinded to the demographic information such as diagnoses, ages, and previous hospitalization experience, prior to watching and scoring the videos. These precautions enabled the principal investigator to score the videos based on playfulness exuded, without having preconceived notions.

Future implications for research

If this study were to be replicated with a larger sample size involving more children, equal numbers of males and females, and children of varying ages and diagnoses, more generalizable information about children's playfulness both at home and in the hospital could be gained. A multiple regression study to evaluate the elements of playfulness may lead to a better prediction of whether a child will demonstrate increased playfulness in the hospital. Evaluating diagnostic features related to the ToP scores may elicit a better understanding of the influence of diagnostic features on playfulness of children who are hospitalized.

Clinical implications

Very few studies performed by occupational therapists have evaluated playfulness among children who were hospitalized. This study added new knowledge about playfulness within the hospital environment. This study, by evaluating playfulness among the same children prior to entering the hospital and during their hospitalization, added support to the notion that playfulness is an expression of a child's level of adaptiveness. This within-child consistency in overall levels of playfulness may reflect personal coping mechanisms and attributes of the child, independent of environment. Since playfulness was also found to increase from admission to discharge, there is evidence to support that when children were introduced to the new situation of this hospital-based feeding program, they were able to adapt to the demands of the environment over time and express this through playfulness.

Occupational therapists work with children to engage in meaningful occupations. Since play is considered a vital childhood occupation, it is important for occupational therapists to recognize the personal attributes that lead to playfulness and support skills required to be playful. At the same time, this study also showed that even children with lower levels of playfulness gained in playfulness from admission to discharge. Occupational therapists can collaborate with child life specialists and other healthcare team members to ensure that children who are hospitalized have opportunities to play adaptively.

Acknowledgements

Contributor acknowledgments: Kara Kennedy, MOT, OTR/L; Anita C. Bundy, ScD, OTR; Glen Jennings, Ed.D.; Gayle Hersch, PhD, OTR; and Gail Poskey, PhD, OTR.

References

Abbot, K. (1990). Therapeutic use of play in the psychological preparation of preschool children undergoing cardiac surgery. *Comprehensive Pediatric Nursing, 13*, 265–277.

American Occupational Therapy Association. (2008). Occupational therapy practice framework: Domain and process. *American Journal of Occupational Therapy, 62*, 625–683.

American Speech-Language and Hearing Association. (2007). Guidelines for speech-language pathologists providing swallowing and feeding services in school. *ASHA Practice Policies.* Retrieved June 11, 2009, from www.ASHA.org

Barnett, L. (1991). The playful child: Measurement of a disposition to play. *Play and Culture, 4*, 51–74.

Board, R. (2005). School-age children's perceptions of their PICU hospitalization. *Pediatric Nursing, 31*(3), 166–175.

Brentnall, J. (2005). *The effect of the length of observation on the test-retest reliability of the Test of Playfulness* (Unpublished honours thesis). University of Sydney.

Bruner, J. S. (1972). Nature and uses of immaturity. *American Psychologist, 27*, 687–708.

Bundy, A. C. (1993). Assessment of play and leisure: Delineation of the problem. *American Journal of Occupational Therapy, 47*(3), 217–222.

Bundy, A. C., Waugh, K., & Brentnall, J. (2009). Developing assessments that account for the role of the environment: An example using the test of playfulness and test of environmental supportiveness. *Occupational Therapy Journal of Research: Occupation, Participation, and Health, 29*(3), 135–143.

Chandler, L. A. (1981). The source of stress inventory. *Psychology in the Schools, 18*, 164–168.

Clatworthy, S. (1999). Child drawing: Hospital – an instrument designed to measure emotional status of hospitalized school aged children. *Journal of Pediatric Nursing, 14*(1), 2–9.

Erikson, E. H. (1963). *Childhood and society.* New York, NY: Norton.

Fleming, K., & Randle, J. (2006). Toys – friend or foe? A study of infection risk in pediatric intensive care unit. *Pediatric Nursing, 18*, 14–18.

Freud, S. (1961). *Beyond the pleasure principle.* New York, NY: Norton.

Gariepy, N., & Howe, N. (2003). The therapeutic power of play: Examining the play of young children with leukaemia. *Child: Care, Health, & Development, 29*(6), 523–537.

Greenspan, S. (2002). *The secure child: Helping children feel safe and confident in an insecure world.* Cambridge, MA: Perseus.

Hamm, E. M. (2006). Playfulness and environmental support of play in children with and without developmental disabilities. *Occupational Therapy Journal of Research: Occupation, Participation, and Health, 26*(3), 88–96.

Harkness, L., & Bundy, A. C. (2001). Playfulness and children with physical disabilities. *Occupational Therapy Journal of Research, 21*, 73–89.

Hess, L. M., & Bundy, A. C. (2003). The association between playfulness and coping in adolescents. *Physical & Occupational Therapy in Pediatrics, 23*(2), 5–17.

Kennedy Krieger Institute. (2011). *Feeding disorders overview.* Retrieved October 7, 2011, from http://www.kennedykrieger.org/patient-care/diagnoses-disorders/feeding-disorders

Kielhofner, G., Barris, R., Bauer, D., Shoestock, B., & Walker, L. (1983). A comparison of play behavior in non-hospitalized and children who are hospitalized. *American Journal of Occupational Therapy, 37*(5), 305–312.

Knox, S. (1974). A play scale. In M. Reilly (Ed.), *Play as exploratory learning: Studies of exploratory behaviors* (pp. 247–266). Beverly Hills, CA: Sage Publications.

Koller, D. (2008). *Child Life Council evidence-based practice statement: Therapeutic play in pediatric health care: The essence of Child Life practice.* Retrieved December 19, 2008, from http://www.childlife.org

Kortesluoma, R. L., Punamaki, R. L., & Nikkonen, M. (2008). Children who are hospitalized drawing their pain: The contents and cognitive and emotional characteristics of pain drawings. *Journal of Child Health Care, 12*(4), 284–300.

Kuntz, N., Adams, J. A., Zahr, L., Killen, R., Cameron, K., & Wasson, H. (1996). Therapeutic play and bone marrow transplantation. *Journal of Pediatric Nursing, 11*, 359–367.

Landreth, G. (2002). *Play therapy: The art of the relationship.* New York, NY: Brunner-Routledge.

Lieberman, J. N. (1977). *Playfulness: Its relationship to imagination and creativity.* New York, NY: Academic Press.

Linacre, M. J. (2011). *Facets. Many-facet Rasch Measurement Program.* Retrieved March 10, 2011, from http://www.winsteps.com/facets.htm

Lindeke, L., Nakal, M., & Johnson, L. (2006). Capturing children's voices for quality improvement. *American Journal of Maternal/Child Nursing, 31*, 290–295.

Miller-Kuhanek, H., Sptizer, S., & Miller, E. (2010). *Activity analysis, creativity, and playfulness in pediatric occupational therapy: Making play just right.* Boston, MA: Jones and Bartlett.

Morgan, H. (2010). Single and shared accommodation for young patients in hospital. *Paediatric Nursing, 22*(8), 20–24.

O'Brien, J. C., & Shirley, R. J. (2001). Does playfulness change over time? A preliminary look using the Test of Playfulness. *Occupational Therapy Journal of Research, 21*, 132–139.

Okimoto, A. M., Bundy, A. C., & Hanzlik, J. (2000). Playfulness in children with and without disability: Measurement and intervention. *American Journal of Occupational Therapy, 54*(1), 73–82.

Parten, M. B. (1932). Social participation among pre-school children. *Journal of Abnormal and Social Psychology, 27*, 243–269.

Pass, M., & Bolig, R. (1993). A comparison of play behaviors in two Child Life program variations. *Children's Health Care, 22*, 5–17.

PLAY AND WELLBEING

Piaget, J. (1962). *Play, dreams, and imitation in childhood* (C. Gattegno & F. M. Hodgson, Trans.). New York, NY: W.W. Norton.

Prellwitz, M., & Skar, L. (2007). Usability of playgrounds for children of different abilities. *Occupational Therapy International, 14*(3), 144–155.

Reed, C. N., Dunbar, S. B., & Bundy, A. C. (2000). The effects of inclusive programming on the playfulness of preschoolers with and without autism. *Physical and Occupational Therapy in Pediatrics, 19*, 73–91.

Rubin, K. H., Watson, K. S., & Jambor, T. W. (1978). Free play behaviours in preschool and kindergarten children. *Child Development, 49*, 534–536.

Runeson, I., Hallstrom, I., Elander, G., & Hermeren, G. (2002). Children's participation in the decision-making process during hospitalization: An observational study. *Nursing Ethics, 9*, 583–598.

Saunders, I., Sayer, M., & Goodale, A. (1999). The relationship between playfulness and coping in preschool children: A pilot study. *American Journal of Occupational Therapy, 53*(2), 221–226.

Schkade, J. K., & Schultz, S. (1992). Occupational adaptation: Toward a holistic approach for contemporary practice, Part 1. *American Journal of Occupational Therapy, 46*(9), 829–837.

Scott, F. C. (2003). *The test-retest reliability of the Test of Playfulness* (Unpublished master's thesis). University of Toronto, ON, Canada.

Shannon, S. (1984). The effects of hospitalization on young children. *Australian Nurses Journal, 13*, 33–34, 48.

Shields, L. (2001). A review of the literature from developed and developing countries relating to the effects of hospitalization on children and parents. *International Council of Nurses: International Nursing Review, 48*, 29–37.

Skard, G., & Bundy, A. C. (2008). Test of Playfulness. In L. D. Parham & L. S. Fazio (Eds.), *Play in occupational therapy for children* (2nd ed., pp. 71–93). St Louis, MO: Mosby Elsevier.

Stagnitti, K. (2004). Understanding play: The implications for play assessment. *Australian Occupational Therapy Journal, 51*, 3–12.

Stefanatou, A. (2008). Use of drawings in children with pervasive developmental disorder during hospitalization: A developmental perspective. *Journal of Child Health Care, 12*(4), 268–283.

Thurber, C. A., Patterson, D. R., & Mount, K. K. (2007). Homesickness and children's adjustment to hospitalization: Toward a preliminary model. *Children's Healthcare, 36*(1), 1–28.

Weisz, J. R., McCabe, M. A., & Denning, M. D. (1994). Primary and secondary control among children undergoing medical procedures: Adjustment as a function of coping style. *Journal of Consulting and Clinical Psychology, 6*, 324–332.

Wikstrom, B. M. (2005). Communicating via expressive arts: The natural medium of self-expression for hospitalized. *Pediatric Nursing, 31*, 480–485.

PLAY AND WELLBEING

Appendix

Test of Playfulness

TEST OF PLAYFULNESS (ToP) (Version 4.0–5/05)

	EXTENT	INTENSITY	SKILLFULNESS
Child (#): _____ Age: _____ Rater: _____ In Out Video Live (Circle)	3 = Almost always 2 = Much of the time 1 = Some of the time 0 = Rarely or never NA = Not Applicable	3 = Highly 2 = Moderately 1 = Mildly 0 = Not NA = Not Applicable	3 = Highly skilled 2 = Moderately skilled 1 = Slightly skilled 0 = Unskilled NA = Not Applicable

ITEM	EXT	INT	SKILL	COMMENTS
Is actively engaged.				
Decides what to do.				
Maintains level of safety sufficient to play.				
Tries to overcome barriers or obstacles to persist with an activity.				
Modifies activity to maintain challenge or make it more fun.				
Engages in playful mischief or teasing.				
Engages in activity for the sheer pleasure of it (process) rather than primarily for the end product.				
Pretends (to be someone else; to do something else; that an object is something else; that something else is happening).				
Incorporates objects or other people into play in unconventional or variable **and** creative ways.				
Negotiates with others to have needs/desires met.				
Engages in social play.				
Supports play of others.				
Enters a group already engaged in an activity.				
Initiates play with others.				
Clowns or jokes.				
Shares (toys, equipment, friends, ideas).				
Gives readily understandable cues (facial, verbal, body) that say, "This is how you should act toward me."				
Responds to others' cues.				
Demonstrates positive affect during play.				
Interacts with objects.				
Transitions from one play activity to another with ease.				

Family play and leisure activities: correlates of parents' and children's socio-emotional well-being

Diana D. Coyl-Shepherd and Colleen Hanlon

Child Development Department, California State University at Chico, Chico, USA

> Guided by systems theory, this mixed-methods study of 98 families examined parent- and child-reported play, exploration, and leisure activities in relation to family members' socio-emotional well-being. Parents and children completed surveys independently and interviews were conducted with a subset of families. Quantitative findings showed that child report of secure exploration with both parents, and mother report of leisure activities, were associated with some couple and parent–child well-being indicators and nearly all child well-being indicators. Father report of play and leisure activities was associated with more couple and parent–child well-being indicators than mother report and showed some differences in associations with child well-being indicators. Interview data provided examples of how families incorporate play and leisure into their busy lives and the perceived benefits and enjoyment derived from these activities. These findings emphasize the importance of family play and leisure involvement for parents' and children's well-being.

A recent clinical report published by the American Academy of Pediatrics focused on the importance of play in promoting healthy child development and strong parent–child bonds. The authors stated,

> Play is essential to the social, emotional, cognitive, and physical well-being of children beginning in early childhood. It is a natural tool for children to develop resiliency as they learn to cooperate, overcome challenges, and negotiate with others. Play also allows children to be creative. It provides time for parents to be fully engaged with their children, to bond with their children, and to see the world from the perspective of their child. (Milteer & Ginsburg, 2012, p. 204)

This statement implies that parent–child play provides benefits and promotes well-being in adults as well as their children. The report mirrors findings from family studies and child development literature that document play-derived gains in cognitive competencies and increased school motivation (Fantuzzo & McWayne, 2002; Fantuzzo, Sekino, & Cohen, 2004; Raver & Ziegler, 1997; Wentzel, 1999), self-advocacy skills (Hurwitz, 2002–2003; McElwain & Volling, 2005), physical health (Campbell & Hesketh, 2007; Cleland & Venn, 2010), as well as social–emotional benefits of child and peer play (Barnett, 1990; Coolahan, Fantuzzo, Mendez, & McDermott, 2000; Fisher,

1992; Pellegrini & Smith, 1998) and family play (e.g. Elkind, 2007; Frost, 2012; Reading, 2007; Roggman, Boyce, Cook, Christiansen, & Jones, 2004; Stevenson & Crnic, 2013; Tamis-LeMonda, Shannon, Cabrera, & Lamb, 2004; Tsao, 2002; Wong, Weiyi, Song, Strober, & Golinkoff, 2008). However, contemporary family lifestyles (e.g. dual-earner parents) and technology-based forms of entertainment and socializing have been associated with increases in children's and adults' sedentary behaviors, poorer diets, and other health problems (Frost & Brown, 2009). Children's mental and emotional health may also be negatively affected by increased multi-media involvement and decreases in outdoor or free play (Gray, 2011; Kaiser Family Foundation, 2010; Sax, 2007). Evidence of the benefits of play for children is abundant (e.g. Brown, 2009; Frost, Wortham, & Reifel, 2012), but limited research has examined how family play and leisure activities may contribute to parents' socio-emotional well-being. The current study employs a mixed-methods design to explore these associations.

Theoretical framework

A systems perspective acknowledges that individual behavior influences other family members (Cox & Paley, 1997; Whitchurch & Constantine, 1993). Studies show reciprocal socialization processes within parent–child relationships (Carson & Parke, 1996; Gault-Sherman, 2011; Manongdo & Garcia, 2011). Happily married parents are reportedly more responsive and affectionate toward children (Fincham & Hall, 2005; Holland & McElwain, 2013) and marital satisfaction is often related to good parenting (Grych, 2002). Child characteristics (e.g. gender, age, temperament) also affect parent–child relationship quality and the martial relationship (Crouter & Booth, 2003; Mehall, Spinrad, Eisenberg, & Gaertner, 2009; Paikoff & Brooks-Gunn, 1991). Both theory and research indicate that positive parent–child involvement, including play, promotes children's cognitive, social, and emotional well-being (Flouri & Buchanan, 2003, 2004; Kazura, 2000; NICHD, 2004; Parke, 2004; Roopnarine & Mounts, 1985; Tamis-LeMonda et al., 2004).

Mother and father involvement practices

Parents' ability to be consistently and positively involved often depends on contextual factors; some factors may deter involvement (e.g. employment conditions or other perceived barriers to involvement; Freeman, Newland, & Coyl, 2008; Kiernan & Huerta, 2008; Milkie, Kendig, Nomaguchi, & Denny, 2010) and some support involvement (e.g. beliefs and motives favoring involvement; Coyl-Shepherd & Newland, 2013; Green, Walker, Hoover-Dempsey, & Sandler, 2007). Changes within US families due to non-marital childbearing, unstable cohabitating relationships, and divorce impact parent involvement, particularly time allotted for play and leisure activities. While many co-residential fathers are more involved with their children today, involvement by non-residential fathers has significantly decreased (Livingston & Parker, 2011; Pleck & Masciadrelli, 2004; Yeung, Sandberg, Davis-Kean, & Hofferth, 2001).

Mothers and fathers may be involved in similar and unique ways, engaging in complementary parenting roles within the family system (Grossmann, Grossmann, Kindler, & Zimmermann, 2008; Newland, Coyl-Shepherd, & Paquette, 2013; Paquette, 2004). More often mother–child relationships involve didactic and caregiving interactions in which maternal warmth and sensitivity are associated with positive child outcomes, while father–child interactions more typically involve playful exchanges that include teasing, rough-and-tumble play (RTP), and encouragement of risk taking (Bretherton, Lambert, & Golby, 2005; Fletcher, 2011; Fletcher, St. George, & Freeman, 2013; Grossman et al., 2002; Kazura, 2000; Lamb, 1997; Newland & Coyl, 2010). Involvement practices are affected by parent and child gender and child age, as well as other contextual influences such as co-parenting practices, couple relationship quality, and parental perspectives on gender roles (Caldera & Lindsey, 2006; Cowan, Cowan, & Mehta, 2009; Newland, Coyl, & Chen, 2010; Raley & Bianchi, 2006).

Family leisure

For over 70 years research has revealed positive relationships between family leisure and beneficial family outcomes such as increased family functioning and family closeness (Hawks, 1991; Orthner & Mancini, 1991). Leisure is an important component of healthy and cohesive relationships within families and many families believe leisure involvement affects parenting and family life (Daly, 2001). Within families these activities can be utilized to enhance well-being (Mannell, 2007). Parents often perceive family leisure activities as providing opportunities to augment children's development through communication, bonding, and learning experiences (Orthner & Mancini, 1991; Shaw & Dawson, 2001). Family leisure time has been shown to facilitate children's development across multiple domains (e.g. social, emotional, and psychological; see Holman & Epperson, 1989).

Some researchers suggest that leisure satisfaction among family members is more important when determining well-being than satisfaction within any other domain (Agate, Zabriskie, Agate, & Poff, 2009; Riddick, 1986) and is a significant predictor of quality of life (Russell, 1990). Studies of married couples' leisure involvement and satisfaction have been related to both marital satisfaction (Holman & Jacquart, 1988; Johnson, Zabriskie, & Hill, 2006; Orthner, 1975) and overall family life satisfaction (Mactavish & Schleien, 1998; Zabriskie & McCormick, 2003). Gender differences have been found between mothers' and fathers' perceptions and individual experiences of family leisure (Larson et al., 1997; Mattingly & Bianchi, 2003; Shaw, 1992). Parent gender differences in leisure activities may mirror differences found in mothers' and fathers' play with children.

Father play

According to Bowlby (1982) fathering involves a particular emphasis on play, mentorship, and encouragement of the child in challenging situations. Play is the only dimension of parenting in which fathers are more involved with children than mothers (MacDonald & Parke, 1986; Power & Parke, 1983). Play styles tend to vary by parent gender. More fathers engage in vigorous, unpredictable, and excitatory physical play, whereas mothers tend to engage in more cognitive object-mediated play and role-playing (e.g. Fletcher, 2011; Schoppe-Sullivan, Kotila, Jia, Lang, & Bower, 2013). While it is possible for mothers and fathers to engage in similar types of play, some research and theory suggests that children may experience similar interactions with mothers versus fathers differently (Bretherton et al., 2005; Dubeau, 1995; Grossmann et al., 2008).

Fathers' propensity for more active, physical play, their teasing during play to challenge children emotionally and cognitively, and their tendency to promote risk-taking open their children to new experiences (Grossman et al., 2002; Kromelow, Harding, & Touris, 1990). This type of play has been linked to children's increased capacity for autonomy and the management of risk-taking during exploration of physical and social environments. It further enhances development of physical and social skills, self-assertiveness, anger management, reduced physical aggression with peers, and academic success (Fletcher, 2011; Newland & Coyl, 2010; Paquette, Carbonneau, Dubeau, Bigras, & Tremblay, 2003; Paquette, Coyl-Shepherd, & Newland, 2013). Recently, this play style has been theorized and described as an *activation* relationship, which promotes children's development and contributes to emotional bonding between fathers and children (see Paquette, 2004). Most studies of father–child activation and RTP have focused on toddler and preschool samples. Limited research has investigated this play style with older children.

Parent well-being

Although numerous studies have examined associations between parent well-being and co-parenting (Caldera & Lindsey, 2006), adult attachment, marital satisfaction (Cowan et al., 2009; Coyl, Newland, & Freeman, 2010), and parent stress (Mitchell & Cabrera, 2009; Saisto, Salmela-Aro, Nurmi, & Halmesmäki, 2008), fewer investigations have specifically examined how the quality and type of parent–child play and leisure involvement may benefit parents. Only limited research has examined parents' perceptions of useful strategies for coping with stress (Kwon, Han, Jeon, & Bingham, 2013); we are unaware of any studies that have specifically examined the use of family playtime to reduce parent stress and enhance marital and parent–child well-being. This study was designed to explore the potential benefits of family play and leisure to the marital and parent–child subsystems. A systems perspective would suggest that experiences in one subsystem (parent–child) are likely to influence other family subsystems (mother–father). Might fathers and mothers perceive greater couple dyadic satisfaction and attachment security associated with their positive involvement in parent–child play and leisure activities? Might these activities reduce parent stress and increase their motives for parent–child involvement and their positive perceptions of the quality of their parent–child relationships?

Research design and study goals

This study used a concurrent triangulation design (see Hanson, Creswell, Clark, Petska, & Creswell, 2005) to address three research goals. Goal 1 was intended to compare mother and father qualitative and quantitative data on play, roughhousing, and leisure involvement, with children's report of secure exploration and roughhousing with each parent. Goal 2 was intended to examine associations of these family play variables with parents' and children's socio-emotional well-being. Our second goal was explored with two research questions. First, are there associations across parent- and child-reported play involvement, parent–child leisure activities, and indicators of child well-being (i.e. locus of control, social stress, depression, inadequacy, self-esteem, self-reliance, positive relations with parents, and interpersonal relations with peers and others)? Second, are there associations among parent- and child-reported play involvement, parent–child leisure activities, and indicators of parent socio-emotional well-being (i.e. dyadic satisfaction, attachment to partner/spouse, parent stress, motives for involvement, and parent–child relationship quality)?

Goal 3 was designed to examine potential mean score differences in parent well-being, parent–child relationship quality, parent motives for involvement, family play and leisure involvement, and child-reported roughhousing and secure exploration, by generating profiles for a subsample of eight families whose children showed low well-being (i.e. children who scored high on indicators of negative well-being) and a subsample of six families whose children showed high well-being (i.e. children who scored high on indicators of positive well-being). Interview data provided additional insight into parents' and children's unique perspectives of play and leisure activities and how these activities were perceived with regard to contributing to family members' well-being.

Method

Data collection and ethical procedures

Institutional Review Board approval, parent consent, and child assent were obtained prior to data collection. Research assistants (RAs) recruited parents within local community networks. Trained

RAs administered all measures and interviews in the participants' homes following a written protocol. Data collection from children included: (a) an explanation of the study in developmentally appropriate language followed by a written child assent form read aloud to each child, (b) children were told they would be providing oral (via interviews) and written (via surveys) responses to questions about parenting styles, their family relationships, self-concept, well-being, and family activities. They were told they could stop or skip items if they chose and there would be no penalty for doing so, (c) there was a period of time to establish rapport between the RA and the child before conducting the semi-structured interview, followed by the administration of the survey measures. For younger children, RAs read items aloud. After each measure the child was asked if they would like a break. If the child showed signs of fatigue, assessments were broken into two assessment periods (e.g. the RA offered to return another day to complete data collection). Data collection from parents also included an explanation of the study followed by a written informed consent letter, which parents read and signed. Parents completed the surveys independently of their partners. A break was provided before the parent interviews were conducted. Parents were also told they could skip items or chose not to respond to queries within the surveys and interview; they were reassured that there would be no penalty for non-responses.

Participants

Participants in this study included families from the Northwestern USA. The families had between 1 and 6 children. This study was designed to examine play and leisure patterns, and social and emotional well-being between parents and a school-age child; thus parents were asked to select one of their children currently in elementary school to participate and to be the focus for their responses. There were 98 mothers (mean age = 37.85), 93 fathers (mean age = 39.95), and 98 school-age children (ages 7–13; mean age = 9.53); 61% of the participating children were female. Child ethnicity was 60% Caucasian, 20% Hispanic, 8% Asian American, and 12% multi-ethnic or 'other'. Approximately 95% were biological mothers; 78% were biological fathers. For family income, 28% reported incomes of <$40,000, 17% reported between $41,000–65,000, and 55% reported >$65,000. Parent education ranged from high school education or less, to graduate or professional degrees; the majority had some college or a four-year degree. The majority of parents worked; mothers' median hours per week were 25 and fathers' were 40.

Parent quantitative measures

Fathers and mothers independently completed scales measuring family play and leisure activities, with items rated on a 5-point scale, either from 'rarely' to '4 or more times per week' or from 'never' to 'always'. Items included: (1) *outdoor games and sports* (5 items, e.g. practicing a sport, riding bikes, outdoor games), and (2) *leisure activity involvement* (10 items, e.g. reading together, crafts or hobbies, playing video or computer games, card and board games, outings with child. These two areas were both adapted from Cabrera et al. (2004). Another single item additionally included was: (3) *roughhousing* (1 item, 'How often do you roughhouse or play tickle games?').

Parents' couple well-being was assessed with a measure of (1) *Dyadic Satisfaction* from *The Dyadic Adjustment Scale* (Spanier, 1976) and (2) *Adult Attachment Scale* (AAS; Simpson, Rholes, & Nelligan, 1992); separate subscale scores for the AAS were created for *Partner Secure, Avoidant and Ambivalent Attachment*. Parent–child well-being was measured by (3) *Parent Stress* (Newland et al., 2010), (4) *Motives for Involvement* (e.g. because it is fun and enjoyable, to relax after work), and (5) *Parent–Child Relationship Quality* (both from Newland, Chen et al., 2013). Reliability coefficients for all variables are reported in Table 1.

PLAY AND WELLBEING

Table 1. Descriptive statistics for parent socio-emotional variables and paired differences for family play and leisure activities.

	Mothers			Fathers				
	M	SD	*α*	*M*	SD	*α*	*t*	Cohen's *d*
Parent socio-emotion variables								
Dyadic satisfaction	5.02	0.63	0.84	4.95	0.64	0.85	0.94	0.11
Secure with partner	4.58	0.58	0.82	4.41	0.75	0.87	2.46*	0.25
Avoidant with partner	1.46	0.68	0.89	1.58	0.73	0.85	−1.51	0.17
Ambivalent with partner	1.45	0.64	0.69	1.68	0.88	0.80	−2.45*	0.30
Parent stress	4.10	1.88	0.80	4.22	1.96	0.80	−0.54	−0.07
Motives for involvement	3.02	0.83	0.84	2.82	0.70	0.76	1.89	0.26
Parent–child relationship quality	4.80	0.36	0.81	4.72	0.50	0.81	1.18	0.18
Parent play and leisure								
Outdoor games and sports	2.32	0.86	0.73	2.36	1.02	0.83	−0.32	0.04
Parent-reported roughhousing	2.66	1.46	–	3.34	1.33	–	−3.94**	0.49
Leisure activities	2.42	0.70	0.84	2.34	0.76	0.85	0.83	0.11
Child exploration and play								
Secure exploration	3.45	0.52	0.83	3.42	0.55	0.83	0.71	0.06
Roughhousing	2.44	1.05	–	3.12	1.11	–	−4.93**	0.63

Note: Parent and child roughing are single items, no alpha.
*$p < .05$.
**$p < .01$.

Child quantitative measures

Children completed an expanded version of the *Children's Relationship Attitudes* (CRA; Roggman, Coyl, Newland, & Cook, 2001), a pictorial measure based on the AAS (Simpson et al., 1992). The CRA contains a new scale titled *Secure Exploration* (Newland et al., 2010). The *Secure Exploration* scale was the portion used in this study; it included four items, which measured the extent to which fathers and mothers were supportive and available when children were nervous or excited, as well as the extent to which they encouraged children to try new things and take risks. Children also responded to one item, 'Father/mother shows they love me by roughhousing or goofing around'. This item was labeled 'child *Roughhousing*'. Reliability coefficients for the secure exploration variables are reported in Table 1.

To assess socio-emotional well-being, children completed the *Behavioral Assessment System for Children*, 2nd ed. (BASC-2), for self-report by children aged 8–11 (Reynolds & Kamphaus, 2004). A few of our participating children ($n = 13$) were outside the 8–11 age range, either slightly younger (age 7) or older (12 and 13 years old) than the age group for which this instrument was designed, but our reliability estimates were found to be within acceptable ranges (between 0.69 to 0.85) and similar to those reported in the BASC-2 manual. Composite *T* scores are reported for negative scales ([external] locus of control, social stress, anxiety, depression, sense of inadequacy) and positive scales (self-esteem, self-reliance, positive relations with parents, and relations with peers).

Qualitative interviews, coding, and analysis

Trained research assistants conducted joint interviews with a subsample of 41 couples, which were demographically representative of the larger sample ($n = 93$). The 60–90-minute interviews were recorded for later transcription. Parents were asked about the types of activities they did with their school-age child, whether the child's gender determined activity type, and if activity

PLAY AND WELLBEING

involvement provided opportunities for emotional closeness. Our decision to interview couples jointly reflects the perspective that parenting practices, including play and leisure, are often coordinated within two-parent families. Joint interviews provided the opportunity for individuals to present a shared perspective in which they could 'corroborate or supplement each other's stories' (Racher, 2003; Taylor & deVocht, 2011, p. 1577). Children also participated, separately, in semi-structured interviews that lasted from 10 to 30 minutes. They were asked about their perceptions of time spent with parents each week, types of parent involvement, and enjoyable aspects of these interactions (see Appendix for child and parent qualitative interview questions).

Procedures for the qualitative data analysis were adapted from Creswell (2002): (1) domains or topics were provided by the interview questions, (2) significant statements were identified from transcripts, (3) these significant statements were organized into themes/categories that were compared across responses for the same question, (4) each transcript was analyzed separately by two research assistants and the principle investigator, who discussed the themes/categories and reached consensus on them, and (5) illustrative quotes were identified to be presented.

Results

Study goal 1: differences in perceptions of family play and leisure activities

Paired t-tests were used to examine mother and father report of couple and parent–child well-being. Effect sizes for all variables ranged from Cohen's $d = 0.04$ to 0.63 (Table 1). There were no statistically significant differences in father- and mother-reported dyadic satisfaction or parent–partner avoidant attachment, parent stress, motives for involvement, or parent–child relationship quality. Mothers did report greater partner secure attachment, while fathers reported greater partner ambivalent attachment.

For quantitative measures of parent play and leisure there were no statistically significant differences in parent-reported outdoor games, sports, and leisure activities. Fathers reported greater involvement in roughhousing; this was the largest effect size for parent variables, Cohen's $d = 0.49$. Children did not report significant differences in secure exploration with each parent. However, they did report significantly greater involvement in roughhousing with their fathers; this was the largest effect size for all family play variables, Cohen's $d = 0.63$.

Study goal 2: associations among play and leisure activities and family socio-emotional well-being

Based on examining child well-being, child report of secure exploration with both parents was associated with all indicators of child well-being, in expected directions, except child anxiety. Child report of roughhousing with mothers was positively correlated with positive relations with parents; with fathers this variable was positively correlated with self-reliance and negatively correlated with social stress. Parents' report of outdoor play was negatively correlated with child's sense of inadequacy. Additionally, father report of outdoor play was also negatively associated with child depression and positively associated with child self-esteem. Parents' report of roughhousing was negatively correlated with child sense of inadequacy, and mother roughhousing was positively associated with child self-esteem, whereas father roughhousing was positively associated with child self-reliance. Overall, parents' report of leisure activities was inversely related to all negative indicators of child well-being (i.e. locus of control, social stress, anxiety, sense of inadequacy, depression). Additionally, mothers' report of leisure activities was positively correlated with all positive indicators of child well-being (self-reliance, positive relations with parents and peers) except self-esteem. Father report of leisure activities was positively correlated with child self-esteem only (Table 2).

In terms of examining mother well-being, there were no statistically significant correlations between child report of secure exploration and roughhousing with mothers and mothers' report of dyadic satisfaction and couple attachment variables. However, secure exploration with mothers was associated with mother report of decreases in parent stress and increases in parent–child relationship quality. Mother report of outdoor play and roughhousing were not associated with couple well-being, but mother report of leisure activities was associated with increases in attachment security and decreases in avoidance. Mother report of outdoor and sport involvement were also associated with increases in both motives for involvement with child and parent–child relationship quality. Mother-reported roughhousing was also positively associated with parent–child relationship quality (Table 2).

With regard to examining father well-being, child report of secure exploration with fathers was associated with father report of decreases in partner avoidant attachment. Child report of roughhousing with fathers was not associated with any father-reported couple or parent–child well-being variables. However, father report of roughhousing was associated with increases in partner attachment security, decreases in both avoidance and ambivalence, and increases in both motives for involvement and parent–child relationships quality. Father report of outdoor play was associated with decreases in partner ambivalent attachment and parent stress, as well as with increases in both motives for involvement and parent–child relationship quality. Father report of leisure activities was not associated with couple well-being, but was associated with decreases in parent stress and increases in motives for involvement. Couple dyadic satisfaction was not associated with any of the family play and leisure variables (Table 2).

Themes in family play and leisure

Outdoor activities and sports

During parent interviews, more fathers discussed outdoor and sports activities and several mothers agreed that fathers undertook these activities more frequently. More fathers reported that they practiced and played sports with their children and engaged in other outdoor activities such as soccer, football, basketball, volleyball, catching a ball, tennis, riding bikes, running, swimming, hunting, and golf. Children also discussed engaging in outdoor activities more with their fathers, including sports participation.

Leisure activities

Most parents reported watching television together as a family. Several also mentioned playing board games (e.g. Scrabble, Monopoly) and card games. More mothers mentioned reading, doing arts and crafts, and cooking with children. Only fathers reported playing video games (e. g. X-Box™ and Wii™) with children; more fathers did this with sons than with daughters. Children reported similar types of leisure activities and specifically mentioned family outings that included shopping and meals out. When describing family play time, children mentioned both non-specific, unstructured play (e.g. 'hang out', 'mess around', 'have fun') and structured activities and plans. One child commented, 'They [parents] usually have a lot of plans for us, so we are never bored.'

Secure exploration and roughhousing

Several fathers indicated that they wrestled and played tickle games with children. More fathers described play with sons (as opposed to daughters) as high energy and physical. One father

Table 2. Correlations among family play and leisure activities and parent and child socio-emotional well-being.

Variable	Child secure explore		Child roughhouse		Outdoor and sports		Leisure activities		Parent roughhouse	
	M	F	M	F	M	F	M	F	M	F
Parent socio-emotion variables										
Dyadic satisfaction	0.08	0.08	0.08	−0.11	−0.01	−0.07	−0.08	−0.03	−0.15	0.09
Secure with partner	0.05	0.18	0.07	0.09	0.11	0.17	0.18	0.05	−0.03	0.22*
Avoidant with partner	−0.01	−0.17	−0.14	−0.02	−0.09	−0.09	−0.15	−0.02	0.11	−0.19
Ambivalent with partner	−0.05	−0.13	0.03	−.013	−0.05	−0.21*	−0.16	−0.06	0.06	−0.21*
Parent stress	0.19	0.01	−0.07	−0.19	−0.10	−0.30**	−0.09	−0.23*	0.01	−0.07
Motives for involvement	0.09	0.03	0.10	0.15	0.16	0.39**	0.46**	0.44**	0.17	0.39**
Parent–child relationship quality	0.18	0.07	−0.13	−0.09	0.18	0.17	0.30**	0.15	0.17	0.28**
Child socio-emotion variables										
Locus of control	−0.22*	−0.25*	−0.02	0.0	−0.01	−0.01	−0.23*	−0.12	−0.07	−0.11
Social stress	−0.24*	−0.25*	−0.02	−0.16	−0.08	−0.08	−0.27**	−0.22*	−0.10	−0.08
Anxiety	−0.11	−0.15	0.04	0.03	0.0	−0.15	−0.20	−0.27**	−0.11	−0.12
Sense of inadequacy	−0.32**	−0.31**	−0.01	−0.16	−0.19	−0.22*	−0.31**	−0.23*	−0.31**	−0.28**
Depression	−0.37**	−0.38**	0.02	−0.14	−0.11	−0.20	−0.23*	−0.17	−0.21	−0.15
Self-reliance	0.25*	0.43**	0.09	0.21*	0.17	0.10	0.21*	0.12	0.14	0.24*
Self-esteem	0.22*	0.24*	0.0	0.07	0.05	0.21*	0.14	0.18	0.26*	0.14
Positive relations with parents	0.34**	0.43**	0.19	−0.01	0.11	−0.02	0.30**	0.05	0.09	0.14
Positive relations with peers	0.35**	0.28**	−0.04	0.04	0.04	0.06	0.22*	0.15	0.11	0.01

*$p < .05$.
**$p < .01$.

admitted, 'I see him at bed time and kinda jump around with him and get him hyper before they are supposed to go to sleep.' Another father described gender differences in play with his son as 'more aggressive activities, more energy'. One father agreed that child gender influenced play, he said, 'Boys in general have more of an aggressive play tactic: wrestling, punching, play fighting …' Some fathers indicated that sons demonstrated a preference for this type of play, with comments such as ' … I think he likes to play rough, you know, motorcycles and stuff'. While another father commented, ' … with my daughter I cannot play the same way I do with him [son]. With her it's different'. Several fathers indicated that they rode motorcycles with their school-age children. All but one of these fathers said they did this with their sons, as opposed to daughters.

Mothers spoke much less about physical play with their children. One mother said, 'I do not play much with him … he likes wrestling. I do not like to play a lot; I don't like to wrestle.' A few fathers indicated that they encouraged their children to participate in activities that they (i.e. the fathers) enjoyed. One father said,

> Well I try to get her into basketball … I try to give her hints on how she practices shooting. She tried out for the basketball team and she made it. We will watch TV together, but sports.

Several fathers discussed playing golf with their children, one said, 'I like golf, so I like it when we go hit golf balls. She seems to like it too.'

Study goal 3: profiles for families with low and high well-being children

Mean scores for key study variables were created for a subsample of eight families whose children showed low well-being, and a subsample of six families whose children showed high well-being. Table 3 provides a comparison of the total sample mean scores ($N = 98$ mothers, $N = 93$ fathers) and for the two subsamples of families.

The results indicate that for mother- and father-reported dyadic satisfaction, secure partner attachment, motives for involvement, parent–child relationship quality, outdoor games, leisure activities, parent- and child-reported roughhousing, and child-reported secure exploration, the mean scores for the subsample of families with child low well-being were lower compared to the total sample and the subsample of families with child high well-being. For parent stress and mother- and father-reported avoidant and ambivalent partner attachment, the mean scores for the subsample of families with child low well-being were higher compared to the total sample and the subsample of families with child high well-being.

In terms of demographics, families with child-reported low well-being were diverse in terms of their family structures (two of the eight couples were the married biological parents of the target child, two were stepparents, one couple was cohabiting, the other was dating). Among these child-reported low well-being families, the majority of parents reported educational levels of two years of college or less, and most reported incomes between $20,00 and $30,000. In contrast, families with child-reported high well-being had less varied family structures (four of the six were the married biological parents of the target child, two were stepparents). Among child-reported high well-being families, more couples reported education levels of four years of college or more, while all but one had incomes of $40,000 or higher.

In interviews, children and parents from both subsamples discussed play and leisure involvement. A few striking differences between the two groups emerged. Children in the low well-being subsample reported spending less time with their parents and engaging in more indoor activities such as watching television, playing games, and reading. They also reported that they did not feel safe playing outside. One of these children said 'Well this is a very bad neighborhood, … they stole all mom's jewelry, … so [its] not very safe.' In contrast, children in the high well-being

PLAY AND WELLBEING

Table 3. A Comparison of mean scores for parent socio-emotional variables, parent play and leisure activities, child exploration and play for the total sample and families with low and high child well-being.

	Child low well-being mean ($n = 8$)	Mother mean ($N = 98$)	Child high well-being mean ($n = 6$)	Child low well-being mean ($n = 8$)	Father mean ($N = 93$)	Child high well-being mean ($n = 6$)
Parent socio-emotion variables						
Dyadic satisfaction	4.78	5.02	5.06	4.52	4.95	4.86
Secure with partner	4.06	4.58	4.65	3.61	4.41	4.32
Avoidant with partner	1.58	1.46	1.13	2.07	1.58	1.54
Ambivalent with partner	2.27	1.45	1.45	2.45	1.68	1.81
Parent stress	4.00	4.10	3.67	5.85	4.22	4.50
Motives for involvement	2.58	3.02	3.28	2.42	2.82	2.89
Parent–child relationship quality	4.46	4.80	4.83	4.56	4.72	4.72
Parent play and leisure						
Outdoor games and sports	2.18	2.32	2.59	1.49	2.36	2.90
Parent-reported roughhousing	1.63	2.66	2.83	2.45	3.34	3.67
Leisure activities	2.05	2.42	2.80	1.59	2.34	2.55
Child exploration and play						
Secure exploration	3.25	3.45	3.71	3.33	3.42	3.79
Roughhousing	2.88	2.44	2.67	3.00	3.12	3.50

Notes. Mother mean scores ($N = 98$) and father mean scores ($N = 93$) are for the total sample. Child low well-being mean scores represent a subset of families ($n = 8$) with child high scores for negative indicators of well-being. Child high well-being mean scores represent a subset of families ($n = 6$) with child high scores for positive indicators of well-being.

subsample described more outdoor play (e.g. riding dirt bikes or playing catch). One child described his father's preferences as, 'He likes natural stuff, so in summer, I've gone bird watching and different places.' Additionally, the high well-being children described their neighborhoods as safe places to play.

Benefits of play for children

Some parents identified child benefits from play to include skill development and confidence building aided by coaching or practicing together. One father said, 'She's not closed off or thinks that she can't do things. I hope that we've instilled in her that she can do and accomplish anything.' Parents described their play and activity involvement as providing opportunities for the entire family to relax together and to enjoy each other's company. When asked what they enjoyed doing with parents, children described similar indoor leisure activities such as playing board games and outdoor activities such as nature walks, sports, and outings. One child said, 'I just like that we can be together, that we can have some time to play and do stuff.' One girl said, 'We go shopping. I enjoy going places with them [parents].'

Benefits for parents

Some parents expressed personal enjoyment in the activities they could engage in with their school-age children. One father cited more involvement as his children grew more capable. He said,

> Now we can go on bike rides through [the park], because I like to be outdoors. And I am looking forward to going on hikes. Now they are more physically able to do it. And with them doing sports, I can coach them.

Another father clearly enjoyed his child's interest in a sport they shared together. This father said, 'I think my favorite is, "Dad I'm just going to go outside and practice my golf swing."'

A few fathers discussed shared activities and hobbies that provided opportunities to interact and feel closer. One said,

> We hit golf balls. I think it brings us closer because he finds a common ground with me. We both like video games. That's kind of a guy thing but that brings us close too because he always wants to find interest in what I'm doing on the computer and he always wants to learn. That comes in second to being an outdoor thing. I would almost rather encourage him to play golf and be outside instead of at the computer but ... Both those things bring us together.

Another father expressed the mutual enjoyment he and his son shared in their playtime, 'We play cars together and build road track for the cars. He likes to build. When he plays with his toys, I will play with him. It makes playing a fun thing to do.'

Several parents commented that this developmental period from 7 to 13 enabled parents and children to select mutually enjoyable activities. A few mothers talked about limitations when their children were younger and how they appreciated that now the whole family could participate in the same activities. One mother said she especially liked, 'Being able to do family activities that we all enjoy. Find stuff that we all enjoy like ... snow skiing and play board games that are of interest to us, and being able to ... share humor.'

A few parents also recognized and appeared to regret that these opportunities would possibly not last. One father said, ' ... I know when they become 16, or so, they're not going to want to hang out with dad.' Another father said, 'I enjoy the fact that she still likes ... to play with dad because I notice the boys, as they get older they don't want to spend near as much time with dad. And that kind of bothers me.' When asked what they most enjoyed about their children at this age, one father said, 'That we play often at this age, and we play together.'

Discussion

This study adds to the current literature on family play and leisure involvement by examining mother, father, and child perspectives of family activities. The mixed-methods research design allowed for quantitative and qualitative data comparisons of family members' perspectives. In addition, the focus on families with school-age children allowed us to capture children's perspectives of family play and leisure that confirmed many of the perspectives and benefits parents' reported. For study goal 1, differences in perceptions of family play and leisure activities, analysis of the quantitative survey data showed that fathers and children reported significantly higher

PLAY AND WELLBEING

levels of father–child roughhousing. This gender difference in play style is consistent with *Activation Relationship Theory* (Paquette, 2004; Paquette & Bigras, 2010; Paquette et al., 2003) and related research on father RTP (Fletcher, 2011, Fletcher et al., 2013). Additionally, more children and fathers reported mutual involvement in outdoor leisure and sport activities.

For study goal 2, associations among play and leisure activities and family socio-emotional well-being, we found that child secure exploration with both parents was associated with all child well-being indicators except anxiety. Additionally, child and father roughhousing was associated with lower child social stress and a sense of inadequacy, and higher levels of self-reliance. These results are also consistent with Paquette's (2004) theory and Fletcher's (2011; Fletcher et al., 2013) research about the benefits of father RTP for children's social competence and developing confidence. Our results also indicated that child roughhousing with mothers was associated with child perceptions of more positive relationships with parents and mothers' report of roughhousing was associated with lower levels of a sense of inadequacy and higher self-esteem for children. Thus mother roughhousing appears to provide some benefits for children that complement fathers' roughhousing (Bretherton et al., 2005; Dubeau, 1995).

For study goal 3, profiles for families with low and high well-being children, the subsamples of families were quantitatively different in expected directions when key study variables were compared across groups. Children with high well-being described more play with parents and more sports involvement and outdoor play; they described their neighborhoods as safe places to play. Children in the low well-being subsample reported less time with parents, less outdoor play, and felt their neighborhoods were not safe to play in.

Similar to previous findings that family leisure involvement increases family life satisfaction and well-being (Mactavish & Schleien, 1998; Zabriskie & McCormick, 2003), our study revealed parent report of leisure activities was associated with lower levels of children's negative indicators (i.e. external locus of control, social stress, anxiety, sense of inadequacy and depression) and higher levels of positive indicators (i.e. self-reliance, self-esteem, relationships with parents and peers). Associations between family play variables and parent well-being did reveal some influences on couple attachment styles, exclusive of dyadic satisfaction. These findings suggest that positive parent–child play and leisure involvement may reduce feelings of ambivalence and avoidance and may increase feelings of security within adult partnered relationships. These results support a systems perspective, that experiences in one family subsystem (parent–child) may affect experiences within another family subsystem (marital). In turn, the findings add to the literature on the benefits of family leisure and play involvement for couple well-being.

We found that parent-reported play, leisure, and roughhousing were associated with positive parent–child relationships (i.e. decreases in parent stress, increases in both motives for involvement and perceptions of parent–child relationship quality); these findings are consistent with research on family leisure satisfaction as a determinant of well-being (Riddick, 1986) and with corresponding family play research (e.g. Coyl-Shepherd & Newland, 2013; MacDonald & Parke, 1986; Newland, Chen et al., 2013). Consistent with past findings, we found gender differences in parents' perceptions and individual experiences of play and family leisure (Larson et al., 1997; Shaw, 1992). In interviews, parents indicated that some activity choices were based on child gender and some on parent preference.

Future directions

Although this study has contributed to the research literature on family play and family well-being, it could be extended in future studies in several ways. Replication with larger and more diverse multicultural samples may provide greater external validity for these findings. Families should be recruited from diverse socio-economic backgrounds and from both rural and urban areas to allow for the examination of how community environments may impact family resources, play, and leisure opportunities.

Our findings regarding the positive associations between parent roughhousing and child wellbeing were relatively robust, by comparison with our measures of secure exploration. Roughhousing was assessed with a single item (i.e. one reported by the child and one reported by each parent), thus reliability for this construct was limited, despite the consistency across both children's and parents' reports of greater levels of RTP between fathers and children. Both our quantitative and qualitative findings for RTP were consistent with previous reports by Paquette et al. (2003) and Fletcher et al. (2013) highlighting the perceived importance of this type of play, particularly for fathers and their children. Expanded measures or multi-methods (e.g. self-report surveys and observational measures) could be further developed to capture and analyze the encouragement of risk-taking, types of interactive, excitatory physical play, and responses of family members to these types of play. Such measures have been developed and tested with young children (toddler and preschoolers; see Fletcher et al., 2013; Paquette et al., 2003) but more work is needed in the development of appropriate measures for use with parents and school-age children. Additionally, an examination of how play and leisure are affected by family structure (e.g. dual parent, single parent), barriers to involvement (e.g. employment circumstances, non-residential parents), and changes in family structure would be important to consider. Finally, longitudinal analyses could potentially provide a developmental perspective upon stability or change in family play patterns and leisure, as children and parents age.

Implications

These findings have implications for parent educators, family counselors, family service professionals, and families themselves. As families today are challenged to balance work and parent–child involvement, it is important to remember that family play and leisure continue to be sources of enjoyment, creating greater closeness, cohesion, and well-being within families. Our findings suggest that children do not exclusively benefit from parents' efforts to engage in these activities, but that parents and their couple relationship quality also benefit. The complementary activity choices of mothers and fathers appear to support different aspects of children's development and provide opportunities for preferred types of engagement for parents.

In an interview with John Bowlby's son (the attachment theorist), Sir Richard Bowlby was asked about the complementary roles of mothers and fathers and the benefits of father play for children. His response, consistent with our results, suggested that these benefits extend beyond the child. He said,

> I believe that we also need to examine the instinctive human need for discovery, enjoyment, and a sense of achievement ... Whether young or old we seem driven to explore and to seek new experiences and there is a potent neurochemical reward when we do, but we need to feel sufficiently safe doing so, or we're too frightened to continue. To optimize our chances of being successful we need two distinct systems in place: the first is to know there is a secure base to return to when the activity ends or goes wrong, and the other is having a trusted companion to show the way. (Newland & Coyl, 2010, p. 28)

References

Agate, J. R., Zabriskie, R. B., Agate, S. T., & Poff, R. (2009). Family leisure satisfaction and satisfaction with family life. *Journal of Leisure Research, 41*(2), 205–223.

Barnett, L. A. (1990). Developmental benefits of play for children. *Journal of Leisure Research, 22*(2), 138–153.

Bowlby, J. (1982). *Attachment and loss. Vol. 1: Attachment* (2nd ed.). New York, NY: Basic Books.

Bretherton, I., Lambert, J. D., & Golby, B. (2005). Involved fathers of preschool children as seen by themselves and their wives: Accounts of attachment, socialization, and companionship. *Attachment and Human Development, 7*, 229–251.

Brown, S. (2009). *Play: How it shapes the brain, opens the imagination, and invigorates the soul*. New York, NY: Avery.

Cabrera, N. J., Shannon, J. D., Vogel, C., Tamis-LeMonda, C., Ryan, R. M., Brooks-Gunn, J., ... Cohen, R. (2004). Low-income fathers' involvement in their toddlers' lives: Biological fathers from the early head start research and evaluation study. *Fathering, 2*, 5–30.

Caldera, Y. M., & Lindsey, E. W. (2006). Coparenting, mother–infant interaction, and infant–parent attachment relationships in two-parent families. *Journal of Family Psychology, 20*(2), 275–283.

Campbell, K. J., & Hesketh, K. D. (2007). Strategies which aim to positively impact on weight, physical activity, diet and sedentary behaviours in children from zero to five years. A systematic review of the literature. *Obesity Reviews, 8*(4), 327–338.

Carson, J. L., & Parke, R. D. (1996). Reciprocal negative affect in parent–child interactions and children's peer competency. *Child Development, 67*(5), 2217–2226.

Cleland, V., & Venn, A. (2010). Encouraging physical activity and discouraging sedentary behavior in children and adolescents. *Journal of Adolescent Health, 47*(3), 221–222.

Coolahan, K., Fantuzzo, J., Mendez, J., & McDermott, P. (2000). Preschool peer interactions and readiness to learn: Relationships between classroom peer play and learning behaviors and conduct. *Journal of Educational Psychology, 29*(3), 458–465.

Cowan, P. A., Cowan, C., & Mehta, N. (2009). Adult attachment, couple attachment, and children's adaptation to school: An integrated attachment template and family risk model. *Attachment & Human Development, 11*(1), 29–46.

Cox, M. J., & Paley, B. (1997). Families as systems. *Annual Review of Psychology, 48*, 243–267.

Coyl, D. D., Newland, L. A., & Freeman, H. (2010). Predicting preschoolers' attachment security from parenting behaviors, parents' attachment relationships and their use of social support. *Early Child Development and Care, 180*(4), 499–512.

Coyl-Shepherd, D. D., & Newland, L. A. (2013). Mothers' and fathers' couple and family contextual influences, parent involvement, and school-age child attachment. *Early Child Development and Care, 183*(3–4), 553–569.

Creswell, J. W. (2002). *Educational research: Planning, conducting and evaluation quantitative and qualitative approaches to research*. Upper Saddle River, NJ: Merrill/Pearson Education.

CrouterA. C., & BoothA. (Eds.). (2003). *Children's influence on family dynamics: The neglected side of family relationships*. Mahwah, NJ: Erlbaum.

Daly, K. J. (2001). Deconstructing family time: From ideology to lived experience. *Journal of Marriage and Family, 63*(2), 283–294.

Dubeau, D. (1995). *Comparaisons des caractéristiques interactives et relationnelles des mères et des pères avec leur enfant d'âge préscolaire* (Thèse de doctorat inedited). Université du Québec à Montréal, Montréal.

Elkind, D. (2007). *The power of play: How spontaneous, imaginative activities lead to happier, healthier children*. Cambridge, MA: De Capo Press.

Fantuzzo, J., & McWayne, C. (2002). The relationship between peer play interactions and family context and dimensions of school readiness for low-income preschool children. *Journal of Educational Psychology, 94*, 79–87.

Fantuzzo, J., Sekino, Y., & Cohen, H. L. (2004). An examination of the contributions of interactive peer play to salient classroom competencies for urban Head Start children. *Psychology in the Schools, 41*(3), 323–336.

Fincham, F. D., & Hall, J. H. (2005). Parenting and the marital relationship. In T. Luster & L. Okagaki (Eds.), *Parenting: An ecological perspective* (2nd ed., pp. 205–233). Mahwah, NJ: Lawrence Erlbaum Associates.

Fisher, E. P. (1992). Impact of play on development: A meta-analysis. *Play & Culture, 5*(2), 159–181.

Fletcher, R. (2011). *The dad factor: How father–baby bonding helps a child for life.* Sydney: Finch Publishing.

Fletcher, R., St. George, J., & Freeman, E. (2013). Rough and tumble play quality [RTP-Q]: Theoretical foundations for a new measure of father–child interaction. *Early Child Development and Care, 183* (6), 746–759.

Flouri, E., & Buchanan, A. (2003). The role of father involvement and mother involvement in adolescents' psychological well-being. *British Journal of Social Work, 33*, 399–406.

Flouri, E., & Buchanan, A. (2004). Early father's and mother's involvement and child's later educational outcomes. *British Journal of Educational Psychology, 74*, 141–153.

Freeman, H., Newland, L. A., & Coyl, D. D. (2008). Father beliefs as a mediator between contextual barriers and father involvement. *Early Child Development and Care, 178*, 803–819.

Frost, J. L. (2012). The changing culture of play. *International Journal of Play, 1*(2), 117–130.

Frost, J. L., & Brown, S. (2009). The consequences of play deprivation. *Playground Magazine, 8*(3), 26–30.

Frost, J. L., Wortham, S. C., & Reifel, S. (2012). *Play and child development* (4th ed.). Boston, MA: Pearson.

Gault-Sherman, M. (2011). It's a two-way street: The bidirectional relationship between parenting and delinquency. *Journal of Youth and Adolescence, 42*(2), 121–145.

Gray, P. (2011). The decline of play and the rise of psychopathology in children and adolescents. *American Journal of Play, 3*(4), 443–463.

Green, C. L., Walker, J. M. T., Hoover-Dempsey, K. V., & Sandler, H. M. (2007). Parents' motivations for involvement in children's education: An empirical test of a theoretical model of parental involvement. *Journal of Educational Psychology, 99*(3), 532–544.

Grossman, K., Grossman, K. E., Fremmer-Bombik, E., Kindler, H., Scheuerer-Englisch, H., & Zimmermann, P. (2002). The uniqueness of the child–father attachment relationship: Fathers' sensitive and challenging play as a pivotal variable in a 16-year longitudinal study. *Social Development, 11*(3), 307–331.

Grossmann, K., Grossmann, K. E., Kindler, H., & Zimmermann, P. (2008). A wider view of attachment and exploration: The influence of mothers and fathers on the development of psychological security from infancy to young adulthood. In J. Cassidy & P. R. Shaver (Eds.), *Handbook of attachment: Theory, research, and clinical applications* (2nd ed., pp. 880–905). New York, NY: Guilford Press.

Grych, J. H. (2002). Marital relationships and parenting. In M. H. Bornstein (Ed.), *Handbook of parenting* (2nd ed., pp. 203–226). Mahwah, NJ: Erlbaum.

Hanson, W. E., Creswell, J. W., Clark, V. L., Petska, K. S., & Creswell, J. D. (2005). Mixed methods research designs in counseling psychology. *Journal of Counseling Psychology, 52*(2), 224–235.

Hawks, S. (1991). Recreation in the family. In S. J. Bahr (Ed.), *Family research: A sixty year review, 1930–1990* (pp. 387–433). New York, NY: Lexington Books.

Holland, A. S., & McElwain, N. L. (2013). Maternal and paternal perceptions of coparenting as a link between marital quality and the parent–toddler relationship. *Journal of Family Psychology, 27*(1), 117–126.

Holman, T. B., & Epperson, A. (1989). Family and leisure: A review of literature with research recommendations. *Journal of Leisure Research, 16*, 277–294.

Holman, T. B., & Jacquart, M. (1988). Leisure activity patterns and marital satisfaction: A further test. *Journal of Marriage and the Family, 50*(1), 69–77.

Hurwitz, S. C. (2002–2003). To be successful-let them play! For parents particularly. *Child Education, 79*(2), 101–102.

Johnson, H. A., Zabriskie, R. B., & Hill, B. (2006). The contribution of couple leisure involvement, leisure time, and leisure satisfaction to marital satisfaction. *Marriage and Family Review, 40*(1), 69–91.

Kaiser Family Foundation. (2010). *Generation M2: Media in the lives of 8-18-year-olds.* Menlo Park, CA: Henry J. Kaiser Family Foundation.

Kazura, K. (2000). Fathers' qualitative and quantitative involvement: An investigation of attachment, play, and social interactions. *Journal of Men's Studies, 9*, 41–57.

Kiernan, K., & Huerta, M. (2008). Economic deprivation, maternal depression, parenting and children's cognitive and emotional development in early childhood. *British Journal of Sociology, 59*, 783–806.

Kromelow, S., Harding, C., & Touris, M. (1990). The role of the father in the development of stranger sociability during the second year. *American Journal of Orthopsychiatry, 60*, 521–530.

Kwon, K., Han, S., Jeon, H. J., & Bingham, G. (2013). Mothers' and fathers' parenting challenges, strategies, and resources in toddlerhood. *Early Child Development and Care*, *183*(3–4), 415–429.

LambM. (Ed.). (1997). *The role of the father in child development* (3rd ed.). New York, NY: Wiley.

Larson, R. W., Gillman, S. A., & Richards, M. H. (1997). Divergent experiences of family leisure: Fathers, mothers, and young adolescents. *Journal of Leisure Research*, *29*(1), 78–97.

Livingston, G., & Parker, K. (2011). *A tale of two fathers: More are active, but more are absent*. Retrieved from Pew Research Center website: http://pewsocialtrends.org/2011/06/15/a-tale-of-two-fathers/

MacDonald, K., & Parke, R. D. (1986). Parent–child physical play: The effects of sex and age of children and parents. *Sex Roles*, *15*, 367–378.

Mactavish, J., & Schleien, S. J. (1998). Playing together growing together: Parents' perspectives on the benefits of family recreation in families that include children with a developmental disability. *Therapeutic Recreation Journal*, *32*, 207–230.

Mannell, R. C. (2007). Leisure, health and well-being. *World Leisure Journal*, *49*(3), 114–128.

Manongdo, J. A., & Garcia, J. I. R. (2011). Maternal parenting and mental health of Mexican American youth: A bidirectional and prospective approach. *Developmental Psychology*, *25*, 261–270.

Mattingly, M., & Bianchi, S. (2003). Gender differences in the quantity and quality of free time: The US experience. *Social Forces*, *81*, 999–1030.

McElwain, N. L., & Volling, B. L. (2005). Preschool children's interactions with friends and older siblings: Relationship specificity and joint contributions to problem behavior. *Journal of Family Psychology*, *19* (4), 486–496.

Mehall, K. G., Spinrad, T. L., Eisenberg, N., & Gaertner, B. M. (2009). Examining the relations of infant temperament and couples' marital satisfaction to mother and father involvement: A longitudinal study. *Fathering*, *7*, 23–48.

Milkie, M. A., Kendig, S. M., Nomaguchi, K. M., & Denny, K. E. (2010). Time with children, children's well-being, and work–family balance among employed parents. *Journal of Marriage and Family*, *72* (5), 1329–1343.

Milteer, R. M., & Ginsburg, K. R. (2012). The importance of play in promoting healthy child development and maintaining strong parent–child bond: Focus on children in poverty. *Pediatrics*, *129*(1), E204–E213.

Mitchell, S. J., & Cabrera, N. J. (2009). An exploratory study of fathers' parenting stress and toddlers' social development in low-income African American Families. *Fathering*, *7*, 201–225.

Newland, L. A., Chen, H.-H., Coyl-Shepherd, D. D., Liang, Y. -C., Carr, E., Dykstra, E., & Gapp, S. C. (2013). Parent and child perspectives on mothering and fathering: The influence of ecocultural niches. *Early Child Development and Care*, *183*(3–4), 534–552.

Newland, L. A., & Coyl, D. D. (2010). Fathers' role as attachment figures: An interview with Sir Richard Bowlby. *Early Child Development and Care*, *180*(1&2), 25–32.

Newland, L. A., Coyl, D. D., & Chen, H. H. (2010). Fathering and attachment in the U.S. and Taiwan: Contextual predictors and child outcomes. *Early Child Development and Care*, *180*(1&2), 173–191.

Newland, L. A., Coyl-Shepherd, D. D., & Paquette, D. (2013). Editorial: Implications of mothering and fathering for children's development. *Early Child Development and Care*, *183*(3–4), 337–342.

NICHD. (2004). Fathers' and mothers' parenting behavior and beliefs as predictors of children's social adjustment in the transition to school. *Journal of Family Psychology*, *18*, 628–638.

Orthner, D. K. (1975). Leisure activity patterns and marital satisfaction over the marital career. *Journal of Marriage and the Family*, *37*, 91–102.

Orthner, D. K., & Mancini, J. A. (1991). Benefits of leisure for family bonding. In B. L. Driver, P. J. Brown, & G. L. Peterson (Eds.), *Benefits of leisure* (pp. 215–301). State College, PA: Venture.

Paikoff, R. L., & Brooks-Gunn, J. (1991). Do parent child relationships change during puberty? *Psychological Bulletin*, *110*, 47–66.

Paquette, D. (2004). Theorizing the father–child relationship: Mechanisms and developmental outcomes. *Human Development*, *47*, 193–219.

Paquette, D., & Bigras, M. (2010). The risky situation: A procedure for assessing the father–child activation relationship. *Early Child Development and Care*, *180*(1–2), 33–50.

Paquette, D., Carbonneau, R., Dubeau, D., Bigras, M., & Tremblay, R. E. (2003). Prevalence of father–child rough-and-tumble play and physical aggression in preschool children. *European Journal of Psychology of Education*, *18*(2), 171–189.

Paquette, D., Coyl-Shepherd, D. D., & Newland, L. A. (2013). Fathers and development: New areas for exploration. *Early Child Development and Care*, *183*(6), 735–745.

PLAY AND WELLBEING

Parke, R. (2004). Development in the family. *Annual Review of Psychology, 55*, 365–399.

Pellegrini, A. D., & Smith, P. K. (1998). The development of play during childhood: Forms and possible functions. *Child Psychology and Psychiatry Review, 3*(2), 39–41.

Pleck, J., & Masciadrelli, B. (2004). Paternal involvement by US residential fathers: Levels, sources, and consequences. In M. Lamb (Ed.), *The role of the father in child development* (4th ed., pp. 222–271). New York, NY: Wiley.

Power, T. G., & Parke, R. D. (1983). Patterns of mother and father play with their 8-month-olds infant: A multiple analysis approach. *Infant Behavior and Development, 6*, 453–459.

Racher, F. (2003). Using conjoint interviews to research the lived experience of elderly rural couples. *Nurse Researcher, 10*(3), 60–72.

Raley, S., & Bianchi, S. (2006). Sons, daughters, and family processes: Does gender of children matter? *Annual Review of Sociology, 32*, 401–421.

Raver, C. C., & Ziegler, E. F. (1997). Social competence: An untapped dimension in evaluating head start's success. *Early Childhood Research Quarterly, 12*, 363–385.

Reading, R. (2007). Review of 'The importance of play in promoting healthy child development'. *Child Care, Health, and Development, 33*(6), 807–808.

Reynolds, C. R., & Kamphaus, R. W. (2004). *Behavior assessment system for children, second edition (BASC-2)*. Circle Pines, MN: AGS.

Riddick, C. C. (1986). Leisure satisfaction precursors. *Journal of Leisure Research, 18*, 259–265.

Roggman, L. A., Boyce, L. K., Cook, G. A., Christiansen, K., & Jones, D. (2004). Playing with daddy: Social toy play, early head start, and developmental outcomes. *Fathering, 2*(1), 83–108.

Roggman, L. A., Coyl, D. D., Newland, L. A., & Cook, G. (2001, August). *Attachment measures in infancy, childhood, adulthood: Reliability, stability, and continuity.* Poster presented at the annual meeting of the American Psychological Association, San Francisco.

Roopnarine, J., & Mounts, N. (1985). Mother–child and father–child play. *Early Child Development and Care, 20*, 157–169.

Russell, R. V. (1990). Recreation and quality of life in old age: A causal analysis. *Journal of Applied Gerontology, 9*(1), 77–90.

Saisto, T., Salmela-Aro, K., Nurmi, J.-E., & Halmesmäki, E. (2008). Longitudinal study on the predictors of parental stress in mothers and fathers of toddlers. *Journal of Psychosomatic Obstetrics & Gynecology, 29*(3), 213–222.

Sax, L. (2007). *Boys adrift: The five factors driving the growing epidemic of unmotivated boys and under-achieving young men.* New York, NY: Basic Books.

Schoppe-Sullivan, S. J., Kotila, L., Jia, R., Lang, S. N., & Bower, D. J. (2013). Comparisons of levels and predictors of mothers' and fathers' engagement with their preschool-aged children. *Early Child Development and Care, 183*(3–4), 498–514.

Shaw, S. M. (1992). Dereifying family leisure: An examination of women's and men's everyday experiences and perceptions of family time. *Leisure Sciences, 14*, 271–286.

Shaw, S. M., & Dawson, D. (2001). Purposive leisure: Examining parental discourses on family activities. *Leisure Sciences, 23*, 317–231.

Simpson, J. A., Rholes, W. S., & Nelligan, J. S. (1992). Support-seeking and support-giving within couple members in an anxiety-provoking situation: The role of attachment styles. *Journal of Personality and Social Psychology, 62*, 434–446.

Spanier, G. B. (1976). Measuring dyadic adjustment: New scales for assessing the quality of marriage and similar dads. *Journal of Marriage and the Family, 38*, 15–28.

Stevenson, M. M., & Crnic, K. A. (2013). Activative fathering predicts later children's behaviour dysregulation and sociability. *Early Child Development and Care, 183*(6), 774–790.

Tamis-LeMonda, C. S., Shannon, J. D., Cabrera, N. J., & Lamb, M. E. (2004). Fathers and mothers at play with their 2- and 3-year olds: Contributions to language and cognitive development. *Child Development, 75*, 1806–1820.

Taylor, B., & deVocht, H. (2011). Interviewing separately or as couples? Considerations of authenticity of method. *Qualitative Health Research, 21*(11), 1576–1587.

Tsao, L. (2002). How much do we know about the importance of play in child development? *Child Education, 78*(4), 230–233.

Wentzel, K. R. (1999). Socio-emotional processes and interpersonal relationships: Implications for understanding motivation at school. *Journal of Educational Psychology, 91*, 76–97.

Whitchurch, G. G., & Constantine, L. L. (1993). Systems theory. In P. G. Boss, W. J. Doherty, R. LaRossa, W. R. Schumm, & S. K. Steinmetz (Eds.), *Sourcebook of family theories and methods: A contextual approach* (pp. 325–355). New York, NY: Plenum Press.

Wong, W., Weiyi, M., Song, L., Strober, D. E., & Golinkoff, R. (2008). Review of 'The power of play'. *Journal of the American Academy of Child and Adolescent Psychiatry, 47*(9), 1099–1100.

Yeung, W. J., Sandberg, J. F., Davis-Kean, P. A., & Hofferth, S. A. (2001). Children's time with fathers in intact families. *Journal of Marriage and Family, 63*, 136–154.

Zabriskie, R. B., & McCormick, B. P. (2003). Parent and child perspectives of family leisure involvement and satisfaction with family life. *Journal of Leisure Research, 35*(2), 163–189.

Appendix

Child interview questions

1. How much time do you spend with your mom and dad each week?
    a. Doing what?
    b. What do you most enjoy about being with your mom and dad?
    c. Is there anything in particular that you do with just mom or just dad?
2. If you could go anywhere you'd like on vacation, where would you go?
    a. If you could go there with an acquaintance (someone you know but not very well) for a week, or spend that week at home with your mom or dad, which would you choose?
    b. Why?
    c. What kinds of things would you do at home with your mom and dad (if that was your choice)?
3. If you had to choose five words to describe your father, what would they be? What five words would best describe your mother?

Parent interview questions

1. How much time do you spend with your child each week?
    Probe: How much time does Mom spend?
    Probe: How much time does Dad spend?
2. What kinds of activities do you do with your child at this age?
    Probe: As a mother, do you share different activities with your child than your partner or husband?
    Probe: As a father, do you share different activities with your child than your partner or wife?
3. Is your child's gender a factor in determining the type of activities you engage in with him or her?
    Probe: Because your child is a … (boy) or (girl) does that influence the type of things you do with him or her?
4. What activities do you do with your child to help you feel close to each other?
    Probe: As a father, what activities do you do with your child that helps you two to feel close?
    Probe: As a mother, what activities do you do with your child that helps you two to feel close?
5. What do you like or enjoy most about parenting your child at this age?
    Probe: The types of activities you can do with your child now?

Using playfulness to cope with psychological stress: taking into account both positive and negative emotions

Po-Ju Chang, Xinyi Qian and Careen Yarnal

Department of Recreation, Park, and Tourism Management, The Pennsylvania State University, USA

> Playfulness increases positive emotions (PEs) and enhances psychological well-being. However, no studies have examined whether playfulness serves as a stress–coping resource, nor assessed both positive and negative emotions (NEs) as coping outcomes. The current study used the Process Model of Stress and Coping to examine whether playfulness helps university students cope with psychological stress. Both PE and NE were examined as immediate coping outcomes, assessing life satisfaction as a more comprehensive outcome. Using structural equation modeling to analyze the data, we found that heightened playfulness was associated with more PE, which led to greater life satisfaction. Heightened playfulness was also related to less NE, partially offsetting the adverse effects of stress. The results contribute to the leisure literature by showing the value of playfulness as a coping resource, the applicability of the Process Model of Stress and Coping, and the importance of examining both emotional and more comprehensive coping outcomes.

Introduction

Playfulness is viewed as engaging in a voluntary leisure activity and/or choosing non-serious behaviors just for fun, enjoyment, satisfaction, involvement, and pleasure (Chick, Yarnal, & Purrington, 2012; Glynn & Webster, 1992; Starbuck & Webster, 1991). Previous research has documented links between playfulness and life satisfaction (Mattei & Schaefer, 2004) as well as between playfulness and positive emotions (PEs) (Qian & Yarnal, 2011). There is also a growing body of literature that links playfulness to stress coping (Harkness & Bundy, 2001; Yarnal & Qian, 2011). In general, playfulness may help people cope with stress and contribute to their life satisfaction.

To understand the role of playfulness in the stress–coping process, it is important to recognize the extensive research on stress coping. Much of the research has been devoted to testing various models that may explain the stress–coping process, including the Mediation Model (Iwasaki, 2003; Pearlin, Mullan, Semple, & Skaff, 1990) and the Process Model of Stress and Coping (DeLongis, Folkman, & Lazarus, 1988). The Mediation Model indicates that the effect of stress on psychological outcomes is transmitted by coping resources, whereas the Process Model of Stress and Coping treats the stress process as more dynamic and accommodates multiple outcomes, which can be positive and negative, immediate and long-term. Despite extensive research on stress coping and the latest finding that playfulness can make a beneficial contribution to the stress–coping process (Qian & Yarnal, 2011), there is a relative lack of research that assesses the potential of playfulness as a coping resource. Another gap in the literature is in regard to how positive and negative emotions (PEs; NEs) as simultaneous and immediate stress–coping outcomes influence more comprehensive coping outcomes such as life satisfaction.

To fill these gaps, the current study used the Process Model of Stress and Coping to examine the effect of playfulness as a stress–coping resource for a sample of students in an American university class. We took advantage of the Process Model to examine both positive and NEs as immediate coping outcomes, but life satisfaction was the more comprehensive outcome of our study. Further, the university students were viewed as being in the stage of emerging adulthood (Arnett, 2000). According to Arnett's theory on emerging adulthood, individuals between 18 and 25 years of age become more independent and explore various life possibilities. However, Arnett failed to provide a conceptual connection between playfulness and emerging adulthood, which may be conducive to the role of exploration and identity development that characterizes this stage. However, the findings of the current study recognize the role of playfulness in the process of emerging adulthood, based on its findings among college students at this life stage.

Literature review

Playfulness and stress coping

Studies have linked playfulness to various positive psychological outcomes, such as PEs (Yarnal, 2006), psychological well-being, and resilience (Mitas, Qian, Yarnal, & Kerstetter, 2011; Saunders, Sayer, & Goodale, 1999). Generally, playfulness has been conceptualized as an individual disposition that is manifested by the qualities or attributes that individuals bring to their environment (Bozionelos & Bozionelos, 1999). Research has also shown that individuals with higher levels of playfulness are more flexible when facing problems (Bundy, 1993), indicating the possible contribution of playfulness to stress coping. At the same time, previous research has found that playfulness is situational (Barnett & Kleiber, 1982; Lieberman, 1975) and is affected by state-based stimuli, such as psychological stress (Qian & Yarnal, 2011; Sutton-Smith, 1997).

Noting that the concepts of play and playfulness are slightly different; play is viewed as having a vital role in human development that 'refers to its behavioral manifestations' (Magnuson & Barnett, 2013, p. 129), whereas playfulness is viewed as 'the predisposition to frame a situation in such a way as to provide oneself with amusement, humor, and entertainment' (Barnett, 2007, p. 955). Thus, play 'is defined by attitudes and behavioral styles', and 'playfulness is the term applied to this style and attitude,' present in play activities (Hess & Bundy, 2003, p. 6). In other words, playfulness is not defined as a specific activity but refers to individuals' experiences during activity (Csikszentmihalyi, 1981). Therefore, as playfulness has been defined, it encompasses individuals engaged in a voluntary leisure activity for fun, enjoyment and pleasure (Chick et al., 2012). Playfulness has been well examined in animals and children (Barnett, 1990), but little is known about adult playfulness in general (Bozionelos & Bozionelos, 1999), or how it relates to emerging adulthood.

Both playfulness and coping have been identified as 'self-directed process[es] that involve creative, multi-strategy approaches, persistence, active engagement, and flexibility, and often produce positive affect' (Saunders et al., 1999, p. 222). Given the complementary characteristics of playfulness and coping, researchers have suggested that playfulness may be a coping resource that helps sustain psychological health in stressful situations (Qian & Yarnal, 2011). For instance, Saunders et al. (1999) indicated that perceiving playfulness improves coping skill and adaptability, that is, playful adolescents like going to school to enjoy social, physical, and outdoor activities because they view school as a place to be playful. Further, playful adolescents reported higher levels of health and fewer problems with their peers. Hess and Bundy (2003) found that a higher level of playfulness was associated with less daily stress and a better sense of well-being among adolescents. More recently, Qian and Yarnal (2011) provided empirical evidence for the benefit of playfulness in the stress–coping process among university students. These researchers found that university students with higher levels of playfulness engaged in social leisure activities to cope with psychological stress, resulting in reduced NEs and sustained psychological well-being. Qian and Yarnal (2011) discussed their findings in light of the Process Model of Stress and Coping as well as the Mediation Model. The two models have been widely examined elsewhere, as well as informing the current study.

Models of stress coping

The Mediation Model of Stress Coping posits that coping resources are the factors that transmit the effects of stress on psychological outcomes (Iwasaki, 2003; Pearlin et al., 1990). Two effects were identified by the Mediation Model: counteractive and deterioration. According to the counteractive effect, stressful experience prompts individuals to mobilize coping resources, which leads to lower distress. For example, individuals may receive support from social gatherings that improves their well-being during major life events (e.g. losing a loved one) (Iwasaki, 2003). The deterioration effect, on the other hand, indicates that stressful encounters deplete resources and thus lead to higher distress. Ensel and Lin (1991) tested the applicability of the counteractive and deterioration effects on the role of positive resources in the life stress process. Their findings supported the deterioration effect, whereby positive resources decreased when life stress increased.

The Process Model of Stress and Coping was developed from the Process Theory of Stress and Coping (DeLongis et al., 1988). According to this theory, a stress process is 'not a simple variable but a system of interdependent processes' (DeLongis et al., 1988, p. 486). The Process Model, therefore, includes not only stress and coping, but also immediate and more comprehensive coping outcomes, capturing the dynamic nature of the stress–coping process more fully. A small number of studies have used the Process Model to assess the effect of leisure coping. For example, Iwasaki and Mannell (2000), used it to demonstrate that leisure helps university students cope with academic and interpersonal stressors by having a significant effect on their immediate coping outcomes, which in turn influenced both emotional and more comprehensive outcomes. More recently, Qian and Yarnal (2011) used the Process Model to examine if playfulness contributes to the process of using leisure to cope with psychological stress among university students. Their findings supported the Process Model, as university students, upon encountering a high level of psychological stress, were prompted by playfulness to engage in leisure coping, which then reduced their NEs. Furthermore, the adverse effect of NEs on their psychological well-being was more than compensated by the positive effect of playfulness. It is important to note that more stress–coping research has examined NE as a coping outcome, with PE receiving much less attention. Folkman (2009) suggested, however, that a new direction in the stress and coping literature should focus on 'the observation that positive and negative emotions co-occur during intensely stressful periods' (p. 75).

Emotional outcomes of stress coping

Multiple studies have examined the negative emotional outcomes of stress coping among university and high school students. For example, Weinstein, Brown, and Ryan (2009), in their study of psychological adjustment among Mexican American university students, found that they reported higher levels of anxiety if they had fewer coping resources (i.e. mindfulness) when dealing with college stress. Kostelecky and Lempers (2009) reported that high school seniors experienced higher levels of distress (e.g. depression and loneliness) during stressful life events if they had fewer coping resources (i.e. family support).

While there has been a strong tradition of studying NEs as stress coping outcomes, PEs have received growing attention in the last decade. Folkman (2008) indicated that meaning-focused coping, including benefit finding, adaptive goal processes, reordering priorities, and infusing positive meaning into ordinary events (e.g. enjoying a movie, dining out), generate PEs in times of stress. PEs, in turn, contribute to sustaining psychological well-being (Folkman, 2008; Folkman & Moskowitz, 2000a). Folkman (2008) also pointed out that the same coping strategy may create different positive and NEs. For example, PEs increased significantly after positive reappraisal had been used as a coping method, but the decrease in NEs was much smaller (Moskowitz, Folkman, Collette, & Vittinghoff, 1996).

It is worth noting that there is a difference between 'emotion' and 'affect.' An emotion is the display/reflection of feelings, which can be genuine or feigned, while an affect is a non-conscious experience of emotions, which is 'the body's way of preparing itself for action in a given circumstance' (Leys, 2011, p. 442). Since the purpose of the current study was to view emotions as outcomes of stress coping, we focused on 'emotion' rather than 'affect.'

Besides emotional outcomes, stress–coping processes also have a significant effect on more comprehensive outcomes, such as quality of life (Iwasaki, 2001) and life satisfaction (Collins, Glei, & Goldman, 2009). Among these outcomes, life satisfaction has been regarded as an important indicator of health and quality of life (Girzadas, Counte, Glandon, & Tancredi, 1993). However, we do not know whether positive and NEs, as immediate coping outcomes, make a difference in life satisfaction. Nor do we know whether playfulness as a coping resource benefits life satisfaction as a more comprehensive coping outcome.

Stress coping and life satisfaction

Life satisfaction is defined as a cognitive judgement process and includes experiencing both satisfaction and pleasure. The level of life satisfaction can vary depending on how individuals evaluate their life quality (Deniz, 2006). Stressful experiences (e.g. losing a loved one) may be one of the factors changing an individual's evaluation of their life quality or satisfaction.

Multiple studies have examined the effects of stress coping on life satisfaction among university students. For example, Barnes and Lightsey (2005) found a negative relationship between discrimination stress and life satisfaction among African American university students, and found that the coping strategies assessed (social support, avoidance, and problem solving) did not help them cope with their stress. The negative effect of stress on life satisfaction was recently replicated by Matheny, Roque-Tovar, and Curlette (2008). In a study of stress–coping and life satisfaction among Turkish college students, Deniz (2006) reported that problem-focused coping and seeking social support were positively associated with life satisfaction.

There is also scattered evidence that experiencing PEs in the stress–coping process contributes to sustaining life satisfaction. In a study of individuals coping with spinal cord injury, Kortte, Gilbert, Gorman, and Wegener (2010) examined the effect of positive affect on life satisfaction during their initial recovery period. These researchers found that those with a greater positive affect reported higher levels of life satisfaction despite their debility.

Given the findings of previous research and the gaps in the literature, the current study used the Process Model of Stress and Coping to assess whether playfulness helps university students cope with psychological stress. We examined both positive and NEs as immediate outcomes of

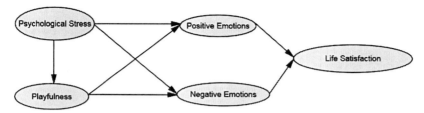

Figure 1. Proposed model.

stress coping as well as life satisfaction as a more comprehensive coping outcome (Figure 1). Specifically, we proposed that playfulness partially mediates the effect of psychological stress on positive and NEs, both of which then influence life satisfaction.

Methods

Research participants

For this study, we used a paper-and-pencil questionnaire to collect data from undergraduate students enrolled in two general education courses at a large Eastern university in the USA. There were two versions of the questionnaire with different orders of items. randomly distributed and completed in class at the beginning of April 2009, four weeks before the end of the semester – a time when students may experience a high level of stress (Iwasaki, 2001) (The appendix reflects one of the questionnaire versions, differing from the other version only in the ordering of items.). Participation in the study was voluntary. Before distributing the questionnaire, the principal investigator gave a brief speech in class, discussing the purpose of the study, the contents of the questionnaire, and issues of anonymity. Students who completed the questionnaire provided informed consent and received an extra credit for the respective course, in conformance to IRB standards. Altogether 195 students (54.87% males; ages 18–34, $M = 20.46$; 14.5% freshmen, 28.5% sophomores, 43% juniors, 13.4% seniors, 0.6% fifth-year undergraduates) provided usable data.

Measures

The respondents were asked to complete the questionnaire based on their experiences in 'the previous week.' Note that the Likert-type rating scale (e.g. 1 = very little, to 10 = a lot) adopted for each measure was the one used when the measure was initially developed. Therefore, different rating scales were used for different measures (e.g. 1–10 for the Playfulness Scale, 0–3 for the Psychological Stress Scale). The correlation coefficients of utilized scales are given in Table 1. The items in each scale can be found in Table 2.

Table 1. Correlation coefficients of scales used.

	1	2	3	4	5
1. Psychological stress	1.00				
2. Playfulness	−0.23*	1.00			
3. PEs	−0.04	0.57*	1.00		
4. NEs	0.44*	−0.14	−0.09	1.00	
5. Life satisfaction	−0.37*	0.43*	0.43*	−0.27*	1.00

*$p < 0.01$

PLAY AND WELLBEING

Table 2. Summary of items and scales: mean, standard deviation, Cronbach's alpha.

Scale/item	Mean	SD	Beta
Playfulness:			
Factor 1: $\alpha = 0.86$			0.904
Sociable	7.41	1.66	0.668
Friendly	7.97	1.60	0.805
Happy	7.68	1.71	0.791
Cheerful	7.25	158	0.867
Factor 2: $\alpha = 0.81$			0.451
Adventurous	7.31	1.61	0.644
Unpredictable	6.34	1.85	0.711
Impulsive	6.77	1.65	0.621
Spontaneous	6.97	1.56	0.900
Factor 3: $\alpha = 0.91$			0.656
Humorous	7.59	1.50	0.890
Funny	7.54	1.51	0.944
Jokes/teases	7.82	1.73	0.754
Clowns around	7.25	1.94	0.740
Factor 4: $\alpha = 0.71$			0.819
Active	7.34	1.59	0.562
Energetic	7.12	1.61	0.930
Psychological stress: $\alpha = 0.83$			
I found it difficult to relax	1.84	0.89	0.769
I felt I was rather touchy	1.72	0.76	0.636
I tended to over-react to situations	1.88	0.83	0.611
I found it hard to wind down	1.74	0.92	0.759
I felt I was using a lot of nervous energy	1.52	0.77	0.740
I was intolerant of anything that kept me from getting on with what I was doing	1.60	0.70	0.550
PEs sub-scale of mDES: $\alpha = 0.81$			
Content	3.45	0.94	0.528
Hopeful	3.54	0.85	0.612
Grateful	3.84	0.93	0.800
Joyous	3.48	0.95	0.779
Proud	3.48	0.91	0.494
Loving	3.82	0.97	0.629
Amused	3.60	0.87	0.499
NEs sub-scale of mDES: $\alpha = 0.83$			
Sad	1.92	0.86	0.726
Angry	2.19	1.02	0.742
Embarrassed	1.90	0.88	0.591
Afraid	1.88	0.92	0.625
Disgusted	1.97	1.00	0.752
Life satisfaction: $\alpha = 0.87$			
In most ways, my life is close to my ideal	4.83	1.23	0.824
The conditions of my life are excellent	5.05	1.18	0.860
I am satisfied with my life	5.51	1.15	0.890
So far I have gotten the important things I want in life	5.28	1.25	0.682
If I could live my life over, I would change almost nothing	4.40	1.71	0.547

Playfulness

For our study, we used the Young Adult Playfulness Scale (Barnett, 2007) to measure playfulness among the university students. We used this scale for two reasons: first, it established playfulness as a meaningful psychological construct in the young adult population; and second, it was developed using a large sample ($N = 694$) of American university students (Barnett, 2007). The scale includes 15 items that encompass four factors: gregarious (Factor 1), uninhibited (Factor 2), comedic (Factor 3), and dynamic (Factor 4). The respondents indicated how they characterized themselves using 15 items rated by a Likert-type scale (1 = very little to 10 = a lot).

Psychological stress

The Stress Sub-scale of the DASS-21 (the short-form of the Depression, Anxiety, and Stress Scale) was used to measure the students' psychological stress. The original DASS includes 42 items (Lovibond & Lovibond, 1995), 14 of which measure psychological stress. Using a sample size of 1794 adults from the general adult population, Henry and Crawford (2005) developed and validated the DASS-21, which includes 21 items, although each of the three sub-scales (depression, anxiety, stress) can be used independently. Participants in the current study rated themselves on the 21 items, using a 0–3 Likert-type scale (0 = did not apply to me at all, to 3 = applied to me very much or most of the time).

Positive and NEs

We used the modified differential emotions scale (mDES; Fredrickson, Tugade, Waugh, & Larkin, 2003) to measure positive and NEs as the students' emotional responses to stress and coping. Because the original differential emotions scale (DES; Izard, 1977) included PE items and mainly focused on high arousal emotions, Fredrickson et al. (2003) added discrete PEs to the original DES, but did not make any change to the NEs Sub-scale. The mDES has 31 items, 15 under the PEs Sub-scale and 16 under the NEs Sub-scale, although the two sub-scales can be used independently. Our respondents rated themselves on the 31 items using a 5-point scale (0 = very slightly or not at all to 5 = extremely).

Life satisfaction

We used the Satisfaction With Life Scale (SWLS; Diener, Emmons, Larsen, & Griffin, 1985) to measure students' life satisfaction, the more comprehensive stress and coping outcome. Diener et al. (1985) used two samples of the undergraduate students to develop the scale and to establish its reliability and validity. The researchers then established the psychometric properties of the SWLS, using a mature population. The scale has five items, forming a single-factor structure. Our respondents rated themselves on the 5 items, using a 7-point scale (1 = strongly disagree to 7 = strongly agree).

Demographic information

At the end of the questionnaire, we asked the age, gender, and class standings of the respondents. Age was measured in years, written on a blank line on the questionnaire. Gender was measured as a categorical variable, indicated by circling 'male' or 'female' on the questionnaire. Class standing was also measured as a categorical variable using one of the following options: freshman, sophomore, junior, senior, or fifth-year undergraduate student. Noting that the above descriptions are only a part of the questions on the questionnaire which was used to examine for the research purpose of the current study.

Analytic strategy

First, PSAW (V18, formerly SPSS) was used to perform descriptive data analyses. Second, confirmatory factor analysis (CFA) was performed using AMOS (V18) to test the factor structure of

PLAY AND WELLBEING

the scales and the fit of the measurement model of the scales. Third, structural equation modeling (SEM) was conducted in AMOS using maximum-likelihood estimation to test the proposed model (Figure 1). Although causality cannot be determined with cross-sectional data, we chose SEM to examine the direct and indirect relationships suggested by the proposed model.

Results

Descriptive statistics and preliminary analysis

The variables were standardized during the preliminary analysis. Each of the five scales was computed using the mean of the items on the scale, and the correlations between the five computed scales were calculated. According to Table 1, psychological stress was positively correlated with NE, and negatively correlated with playfulness and life satisfaction. However, there was no significant correlation between psychological stress and PE. Playfulness had significant positive correlations with PEs and with life satisfaction, but its correlation with NE was non-significant. Positive and NEs had significant correlations with life satisfaction, but were not significantly correlated with each other.

Next, we examined whether there were significant gender, age, or class standing differences in psychological stress, playfulness, PEs, NEs, and life satisfaction. We conducted an analysis of variance and found no significant gender or class standing differences on any of the five computed scales, nor was there a gender-class standing interaction effect on any of the scales. The five computed scales were also regressed by age, respectively, but no significant relationship was identified. Thus, subsequent analyses used the entire sample.

Measurement models: CFAs

We conducted a CFA to verify the factor structure for each of the five scales. One item ('agitated') had a non-significant loading in the Stress Sub-scale of the DASS-21. Hence, the stress measure used in the subsequent analyses consisted of six, rather than seven, items. According to Barnett (2007), the Young Adult Playfulness Scale has 15 items that form four factors. However, the CFA showed that one item ('outgoing') from factor one loaded high on two other factors. Therefore, 'outgoing' was eliminated, and we adopted a 14-item/4-factor structure for the Playfulness Scale in subsequent analyses. In the PEs Sub-scale, one item ('awed') had a non-significant factor loading, while another ('compassionate') had a highly significant covariance with three other items. These two items were eliminated, and the PEs Sub-scale used in subsequent analyses consisted of seven, rather than nine, items. One item ('contemptuous') had a non-significant loading on the NEs Sub-scale. Hence, this sub-scale was used in subsequent analyses consisting of five, rather than six, items. Finally, all five items of the Satisfaction With Life Scale survived the CFA. Table 2 shows the mean, standard deviation, and standardized Beta loading of each item on the respective scale. Cronbach's alpha of each (sub-) scale is also reported in Table 2. All the scales used in the current study showed acceptable to high alpha reliability coefficients (0.71–0.91).

We then tested the measurement model in Figure 2, assuming that the five scales were correlated with each other. All the correlations, except between psychological stress and PEs, were significant.

To select specific goodness-of-fit indices, Bollen (1989) suggested that the chi-square always be reported while it is necessary to use other fit indices simultaneously. However, since chi-square is sensitive to sample size, relative chi-square (χ^2/df) has been used as a fit index (Bollen, 1989). According to Hu and Bentler (1999), Kline (2005), Bryant, King, and Smart (2007), as well as Lei and Wu (2007), a good model fit exists when the relative chi-square (χ^2/df) is smaller than 3 or 2,

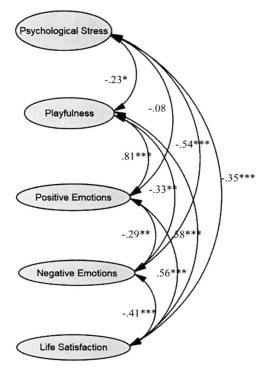

Figure 2. Measurement model.
Note: *$p < 0.05$, **$p < 0.01$, ***$p < 0.001$.

Table 3. CFA model fit.

	Chi-square	df	CMIN/DF	CFI	SRMR	RMSEA
Playfulness	137.5	69	1.99	0.96	0.059	0.072
Psychological stress	10.4	9	1.15	0.99	0.026	0.028
PEs	29.92	14	1.49	0.98	0.036	0.050
NEs	8.6	4	2.16	0.99	0.027	0.075
Life satisfaction	9.93	5	1.99	0.99	0.021	0.071
Measurement model	931.12	610	1.53	0.91	0.068	0.052

the comparable fit index (CFI) is greater than 0.90, the standardized root mean square residual (SRMR) is smaller than 0.08, and the root mean square of approximation (RMSEA) is smaller than 0.075. Using these goodness-of-fit indices, Table 3 shows that the factor structure of all the scales had a good CFA fit, and the fit of the Measurement Model (Figure 2) was also good.

Testing the model: SEM

We first tested the proposed model (Figure 1). Two paths in this model were not significant: the path from psychological stress to PEs and the path from NEs to life satisfaction. We, therefore, eliminated both paths and re-tested the model. Since these two models (one with both paths, the other without) were nested, a difference in chi-square was used to test if eliminating the

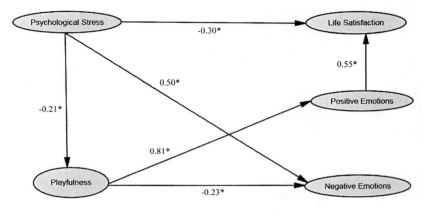

Figure 3. Final model with standardized beta coefficients.
Note: *p < 0.05.

two paths led to a significantly worse-fitting model. Subsequent changes in the chi-square value indicated that eliminating the paths did not lead to a significantly worse fitting model. Hence, the two paths were dropped. At the same time, the modification index indicated a direct path from psychological stress to life satisfaction. When this path was added, the path coefficient was significant. Therefore, the path from psychological stress to life satisfaction was kept in the model.

We also found significant indirect effects from psychological stress to PEs (mediated by playfulness), and from playfulness to life satisfaction (mediated by PEs). Thus, we decided that this would be the final model (Figure 3), with all the direct and indirect effects making conceptual sense and no outstanding issue being indicated by modification indices. The fit of the final model was good (Bryant et al., 2007; Hu & Bentler, 1999; Kline, 2005; Lei & Wu, 2007): Chi-square = 941.79, df = 614, CMIN/DF = 1.53, CFI = 0.91, RMSEA = 0.052 (90% CI: 0.046, 0.059), SRMR = 0.07.

The Final Model (Figure 3) partially confirmed the Proposed Model (Figure 1), since there were significant direct effects from psychological stress to playfulness and NEs, from playfulness to both positive and NEs, and from PEs to life satisfaction. However, the effect from psychological stress to PEs was not significant, nor was the effect from NEs to life satisfaction. At the same time, we found a significant direct effect from psychological stress to life satisfaction.

Discussion of the findings and future directions

The current study used the Process Model of Stress and Coping to examine whether playfulness contributes to coping with psychological stress among a sample of university students. By using the Process Model, we were able to take into account both positive and NEs as immediate outcomes as well as more comprehensive outcomes such as life satisfaction. We found that, when faced with high psychological stress, university students became less playful, experienced more NEs, and reported lower life satisfaction. However, those with a higher level of playfulness were able to experience more PEs and less NEs, thus partially remedying the adverse emotional effects of psychological stress. This finding provides additional evidence to support recent playfulness literature indicating that playfulness is affected by psychological stress (Qian & Yarnal, 2011; Sutton-Smith, 1997), viewing individual characteristics as influenced by their experiences (Barnett, 2007). Moreover, an increase in PEs was associated with an increase in life satisfaction, hence offsetting the negative effect of psychological stress on life satisfaction. Our findings contributed to the literature in at least four ways. First, by showing the benefit of playfulness as a coping resource; second, by demonstrating the value of the process model of stress coping; third, by highlighting the importance of examining both emotional and more comprehensive outcomes of stress coping; and finally, by recognizing the role of playfulness in the emerging adulthood process among this university student sample.

Our first contribution was in directly testing whether playfulness serves as a stress coping resource. Previous research found that more playful adults demonstrated greater flexibility when faced with problems (Bundy, 1993), whereas more playful adolescents reported less daily stress and a better sense of well-being (Hess & Bundy, 2003). These findings have led researchers to suggest that playfulness may contribute to stress coping (Staempfli & Mannell, 2005). Indeed, more recent research (Qian & Yarnal, 2011) provided empirical evidence that playfulness prompted university students to engage in leisure activities as a strategy to cope with psychological stress. However, no research had examined whether playfulness itself serves as a coping resource for this population. The findings of the current study filled this gap by showing that playfulness, as a meaningful psychological construct, serves as a coping resource that undergraduate students can draw on when experiencing psychological stress. It is possible that, by offering greater flexibility in stressful situations (Bundy, 1993), playfulness affords university students the capacity to process stressful situations, thus helping them effectively cope with the stress.

Meanwhile, in the results of our study, the decrease in NEs associated with playfulness was smaller than the increase in NE caused by psychological stress. In other words, playfulness could not fully offset the adverse emotional effects of the students' psychological stress. To reduce NE caused by psychological stress, it is not realistic to rely on playfulness alone. Other coping resources would also need to be mobilized.

Equally important to note is the finding that the level of playfulness was diminished by psychological stress, supporting the previous research finding that playfulness is situational (Barnett & Kleiber, 1982; Lieberman, 1975) and can be suppressed by stressful situations (Qian & Yarnal, 2011; Sutton-Smith, 1997). This finding also provided evidence for the deterioration effect, since psychological stress, rather than prompting a surge in playfulness, was associated with a reduced level of playfulness. This result agrees with Ensel and Lin's (1991) finding which supported the deterioration effect. Taken together, our findings indicate that psychological stress depletes playfulness as a coping resource to some extent. At the same time, those who were able to retain a considerable 'reserve' of playfulness as a coping resource fared better emotionally.

Our second contribution was in providing further evidence for the value of the Process Model of Stress and Coping. Using this model enabled us to assess how playfulness as a coping resource influences multiple coping outcomes directly and indirectly. Our finding that playfulness indirectly contributed to the students' life satisfaction by increasing their PEs extends previous research findings that the Process Model accommodates the dynamic nature of stress coping (Iwasaki & Mannell, 2000; Qian & Yarnal, 2011). Using this model to examine both emotional and more comprehensive coping outcomes also allowed us to reveal where the strength of playfulness as a coping resource lies. Playfulness prompted PEs to more than compensate for the negative effect of perceived stress on life satisfaction, but was not enough to offset the adverse effect of perceived stress on NEs.

Our third contribution was in revealing the fruitfulness of assessing both emotional and more comprehensive outcomes of stress coping. We answered the call by Qian and Yarnal (2011) to simultaneously examine PEs and NEs as immediate coping outcomes. PE and NE were responses to playfulness as a coping resource, dealing with psychological stress in different ways, which supported earlier findings that PE and NE may respond differently to the same coping strategy (Folkman, 2008; Moskowitz et al., 1996). Although playfulness had a significant effect on both PE and NE, its PE-enhancing effect was much stronger than its NE-reducing effect. Such differential effects were not surprising, given the four dimensions of young adult playfulness (gregarious, uninhibited, comedic, and dynamic). More importantly, the finding that playfulness significantly reduced NE indicated that the benefits of playfulness can go beyond facilitating positive outcomes that past studies have repeatedly demonstrated (Mitas et al., 2011; Saunders et al., 1999; Yarnal, 2006). Playfulness as a coping resource also has the capacity to mitigate negative outcomes.

In terms of a more comprehensive coping outcome, we found that the students' life satisfaction was hampered by their psychological stress. Past studies have also identified the adverse effect of stressful experience on life satisfaction (Barnes & Lightsey, 2005; Matheny, Roque-Tovar, & Curlette, 2004), and we provided further evidence in this regard. At the same time, in our study, life satisfaction was boosted by PE but not affected by NE, and the beneficial effect of PE was larger than the negative effect of psychological stress. Our findings provide a strong support for the argument that sustaining PEs in times of stress contribute to protecting well-being (Folkman & Moskowitz, 2000b). Our findings also imply that sustaining PE is critical for counteracting the detrimental effects of psychological stress on life satisfaction. Moreover, we contributed to the literature by identifying a coping resource – playfulness – which is capable of increasing PE in stressful situations. The counteracting effect of PE, coupled with the lack of adverse effects by NE, signals that promoting such positive outlooks as optimism and positivity are important for sustaining life satisfaction in times of stress.

Our fourth and last contribution was in providing additional evidence that playfulness may be a well-being intervention at the college level – contributing to the emerging adulthood literature – and may have a strong public health impact on students and the college community. For example, providing a school environment or prevention program in which students can be playful, improving their PEs and reducing their NEs, may help decrease the rate of risky behaviors related to drug and alcohol use (Hingson, 2010), as well as build their self-identity during emerging adulthood.

Additionally, our sample was American university students, whose stress–coping resources, including playfulness had not been studied. Previous research has offered different definitions of playfulness across age groups and cultural contexts (Armstrong, 1991; Chick et al., 2012; Yarnal & Qian, 2011). For example, Armstrong discussed playfulness and cultural differences suggesting that the study of playfulness 'requires differences as well as similarities' (p. 163). However, Armstrong claimed that playfulness is 'a Western ethnocentric concept' (p. 167), existing mainly in the Western tradition. Therefore, although our results contributed to the understanding of playfulness in relation to coping with stress in Western culture, it may not be possible to replicate them in other societies.

Despite its promising findings, the present study was not without limitations. First, the sample was quite homogenous and relatively small ($N = 195$) for an SEM. Therefore, we did not assess whether demographic and personality factors made differences in the stress–coping process. Second, there may have been recall bias when the participants were asked to report their experiences in the previous week (Stone & Shiffman, 2002). The participants' answers to the survey may also have been influenced by their immediate circumstances when answering the survey. Third, our study used a traditional cross-sectional survey design to collect the data. Therefore, our analysis was strictly a between-person comparison, and did not offer any insight into how the stress–coping process unfolds within-person over time. Finally, our study assessed the participants' sense of playfulness according to Csikszentmihalyi's (1981) definition of playfulness; accordingly playfulness was not defined as a specific activity but by individuals' experiences; but we did not ask them about specific activities, such as playing video games or attending social gatherings.

In light of these limitations, we provide four suggestions for future research. First, we urge further research with a repeated-measure design to collect data from the same participants at multiple times to capture their within-person processes of using playfulness to cope with psychological stress. A repeated-measure design may also reduce the risk of recall bias, since this design would make it possible for the time of data collection to be closer to the time of the experience. Second, we encourage future studies to collect data in different ways, or from a larger and more diverse sample. For one thing, giving course credit to our study participants may have influenced their answers, even though they were assured anonymity. A different data collection method may produce different results. The Experiential Sampling Method may be helpful to collect data from an unbiased sample because it asks the participants to stop at random times to record their temporal feelings in the moment. Additionally, American college students may perceive playfulness differently than Asian or other college students. Further, college students and children may have different perceptions of playfulness. A more diverse sample may allow researchers to assess whether the stress–coping process differs by factors such as age, personality traits, or cultural influences. Third, the current study was focused on the psychological outcomes of stress coping. Although it is not inherently a limitation, the practice did leave out physical health factors. Therefore, we suggest assessing physical health as another stress–coping outcome to provide a comprehensive picture for the value of playfulness as a stress–coping resource. Fourth, playfulness may occur in different circumstances. Examining ways that playfulness might be provided, such as through specific leisure activities, may result in a more comprehensive understanding of the effects of playfulness on stress coping.

References

Armstrong, P. B. (1991). Play and cultural differences. *The Kenyon Review, 13*(1), 157–171.

Arnett, J. (2000). Emerging adulthood: A theory of development from late teens to early twenties. *American Psychologist, 55*(5), 469–480.

Barnes, P. W., & Lightsey, Jr., O. R. (2005). Perceived racist discrimination, coping, stress, and life satisfaction. *Journal of Multicultural Counseling and Development, 33*(1), 48–61.

Barnett, L. A. (1990). Playfulness: Definition, design, and measurement. *Play & Culture, 3*, 319–336.

Barnett, L. A. (2007). The nature of playfulness in young adults. *Personality and Individual Differences, 43*, 949–958.

Barnett, L. A., & Kleiber, D. A. (1982). Concomitants of playfulness in early childhood: Cognitive abilities and gender. *Journal of Genetic Psychology, 141*, 115–127.

Bollen, K. A. (1989). *Structural equations with latent variables.* New York, NY: Wiley.

Bozionelos, N., & Bozionelos, G. (1999). Playfulness: Its relationship with instrumental and expressive traits. *Personality and Individual Differences, 26*, 749–760.

PLAY AND WELLBEING

Bryant, F. B., King, S. P., & Smart, C. M. (2007). Multivariate statistical strategies for construct validation in positive psychology. In A. D. Ong & M. van Dulmen (Eds.), *Oxford handbook of methods in positive psychology* (pp. 61–82). Oxford: Oxford University Press.

Bundy, A. C. (1993). Assessment of play and leisure: Delineation of the problem. *American Journal of Occupational Therapy, 47*, 217–222.

Chick, G., Yarnal, C., & Purrington, A. (2012). Play and mate preference: Testing the signal theory of adult playfulness. *American Journal of Play, 4*(4), 407–440.

Collins, A. L., Glei, D. A., & Goldman, N. (2009). The role of life satisfaction and depressive symptoms in all-cause mortality. *American Psychological Association, 24*, 696–702.

Csikszentmihalyi, M. (1981). *The meaning of things: Domestic symbols and the self.* Boston: Cambridge University Press.

DeLongis, A., Folkman, S., & Lazarus, R. S. (1988). The impact of daily stress on health and mood: Psychological and social resources as mediators. *Journal of Personality and Social Psychology, 54* (3), 486–495.

Deniz, M. E. (2006). The relationships among coping with stress, life satisfaction, decision-making styles and decision self-esteem: An investigation with Turkish university students. *Social Behavior and Personality, 34*(9), 1161–1170.

Diener, E., Emmons, R. A., Larsen, R. J., & Griffin, S. (1985). The satisfaction with life scale. *Journal of Personality Assessment, 49*, 71–75.

Ensel, W. M., & Lin, N. (1991). The life stress paradigm and psychological distress. *Journal of Health and Social Behavior, 32*(4), 321–341.

Folkman, S. (2008). The case for positive emotions in the stress process. *Anxiety, Stress, and Coping, 21*(1), 3–14.

Folkman, S. (2009). Questions, answers, issues, and next steps in stress and coping research. *European Psychologist, 14*(1), 72–77.

Folkman, S., & Moskowitz, J. T. (2000a). Stress, positive emotion, and coping. *Current Directions in Psychological Science, 9*(4), 115–118.

Folkman, S., & Moskowitz, J. T. (2000b). Positive affect and the other side of coping. *American Psychologist, 55*(6), 647–654.

Fredrickson, B., Tugade, M., Waugh, C., & Larkin, G. (2003). What good are positive emotions in crises? A prospective study of resilience and emotions following the terrorist attacks on the United States on September 11th, 2001. *Journal of Personality and Social Psychology, 84*(2), 365–376.

Girzadas, P. M., Counte, M. A., Glandon, G. L., & Tancredi, D. (1993). An analysis of elderly health and life satisfaction. *Behavior, Health, and Aging, 3*(2), 103–117.

Glynn, M. A., & Webster, J. (1992). The adult playfulness scale: An initial assessment. *Psychological Reports, 71*, 83–103.

Harkness, L., & Bundy, A. C. (2001). The test of playfulness and children with physical disabilities. *Occupational Therapy Journal of Research, 21*(2), 73–89.

Henry, J., & Crawford, J. (2005). The short-form version of the Depression Anxiety Stress Scales (DASS-21): Construct validity and normative data in a large non-clinical sample. *The British Journal of Clinical Psychology, 44*, 227–239.

Hess, L. M., & Bundy, A. C. (2003). The association between playfulness and coping in adolescents. *Physical & Occupational Therapy in Pediatrics, 23*(2), 5–17.

Hingson, R. W. (2010). How are colleges doing six years later? *Alcoholism: Clinical and Experimental Research, 34*(10), 1694–1699.

Hu, L., & Bentler, P. M. (1999). Cutoff criteria for fit indexes in covariance structure analysis: Conventional criteria versus new alternatives. *Structural Equation Modelling, 6*, 1–55.

Iwasaki, Y. (2001). Testing an optimal matching hypothesis of stress, coping and health: Leisure and general coping. *Society and Leisure, 24*, 163–203.

Iwasaki, Y. (2003). Examining rival models of leisure coping mechanisms. *Leisure Sciences, 25*(2), 183–206.

Iwasaki, Y., & Mannell, R. C. (2000). The effects of leisure beliefs and coping strategies on stress–health relationships: A field study. *Leisure/Loisir, 24*(1–2), 3–57.

Izard, C. E. (1977). *Human emotions.* New York, NY: Plenum.

Kline, R. B. (2005). *Principles and practice of structural equation modelling.* New York, NY: Guilford.

Kortte, K. B., Gilbert, M., Gorman, P., & Wegener, S. T. (2010). Positive psychological variables in the prediction of life satisfaction after spinal cord injury. *Rehabilitation Psychology, 55*(1), 40–47.

Kostelecky, K. L., & Lempers, J. D. (2009). Stress, family social support, distress, and well-being in high school seniors. *Family and Consumer Sciences Research Journal, 27*(2), 125–145.

Lei, P. W., & Wu, Q. (2007). Introduction to structural equation modelling: Issues and practical considerations. *Educational Measurement: Issues and Practice, 26*, 33–43.

Leys, R. (2011). The turn to affect: A critique. *Critical Inquiry, 37*, 434–472.

Lieberman, J. (1975). *Playfulness, cognitive style, and leisure, or 'Do we need to educate for leisure?'* Paper presented at the 83rd Annual Convention of the American Psychological Association, Chicago, August 30 to September, 2, 1975.

Lovibond, P., & Lovibond, S. (1995). The structure of negative emotional states: Comparison of the Depression Anxiety Stress Scales (DASS) with the beck depression and anxiety inventories. *Behavior Research and Therapy, 33*(3), 335–343.

Magnuson, C. D., & Barnett, L. A. (2013). The playful advantage: How playfulness enhances coping with stress. *Leisure Sciences, 35*(2), 129–133.

Matheny, K. B., Roque-Tovar, B. E., & Curlette, W. L. (2004). Coping resources, perceived stress, and life satisfaction among Turkish and American university students. *International Journal of Stress Management, 9*(2), 81–97.

Matheny, K. B., Roque-Tovar, B. E., & Curlette, W. L. (2008). Perceived stress, coping resources, and life satisfaction among U.S. and Mexican college students: A cross-cultural study. *Annals of Psychology, 24* (1), 49–57.

Mattei, D., & Schaefer, C. E. (2004). An investigation of validity of the subjective happiness scale. *Psychological Report, 94*, 288–290.

Mitas, O., Qian, X. L., Yarnal, C., & Kerstetter, D. (2011). 'The fun begins now!': Broadening and building processes in Red Hat Society participation. *Journal of Leisure Research, 43*(1), 30–55.

Moskowitz, J. T., Folkman, S., Collette, L., & Vittinghoff, E. (1996). Coping and mood during AIDS-related caregiving and bereavement. *Annals of Behavioral Medicine, 18*, 49–57.

Pearlin, L., Mullan, J. T., Semple, S. J., & Skaff, M. M. (1990). Caregiving and the stress process: An overview of concepts and their measures. *The Gerontologist, 30*(5), 583–594.

Qian, X. L., & Yarnal, C. (2011). The role of playfulness in the leisure stress–coping process among emerging adults: An SEM analysis. *Leisure/Loisir, 35*(2), 191–209.

Saunders, I., Sayer, M., & Goodale, A. (1999). The relationship between playfulness and coping in preschool children: A pilot study. *American Journal of Occupational Therapy, 53*(2), 221–226.

Staempfli, M., & Mannell, R. C. (2005). *Adolescent playfulness and well-being.* Nanaimo, BC: Eleventh Canadian Congress on Leisure Research.

Starbuck, W. H., & Webster, J. (1991). When is play productive? *Accounting, Management & Information Technologies, 1*, 1–20.

Stone, A. A., & Shiffman, S. (2002). Capturing momentary, self-report data: A proposal for reporting guidelines. *Annual Behavioral Medicine, 24*, 236–243.

Sutton-Smith, B. (1997). *The ambiguity of play.* Cambridge, MA: Harvard University Press.

Weinstein, N., Brown, K. W., & Ryan, R. M. (2009). A multi-method examination of the effects of mindfulness on stress attribution, coping, and emotional well-being. *Journal of Research in Personality, 43*, 374–385.

Yarnal, C., & Qian, X. (2011). Older-adult playfulness: An innovative construct and measurement for healthy aging research. *American Journal of Play, 4*(1), 52–79.

Yarnal, C. M. (2006). The red hat society: Exploring the role of play, liminality, and communitas in older women's lives. *Journal of Women & Aging, 18*(3), 51–73.

PLAY AND WELLBEING

Appendix. Questionnaire

Dear RPTM 120 student,

We are trying to learn more about college students and would like your help. Enclosed are several scales which will tell us a variety of things about you – certain aspects of your personality, your leisure behavior, and your health. In RPTM 120, we discuss how personality, leisure behavior, and health are related. Your participation in this research study contributes to how much we know about these relationships.

The scales are all very easy to complete and won't require you to do much writing at all. It should take you less than 20 minutes to complete all of them. You will receive extra credit in your class for completing all of them. If you've already filled out the scales to obtain credit in another class besides this one, please do these again to obtain credit in this course.

Please answer all of the scales completely, and be very honest and truthful in your responses. If there are any questions you feel uncomfortable about, you may skip them.

Your identity will **not** be connected to the answers you give, and all of the responses will be totaled to show group scores so that no one person's scores will be known to anyone. We ask for the first four digits of your PSU student ID only to connect your responses to this survey to your responses to an identical one later in the semester. We will not use these digits to look up any personal or identifying information about you.

This research study has been approved by the University's Institutional Review Board. If you have any questions at all about this research study, or about any of the questionnaires, please feel free to e-mail (cmy122@psu.edu) or telephone me (863-5559).

Thanks for your participation!

Careen Yarnal, Ph.D.

First four digits of your PSU student ID# _____

PLAY AND WELLBEING

Please indicate how you would characterize yourself on the qualities listed below. Circle the correct number to show if you think you have very little or a lot of each quality listed.

	Very little									A lot
Active	1	2	3	4	5	6	7	8	9	10
Sociable	1	2	3	4	5	6	7	8	9	10
Energetic	1	2	3	4	5	6	7	8	9	10
Friendly	1	2	3	4	5	6	7	8	9	10
Adventurous	1	2	3	4	5	6	7	8	9	10
Cheerful	1	2	3	4	5	6	7	8	9	10
Impulsive	1	2	3	4	5	6	7	8	9	10
Jokes/teases	1	2	3	4	5	6	7	8	9	10
Funny	1	2	3	4	5	6	7	8	9	10
Spontaneous	1	2	3	4	5	6	7	8	9	10
Humorous	1	2	3	4	5	6	7	8	9	10
Unpredictable	1	2	3	4	5	6	7	8	9	10
Happy	1	2	3	4	5	6	7	8	9	10
Outgoing	1	2	3	4	5	6	7	8	9	10
Clowns Around	1	2	3	4	5	6	7	8	9	10

PLAY AND WELLBEING

> Please think back to the most stressful event **in the past year** and recall how you coped with this event. Then rate how you coped with this event on the following items.

	very strongly disagree	strongly disagree	somewhat disagree	neither disagree nor agree	somewhat agree	strongly agree	very strongly agree
My leisure allowed me to be in the company of supportive friends.	1	2	3	4	5	6	7
Socializing in leisure was a means of managing stress.	1	2	3	4	5	6	7
I dealt with stress through spending leisure time with my friends.	1	2	3	4	5	6	7
Engaging in social leisure was a stress-coping strategy for me.	1	2	3	4	5	6	7
Lack of companionship in leisure prevented me from coping with stress.	1	2	3	4	5	6	7
One of my stress-coping strategies was participation in social leisure.	1	2	3	4	5	6	7
I engaged in a leisure activity to temporarily get away from the problem.	1	2	3	4	5	6	7
Escape through leisure was a way of coping with stress.	1	2	3	4	5	6	7
Leisure was an important means of keeping myself busy.	1	2	3	4	5	6	7
Engagement in leisure allowed me to gain a fresh perspective on my problem(s).	1	2	3	4	5	6	7
By escaping from the problem through leisure, I was able to tackle my problem(s) with renewed energy.	1	2	3	4	5	6	7
I took a brief break through leisure to deal with the stress.	1	2	3	4	5	6	7
My leisure helped me feel better.	1	2	3	4	5	6	7
I gained a positive feeling from leisure.	1	2	3	4	5	6	7
I maintained a good mood in leisure.	1	2	3	4	5	6	7
My leisure involvements failed to improve my mood.	1	2	3	4	5	6	7
Leisure made me feel miserable.	1	2	3	4	5	6	7
Leisure helped me manage my negative feeling.	1	2	3	4	5	6	7

PLAY AND WELLBEING

Each item on this page is a statement that a person may either agree with or disagree with. For each item, indicate how much you agree or disagree with what the item says. Please respond to all the items; do not leave any blank. Choose only one response to each statement. Please be as accurate and honest as you can be. Respond to each item as if it were the only item. That is, don't worry about being "consistent" in your responses.

	very false for me	somewhat false for me	somewhat true for me	very true for me
A person's family is the most important thing in life.	1	2	3	4
Even if something bad is about to happen to me, I rarely experience fear or nervousness.	1	2	3	4
I go out of my way to get things I want.	1	2	3	4
When I'm doing well at something I love to keep at it.	1	2	3	4
I'm always willing to try something new if I think it will be fun.	1	2	3	4
How I dress is important to me.	1	2	3	4
When I get something I want, I feel excited and energized.	1	2	3	4
Criticism or scolding hurts me quite a bit.	1	2	3	4
When I want something I usually go all-out to get it.	1	2	3	4
I will often do things for no other reason than that they might be fun.	1	2	3	4
It's hard for me to find the time to do things such as get a haircut.	1	2	3	4
If I see a chance to get something I want I move on it right away.	1	2	3	4
I feel pretty worried or upset when I think or know somebody is angry at me.	1	2	3	4
When I see an opportunity for something I like I get excited right away.	1	2	3	4
I often act on the spur of the moment.	1	2	3	4
If I think something unpleasant is going to happen I usually get pretty "worked up."	1	2	3	4
I often wonder why people act the way they do.	1	2	3	4
When good things happen to me, it affects me strongly.	1	2	3	4
I feel worried when I think I have done poorly at something important.	1	2	3	4
I crave excitement and new sensations.	1	2	3	4
When I go after something I use a "no holds barred" approach.	1	2	3	4
I have very few fears compared to my friends.	1	2	3	4
It would excite me to win a contest.	1	2	3	4
I worry about making mistakes.	1	2	3	4

PLAY AND WELLBEING

For each of the statements below, please circle the number which best indicates how much the statement applied to you **over the past week**. There are no right or wrong answers. Do not spend too much time on any one statement.

	Did not apply to me at all	Applied to me to some degree, some of the time	Applied to me to a considerable degree, or a good part of the time	Applied to me very much, or most of the time
I found it difficult to work up the initiative to do things.	0	1	2	3
I felt I wasn't worth much as a person.	0	1	2	3
I tended to over-react to situations.	0	1	2	3
I was aware of dryness of my mouth.	0	1	2	3
I felt downhearted and blue.	0	1	2	3
I felt that I was rather touchy.	0	1	2	3
I experienced breathing difficulty (e.g., excessively rapid breathing, breathlessness in the absence of physical exertion).	0	1	2	3
I felt I had nothing to look forward to.	0	1	2	3
I found myself getting agitated.	0	1	2	3
I was aware of the action of my heart in absence of physical exertion (e.g., sense of heart rate increase, heart missing a beat).	0	1	2	3
I experienced trembling (e.g., in the hands).	0	1	2	3
I found it difficult to relax.	0	1	2	3
I was unable to become enthusiastic about anything.	0	1	2	3
I found it hard to wind down.	0	1	2	3
I felt I was close to panic.	0	1	2	3
I was worried about situations in which I might panic and make a fool of myself.	0	1	2	3
I felt I was using a lot of nervous energy.	0	1	2	3
I was intolerant of anything that kept me from getting on with what I was doing.	0	1	2	3
I couldn't seem to experience any positive feeling at all.	0	1	2	3
I felt that life was meaningless.	0	1	2	3
I felt scared without any good reason.	0	1	2	3

PLAY AND WELLBEING

Please rate yourself on the following statements.

	much less than others	less than others	neither less or more than others	more than others	much more than others
Act without planning	1	2	3	4	5
Am always in the same mood	1	2	3	4	5
Am willing to make compromises	1	2	3	4	5
Avoid company	1	2	3	4	5
Avoid contacts with others	1	2	3	4	5
Can easily link facts together	1	2	3	4	5
Can take my mind off my problems	1	2	3	4	5
Copy others	1	2	3	4	5
Do things according to a plan	1	2	3	4	5
Do things at the last minute	1	2	3	4	5
Do what others do	1	2	3	4	5
Follow the crowd	1	2	3	4	5
Get overwhelmed by emotions	1	2	3	4	5
Have crying fits	1	2	3	4	5
Impose my will on others	1	2	3	4	5
Invent problems for myself	1	2	3	4	5
Keep apart from others	1	2	3	4	5
Laugh aloud	1	2	3	4	5
Like to follow a regular schedule	1	2	3	4	5
Love to chat	1	2	3	4	5
Make a mess of things	1	2	3	4	5
Order people around	1	2	3	4	5
Readily overcome setbacks	1	2	3	4	5
Respect others' feelings	1	2	3	4	5
Slap people on the back	1	2	3	4	5
Take others' interests into account	1	2	3	4	5
Think quickly	1	2	3	4	5
Use others for my own ends	1	2	3	4	5
Want to form my own opinions	1	2	3	4	5
Work according to a routine	1	2	3	4	5

PLAY AND WELLBEING

This scale consists of a number of words that describe different feelings and emotions. Read each item and then circle the appropriate answer. Indicate to what extent you generally feel this way, that is, how you feel on the average.

	very slightly or not at all	a little	moderately	quite a bit	extremely
interested	1	2	3	4	5
irritable	1	2	3	4	5
distressed	1	2	3	4	5
alert	1	2	3	4	5
excited	1	2	3	4	5
upset	1	2	3	4	5
inspired	1	2	3	4	5
strong	1	2	3	4	5
nervous	1	2	3	4	5
guilty	1	2	3	4	5
determined	1	2	3	4	5
attentive	1	2	3	4	5
jittery	1	2	3	4	5
active	1	2	3	4	5
ashamed	1	2	3	4	5
amused	1	2	3	4	5
loving	1	2	3	4	5
contemptuous	1	2	3	4	5
embarrassed	1	2	3	4	5
proud	1	2	3	4	5
joyous	1	2	3	4	5
grateful	1	2	3	4	5
angry	1	2	3	4	5
hopeful	1	2	3	4	5
sad	1	2	3	4	5
afraid	1	2	3	4	5
disgusted	1	2	3	4	5
awed	1	2	3	4	5
guilty	1	2	3	4	5
content	1	2	3	4	5
compassionate	1	2	3	4	5

PLAY AND WELLBEING

This assessment asks how you feel about your quality of life, health, or other areas of your life. Please answer all the questions. If you are unsure about which response to give to a question, please choose the one that appears most appropriate. This can often be your first response. Please keep in mind your standards, hopes, pleasures, and concerns. We ask you to think about your life in the **last two weeks**.

	very poor	poor	neither poor nor good	good	very good
How would you rate your quality of life?	1	2	3	4	5

	very dissatisfied	dissatisfied	neither dissatisfied nor satisfied	satisfied	very satisfied
How satisfied are you with your health?	1	2	3	4	5

	not at all	a little	a moderate amount	very much	an extreme amount
To what extent do you feel that physical pain prevents you from doing what you need to do?	1	2	3	4	5
How much do you need any medical treatment to function in your daily life?	1	2	3	4	5
How much do you enjoy life?	1	2	3	4	5
To what extent do you feel your life to be meaningful?	1	2	3	4	5
How well are you able to concentrate?	1	2	3	4	5
How safe do you feel in your daily life?	1	2	3	4	5
How healthy is your physical environment?	1	2	3	4	5

	not at all	a little	moderately	mostly	completely
Do you have enough energy for everyday life?	1	2	3	4	5
Are you able to accept your bodily appearance?	1	2	3	4	5
Have you enough money to meet your needs?	1	2	3	4	5
How available to you is the information that you need in your day-to-day life?	1	2	3	4	5
To what extent do you have the opportunity for leisure activities?	1	2	3	4	5

	very poor	poor	neither poor nor good	good	very good
How well are you able to get around?	1	2	3	4	5

	very dissatisfied	dissatisfied	neither dissatisfied nor satisfied	satisfied	very satisfied
How satisfied are you with your sleep?	1	2	3	4	5
How satisfied are you with your ability to perform your daily living activities?	1	2	3	4	5
How satisfied are you with your capacity for work?	1	2	3	4	5

PLAY AND WELLBEING

	very dissatisfied	dissatisfied	neither dissatisfied nor satisfied	satisfied	very satisfied
How satisfied are you with yourself?	1	2	3	4	5
How satisfied are you with your personal relationships?	1	2	3	4	5
How satisfied are you with your sex life?	1	2	3	4	5
How satisfied are you with the support you get from your friends?	1	2	3	4	5
How satisfied are you with the conditions of your living place?	1	2	3	4	5
How satisfied are you with your access to health services?	1	2	3	4	5
How satisfied are you with your transport?	1	2	3	4	5
How often do you have negative feelings such as blue mood, despair, anxiety, depression?	1	2	3	4	5

Below are several statements you may agree or disagree with. Please indicate your agreement with each of these statements by circling the appropriate number on the 7-point scale.

	strongly disagree	disagree	slightly disagree	neither agree nor disagree	slightly agree	agree	strongly agree
In most ways my life is close to my ideal.	1	2	3	4	5	6	7
The conditions of my life are excellent.	1	2	3	4	5	6	7
I am satisfied with my life.	1	2	3	4	5	6	7
So far I have gotten the important things I want in life.	1	2	3	4	5	6	7
If I could live my life over, I would change almost nothing.	1	2	3	4	5	6	7

Finally, please tell us a little bit about yourself.

Age: _____ years   Gender: ☐ male   ☐ female
Are you currently employed?   ☐ yes, full-time ☐ yes, part-time ☐ no
If yes, how much do you work in a typical week? _____ hours   In how many credits are you currently enrolled? ____ credits
Year in school: ☐ freshman   ☐ sophomore ☐ junior   ☐ senior   ☐ supersenior   ☐ grad
What is your major? _____ How long have you been in this major? _____ #semesters   cumulative GPA_____

Thank you for you time and your thoughts. Your participation is very helpful and much appreciated!

Books worth (re-)reading: *The act of creation* by Arthur Koestler (1969)

Cindy Dell Clark

Department of Sociology, Anthropology and Criminal Justice, Rutgers University, Camden, USA

The late comedian George Carlin, who knew a thing or two about how cartharsis derives from humor and playfulness, admired and recommended Koestler's book *The act of creation*. Published in 1964 in two volumes – the second volume was dropped in later printings – *The act of creation* was widely read in the 1960s and 1970s. Those decades were a time of pronounced cultural transformation, when creative shifts were societal as well as personal. In our present millennium, despite a crying need for creative approaches to nagging problems, *The act of creation* has fallen out of print. But Koestler's work on creativity is not forgotten by any means. In a recent list of the most frequently requested out-of-print books, *The act of creation* stands at #53 on the list, and is regularly in the top 100.

My copy (a 1969 version including volume one only) has become as cover-worn as a child's beloved toy bear. Its back cover announces that *The act of creation* is a book from the discipline of philosophy. But the Hungarian-British Arthur Koestler (1905–1983) was much more than a philosopher. He wrote a trilogy of anti-totalitarian novels known as *Darkness at noon*, chronicled the history of science, was fascinated by mysticism, took drugs with the famed LSD experimenter Timothy Leary, started the KIB Society for the study of paranormal research, and studied psychology. He was unorthodox for his time even in his manner of death; he and his wife committed suicide together, after he (already handicapped by Parkinson's disease) was diagnosed with terminal cancer.

The act of creation deals with expressive subject matter, including humor, art, ritual, music, dance, and poetry. It also recounts cases of paradigm-changing scientific insight. Koestler addresses clowning as a creative act as well, even if not specifically mentioning children or children's use of therapeutic play. Koestler's concept of *bisociation*, illustrated copiously among adults across numerous contexts, provides a model that traces how creative acts, by incorporating playful excursions across distinct domains of thought, work to yield dynamic, transformative power. It is not a stretch to extrapolate bisociation for relevance to acts of therapeutic playful exchange, some of which are showcased in this volume. Play as a healing act relies fundamentally on the imaginative reframing of experience, as any play therapist, child life specialist, or hospital clown can attest.

Creativity, in Koesler's view, is a counter force to the human habit of tracking experience within a single matrix of cultural or disciplinary convention, as typifies set schools of thought such as behaviorism or psychoanalysis. Causal chains conceived within a single matrix or plane of thinking have the advantage of being automatic and expected, but there is also a disadvantage – ready-made framing serves to limit adaptability and flexibility. Bisociation occurs when someone gathers meaning simultaneously from disparate modes of thought, in effect, placing in confrontation multiple planes of reference. The act of creation, for Koestler, involves two planes of meaning, two paradigmatic framings coming into meaningful collision. Bisociation is a connection of separate planes of significance, a meeting of different frames of reference – culminating in insight, laughter, or profound poetic or a esthetic appreciation. Jokes, of course, combine double meanings routinely; appreciating a joke and laughing at it is largely a response to 'getting' the bisociated meanings. Consider a brief doctor-doctor joke included in Judy McKinty's article in this volume titled 'From playground to patient: Reflections on a traditional games project in a pediatric hospital.'

> Doctor, doctor I've only got 59 minutes to live.
> Hang on, I'll be with you in a minute.

To appreciate this joke, the listener must consider a literal plane of meaning in which time is specified precisely ('59 minutes') at the same time as a figurative or idiomatic frame of meaning germane to medical, bureaucratic environments ('I'll be with you in a minute'). When these contrasting modes are conjoined by an interpretive listener, a pulsation of amused response arises. The humorous response carries thrust, for it is situated upon a serious and charged dilemma of significance: that medical intervention must be timely or death might not be obviated.

The figure below, adapted by Chris Thornton (2009) from an illustration in *The act of creation*, visually represents an event of bisociation. The planes of M_1 and M_2 find some sort of connection as might occur in a double-entendre joke or pun. One plane of meaning is brought into connection with another plane of meaning, and a sense of concentrated explosiveness comes about as the meanings collide.

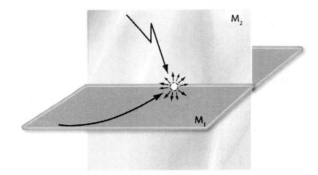

Many stories or performances, of course, involve a series of such bisociations, which Koestler described as a 'series of minor explosions or a continuous state of mild amusement'. The humor response can consist, over time, of oscillating comic references that cause the hearer to experience a sustained pattern of 'getting it', that is, continually approaching one frame of reference in terms of the other. Getting a joke is, in a sense, a cathartic release in response to a coincident anomaly, or a series of related coincident anomalies. Laughter gives physical relief upon relinquishing singular meaning, as the interpreter cognitively and affectively grasps a bisociation. The impulse that powers a smile or laugh occurs as the thinker flips from a singular mode of thought toward consideration of multiple framings in unison.

Put another way, Koestler's concept of bisociation maps how a tension of linked meanings is fundamental to amused laughter. In therapeutic humor, the tension or collision of meanings often comes at just the point where significance needs remaking, the point where a singular notion of reality perhaps has become frozen or problematic. In a camp for children suffering from severe asthma I studied (Clark, 2003), children incorporated humor into a dramatic skit they prepared to show all the asthmatic children in the camp. They juxtaposed two domains in their skit, drawing on the traditional story *The three little pigs*, but colliding this story with a separate interpretive realm, that of asthma treated by biomedicine. They imagined a wolf who had asthma and who underwent biomedical treatment. In their version of the story, the wolf could not 'huff and puff and blow the pig's house down' as he threatened to do, due to wheezing and poor breathing. When the skit was performed for the whole camp, the laughter was particularly pronounced (with quite a few tears from laughter) at certain points in the narrative. Children laughed as if they saw how the wolf's power-seeking intent was hampered by his inability to exhale adequately. Children roared with laughter when the wolf had his breathing measured with a peak flow meter, a device measuring quality of breath that was familiar and used daily at the camp; the wolf's peak flow measurement was dramatized as so low, no actual person would be able to sustain life with such poor breathing. An explosion of laughter at this point in the story indicated that children profoundly enjoyed the chance to take lightly, through the wolf's ironic character, a source of deep anxiety: inadequate breathing implicates suffocation. At root, therapeutic humor brings relief through an instantaneous change of 'scene' or context, a referential escape hatch to another realm of meaning through which hardships or calamity have an opportunity to be laughed off. The point of reframing is often a point of catharsis that aids coping. Fun brings about bisociation, locates a mini-explosion of remade significance and with it, a shifted vantage point in the here and now.

Koestler also applied the concept of bisociation to creative leaps of discovery, moments of truth-seeing when a hidden analogy comes into view and changes how a scientist or artist frames a problem. Conventional procedures and rules may be tried and true, but they can also prove to be too rigid, too stereotypic for a satisfactory solution to newly presented challenges. Innovation involves breaking with stale modes of logic or frames of thought, for these keep to a narrow, inflexible groove the array of approaches. Such a break with convention may come in a dream, or at a time when a scientist is taking a break from usual modes of scientific thought. Frederick August von Kekule dreamt in 1865 about a snake biting its tail, and awoke realizing that molecules of certain compounds are not open, but rather are closed chains or 'rings', the shape of the snake swallowing its tail.

Pretend play is inherently an act of bisociation, I might argue. In pretense, an object is treated as something else, such as a banana for a telephone or a spoon for a microphone. In pretense, collisions of reference are inherent and pervasive. Bisociation offers an explanatory template for a phenomenon that has been challenging to explain – the dynamic by which pretense and metaphor drive healing in formal play therapy. Adult play therapists provide a safe, emotionally supportive context rich in play resources – a context in which children can move their play from domain to domain, in a sense exploring successive representative planes of meaning at will. As the therapist shores up the child's playful moves, there is support in place when a collision of meaning touches close to a child's core problems. Therapeutic breakthroughs, marked by a sense of relief and remade meaning, gain propulsion from a bisociative discharge or impulse, facilitated through play and its propensity to cross-cut domains. This may explain why play therapy often succeeds to free up a stuck child who has not been able to adapt within the routines of his or her environment. Play in formal therapy is a medium for fertilizing cross-domain connection and protecting the new awareness that comes about when meanings bisociate.

In an era when fun is too often dismissed as trivial, Koestler's book reminds us of a view worth reinforcing, that playful openness is crucial for reaching creative break-through. His treatise supports that the comic, the poetic, and the capacity to synthesize across domains are essential for human flexibility.

Koestler's insight, of course, traces to Koestler's own adeptness at bisociated thinking. Across fields of comedy, clowning, poetry, dramatics, and science, Koestler's book is a demonstration of his own premise that insights come about by crossing domains. The collisions and insights he describes make *The act of creation* a book needed now, no less than when it appeared.

References

Clark, C. D. (2003). *In sickness and in play.* New Brunswick: Rutgers University Press.
Koestler, A. (1969). *The act of creation.* London: Picador Press.
Thornton, C. (2009). *Generative creativity lecture 15: Analogie.* Retrieved 19 September, 2013, from http://www.sussex.ac.uk/Users/christ/crs/gc/lec15.html

Index

Note: Page numbers in *italics* represent tables
Page numbers in **bold** represent figures
Page numbers followed by 'n' refer to notes

Abbs P. 23, 24
Aborigine 35
Act of creation, The (Koestler) 3, 4, 139–42
Activation Relationship Theory (Paquette *et al.*)
   98, 108
active listening 56
activities: parenting 101
adaptive skills 46, 80, 83, 90
adjacency pairs 48
Adult Attachment Scale (AAS Simpson, Rholes &
   Nelligan) 100, 101, *101*
adult-child interaction 45
adulthood: emerging 116
adults 125; play 45
aesthetic engagement 23, 24
aftershocks 47
aged care 17, 18
agency: children's 45, 55
alcohol 126
Alexander, K. 3
All we are saying is give peace a chance (Beatles)
   11, 12, 13
Alzheimer's Australia 18
American Academy of Pediatrics (AAP) 96
American Speech-Language and Hearing
   Association (ASHA) 85
AMOS 121, 122
anthropology 14, 65
anxiety 83, *see also* stress
applied theatre 19, 21, 23
Armstrong, P.B. 126
Arnett's theory 116
arts-based responses 18

Association for the Study of Play, The (TASP) 14
Association for the Wellbeing of Children in
   Healthcare (AWCH) 30
asthma 141
Australia 17, 18, 29, 31; dementia 18; gross
   domestic product 18; Humour Foundation 19;
   SMILE 19
Australian Children's Folklore Collection (ACFC)
   32, 36, 41n
Australian Research Council 17
autonomy 82, 98

back gardens 66, *66*, 67, **67**, 75, 85
background knowledge 22
Balfour, M.: *et al.* 16–28
barriers to play 49, 73, 75, 86, 109; natural 86;
   perceived 97
Barron, C. 62–76
Bateman, A.: Danby, S. and Howard, J. 44–59
Beatles 11, 12, 13
bedside games 40
Behavioral Assessment System for Children
   (BASC–2) 101
behaviour 45, 49
belief: religious 82
benefits: play 106–7
Big Apple Circus Clown Care Unit (New York) 7
biographical information 23, 24, 25
bisociation 3, 14, 139–42
board games 103, 106–7
body mass index (BMI) 63
boredom 35, 38, 81, 83
Bowlby, Sir Richard 109

INDEX

boys 69; gender-related differences 75; in hospital 29; tether lengths 72–3
Brook, P. 23, 24
bulimia 9
bullying 8, 9
Bundy, Dr A.C. 23, 88, 90, 91, 117
Bundy's Model of Playfulness 87
Bush, George 8

Cambodia 6
cameras 19, **20**, 65
Candler, C.: and Ryan-Bloomer, K. 79–95
capitalism 6
care: aged 17, 18; disease-orientated 30; patient-orientated 30
Carlin, George 139
cat's cradle 32, 37
Chang, Po-Ju: Qian, X., and Yarnal, C. 115–27
charity 7
chasing games 62, 70–1
chatterboxes 39
chi-square 122
Child Cohort 64
child life playroom 86, **87**
child life therapist 81, 85
child-centred anthropology 65
childbearing 97
Childhood Environment Rating Scale-Revised 83
children 13, 79–92; adaptiveness 80, 83, 90; asthma 141; autonomy 82, 98; disabilities 89; emotions 30, 44, 45, 97; everyday experiences 48; individual differences 89; internal control 80; intrinsic motivation 80; leisure activities 103; mental health 97; mobility 67, 73, 75; narrative 46; nature 73–4; nutrition 85; occupations 79, 92; photography by 65, 66; physical activity 62; playfulness 116; playing family relationships 57–8; preferred play spaces 75; social interactions 82; social rules 54–5; stress 80; traumatic events 44–58; well-being 64, 96, 105–6, *see also* hospitalized children
children's agency 45, 55
Children's Museum 31
Children's Relationship Attitudes (CRA Roggman, Coyl, Newland & Cook) 101
Civilization and its discontents (Freud) 6
Clark, C.D. 3–4, 5–15, 139–42
climbing 62

clowning 88, 139
clowns 19
cognitive behavioural therapy (CBT) 46
cognitive development 79
cognitive spontaneity 20, 21, 25
cohabitation 97
communal green areas 65, 70, 75; girls' marginalized 70, 75
communal living 9–10
communication 48
community clinic 9
compassion 8
concurrent triangulation design 99
confirmatory factor analysis (CFA) 121, 122, *123*
control: internal 80, 90
Cooke, M.: *et al.* 16–28
coping skills 80, 89, 116, 118–19, **119**, 125; emotions 125–6; high school seniors 118; life satisfaction 118–19; playfulness 125, 126; stress 115, 117; university students 117–18
costumes 5, 18
Country Women's Association of Australia (CWAA) 35
Coyl-Shepherd, D.D.: and Hanlon C., 96–109
creativity 13–14, 80, 139
Cronbach's alpha *120*, 122
Crystal, C. 18, 22; *et al.* 16–28
Csikszentmihalyi, M. 20, 116, 126
cultural differences 126
culture: play 29, 30
cystic fibrosis 37

Danby, S.: Howard, J. and Bateman, A. 44–59
Darkness at noon (Koestler) 139
death 10, 12
Dementia Research Centre (DRC) 18
demographic information 105, 121, 127
depression 18, 81, 99, *104*, 108, 118, 121; child 101, 102; and dementia 18
Depression, Anxiety, and Stress Scale (DASS) 121, 122
development: cognitive 79; motor skills 33; psychosocial 79; rural 72; urban 72
diabolo 38, 42n
diet 63, 85, 97
diphtheria 29
disabilities 89
disasters: natural 44–58
disease-orientated care 30

INDEX

disposable cameras 65
distraction 51
diversional activity deficit 81
divorce 97
doctor-doctor jokes 36, 140
doctors 13
Dr Fart: brand fart machine/sound effect 8
dramatic elements 22–3
drug use 126
Dunn, J.: *et al.* 16–28
Dyadic Adjustment Scale (Spanier) 100
dyadic satisfaction 99, 100, *101*, 102, 103, *104*, *106*;
    father-reported 105; mother-reported 102, 103

El Salvador 6
Elderflowers project 18
emerging adulthood 116
emotional health 44, 45
emotions 116, 117–18, **119**, 121, 125–6; life
    satisfaction 119, 124
entertainment: multi-media 97
Epstein, June 35, **36**, 41n
equipment: playgrounds 67
equipment, play 75, 85–6; hospitals 86–7;
    movable 68
ethical considerations 49
ethnic diversity 91, 100
ethnography 65
ethnomethodological analysis 48
European childhood mobility studies 75
European Union (EU) 64
everyday activities 20
exercise 63
exhibitions 30–1
experiences: traumatic 44, 45, 46, 47–8, 55, 58
Experiential Sampling Method 127
expressive caution 56
eye contact 26, 57

Facets Rasch analysis statistical program (Linacre) 88
Factor, Dr June 31
family lifestyles 97, 99, 108, 109; leisure activities
    98, 100, *101*, *104*; and play 106
family relationships: playing 57–8
family roles 57
family therapy 46
fart jokes 5
fathering 97, 98, 107; roughhousing 102, 103, 105,
    108; well-being 103

fathers 98
Featherston, Mary 31
feeding: disorders 84–5, *84*; inpatient 84–5, 86,
    86, **87**, 89, 91
fictitious kinship 10–11
fighting: play 70–2
fortune tellers 39
framing 80, 90, 139, 140
free play 45–6, 49, 85, 97
Freud, S. 6
friendship 29–30, 37–8
frog cups 36
front gardens 67–8, **68**, 75, 85

games 40, 71–2; board 103, 106–7; chasing 62,
    70–1
gardens 66–8, *66*, **67**, **68**, 75, 85
gastrostomy tube 85
Gaulier, P. 18
gender-related differences 70, **71**, 75, 105, 108;
    tether lengths 72–3
Gesundheit Institute 6
girls 70, **71**, 72–3, 75
global mortality 63
Global Strategy on Diet, Physical Activity and
    Health (WHO, 2009) 63
goodness-of-fit indices 122–3
gratitude 10–11
green areas: communal 65, 70, 75
Gro Pro camera 19, **20**
Growing Up in Ireland longitudinal study 64
Gryski, C. 7
Guatemala 10, 13

Hadden Place Day Respite Centre (Brisbane) 19
Haiti 6
Hanlon, C.: and Coyl-Shepherd, D.D. 96–109
healing 7, 139
health: emotional 44, 45; mental 6, 63, 64, 97;
    physical 63
heightened status 24
Hendriks, R. 19
high school seniors 118
holistic approach 45
home recordings 85–6
hospitalized children 7, 80–95; caregivers 81;
    friendships 37; jokes 37; language 36–7; play
    knowledge 37; social interactions 82; stress 80;
    subculture 36–7

INDEX

hospitals: paediatric 29–30, 81–2; play culture 29, 30; play space 86, **87**; procedures 37
housing design 65, 75
Howard, J.: Bateman, A. and Danby, S. 44–59
humanist values 6
humour 17, 20, 22, 23, 37, 140, 141
Humour Foundation 19
Hurricane Katrina 46

Incredible Times, The 37
index of child well-being 64
infection control 81, 82
information: biographical 23, 24, 25
inpatient feeding program 84–5, 89; play mobility 91; play space 86, **86**, **87**
interaction 82; adult-child 45; verbal 24
interactional resource 53
internal control 80, 90
International Obesity Task Force 63
intrinsic motivation 80, 90
Iraq invasion 8
Ireland 64, 66
isolation: social 18

jacks 32, 33, 34, 37, 41n
Jackson, Michael 11, 12
Jennings Carmichael, Sister Grace 29, 30, 37
jokes 5, 36, 37, 140
joy 20, 21, 22

KIB Society for the study of paranormal research 139
Killick, J. 22
kinship: fictitious 10–11
knowledge: background 22; play 37
Koestler, A. 3, 14, 139–42
Kosovo 6

Lamington, Dumpling 16–17, 19–20, **20**, 21; case studies 24–6
Lamington, Tiny 16–17, 19–20, **20**, 21; case studies 24–6
language 36–7, 51; scatological 51
laughter 13, 19, 24, 140, 141
Learning Story books 44, 45, 46, 52, 58; earthquake experiences 49; rules about 51
learning through play 44
Leary, Timothy 139
leisure activities 103; family 98, 100, *101*, *104*

Lennon, John 11
leukaemia 83
Levi-Strauss, C. 13
Lieberman's Playfulness Scale (Lieberman) 20, 82
life satisfaction 118–19, 124
lifestyles: family 97, 98, 99, 100, *101*, *104*, 106, 108, 109
Likert-type rating scale 119, *119*, *120*, 121
listening: active 56
loneliness 6, 8, 9, 18, 118
love 8, 10–12, 13; motherly 10–12, 13, 97
lullabies 10, 13

McDonald's 7
McKinty, J. 29–41, 140
make-believe 12, 21
Manhunt (game) 71–2
manifest joy 20, 22
marbles 32, 33, 37, **39**
Marcuse, H. 23–4
marginalization: girls 70, 75
marital satisfaction 97, 99
Martin, K.: *et al.* 16–28
meaning-focused coping 118
meaning-making 23, 52
Measurement model 123, **123**
mediated symbolism 14
mediation 10–12, 13
Mediation Model (Iwasaki *et al.*) 115, 117
medicine: and societal change 8
Melbourne Hospital for Sick Children (now *Royal Children's Hospital (RCH)*) 29, **31**, 41, 41n
mental health 6, 63, 64, 97
metabolic activity 62
miMakker elderclowns 19
mindfulness 118
mischief and clowning 88
mobility 67, 73, 75, 91
modified differential emotions scale (mDES) 121
mortality: global 63
mother-son relationship 10–12
motherly love 10–12, 13, 97
mothers 10–12, 97, 103; play styles 98; roughhousing 102, 103, 108
motivation 80, 90
Motives for Involvement (Newland, Chen *et al.*) 100, *101*
motor skills 33
Moyle, W.: *et al.* 16–28

INDEX

multi-media entertainment 97
multidisciplinary research 17
music 16, 21

narrative 46
National Association of Health Play Specialists (NAHPS) 30
natural disasters 44–58
nature 73–4, **74**
neglected aspect of play 62, 63
Netherlands 19
neuroses 45
New Brighton Preschool 47
New York 7
New Zealand 44–58
non-profit charity 7
nutrition 85

observations: play 83
occupational therapist 81
occupational therapy 80, 84, 85, 91, 92
occupations 79, 92
opportunities: play 65
outdoor play spaces 53, 62, 66, *66*, 75, 85, 102, 103; decrease in 97; roads 69–70, **69**, **70**; safety 105–6, 108; seasonal variation *66*, 67

paediatric hospitalization 83; room occupancy 82
paediatric hospitals 29–30, 37, 80–2, 86, **87**
Pagneaux, M. 18
Parent Stress (Newland *et al.*) 100, *101*
parent-child: bonds 96; relationship 38
Parent-Child Relationship Quality (Newland, Chen *et al.*) 100, *101*
parental restrictions 72–3
Parenti, S. 5, 8
parenting 97, 98, 99; activities 101; benefits 107; stress 99, *101*, 105; well-being 99
patient-orientated care 30
patients 8; children 13
Patte, M. 5, **6**
peace 11, 12, 13
perception: of play 64
Peru 6
philosophy: relationship-centred 18
photo elicitation 65, 74
photography 65; outdoor images 66
physical activity 62
physical health 63

physical limitations 32, 39, 40
physical play 98
physical spontaneity 20, 21, 24
play baskets 34, **34**, 38
play fighting 70–2
Play Specialists 34–5, 38, 40
Playful Engagement Project 17–18, 19, 24
playfulness 8, 13, 14, 19, 116; and adults 125; benefits 9; distraction 51; everyday activities 20; five dimensions of 20; limitations 25
playgrounds 66, **67**; equipment 67; girls' marginalized 70, 75
playroom: child life 86, **87**
point fix (silences) 24
politics 8–9
post-disaster behaviour 45, 49
post-earthquake events 47
pre-admission videos 84
preferences: play 26, 27
Preschool Play Scale (Knox) 82
pretend play 80, 141
problem solving 46, 57; and play 80; and playfulness 116
Process Model of Stress and Coping 116, 117, 118, 124, 125
props 8, 21
Prozac 9
psychiatric wards 39
psychological stress *120*, 121, 122, 124, 126
psychosocial development 79
pump-action top 40
puppetry 26, 33, 35, **36**

Qian, X.: Yarnal, C. and Chang, Po-Ju 115–27
quality of life (QOL) 17, 18, 98, 118
quantitative repeated measures design 83–4
questionnaires 119, 130–8

Rasch analysis 88
rating scales 119, *119*, *120*, 121, 122
RCH Foundation 31
re-enactment 45, 46, 55
reading 35
reality suspension 80, 90
reciprocal relationships 53
record-keeping 14, 17, 31
recordings: home 85–6; video 88, 91
red noses 16, 18
reflective talk 48, 51

INDEX

relationship building 21, 27, 40, 45; children and teachers 48; creating connections 26; and trust 22

relationship-centred philosophy 18

relationships: mother-son 10–12; parent-child 38; playing family 57–8; reciprocal 53; reversal 39

religious belief 82

responsiveness 21, 22, 24

Rickards, Dorothy 35, **36**, 41n

risk-taking 97, 98

roads 69–70, **69**, **70**

Romania 6

Ronald McDonald 7

Ronald McDonald House 7

room entrances 26

rough-and-tumble play (RTP) 97, 99, 108, 109

roughhousing 102, 103, 105, 108

Royal Children's Hospital (RCH), Melbourne 29, **31**, 41, 41n; Play Specialists 34

Ruben Play Scale (Rubin, Watson & Jambor) 83

rules: social 54–5

rural development 72

Russell, Heather 36–7, 40, 42n

Russia 9

Ryan-Bloomer, K.: and Candler, C. 79–95

safety 105–6, 108

satire 14

satisfaction: life 118–19, 124; marital 97, 99, *see also* dyadic satisfaction

Satisfaction With Life Scale (SWLS) 121, 122

Saunders, Amy 35, 41n

scatological language 51

scent potions 8

schooling 23, 37, 38, 74

secure exploration *101*, 102, 103–4, 105, *106*, 108; child report of 96, 99, 101, *101*, 102, 103, 105

Secure Exploration scale 101

Self-Distress Measure (Weisz, McCabe & Denning) 83

self-esteem 41, 44

sense of humour 20, 22

sensitivity 12

sensory processing 85

shamans 7, 12, 13, 14

shared experiences 40, 49, 50–1, 58

shared performance philosophy 20–1

sibling rivalry 21, 22, 25

silence 26

skills: adaptive 46, 80, 83, 90; motor 33; social 79, 98, *see also* coping skills

slang terms 36, 37

slapstick comedy 21

SMILE 19

soccer 69

social isolation 18

social rules 54–5

social skills 79, 98

social spontaneity 22, 24, 25, 26

societal change 8

soft furnishings 33, 41

songs 21–2

spaces: play 86, **86**, **87**, *see also* outdoor play spaces

Spearman rank tests 88, 89

spinning top 40

spontaneity 20, 26; cognitive 21–2, 25, 26; physical 21, 24, 26; social 22, 24, 25, 26

spontaneous play 41, 56

sports 62

Sri Lanka 6

status 24; dropping (as tool for humour) 17, 23

story attachments 3

storytelling 32, 35; with puppets 35, **36**; shared experiences 50–1

Storytelling Guild of Victoria 35

stranger danger 73, 75, 108

strategic mediation 13

strategic sensitivity 12

street play 68–9, 74–5

stress 83, 117, **119**; life satisfaction 118, 126; parenting 99, *101*, 105; psychological *120*, 121, 122, 124, 126

Stress Inventory (Chandler) 83

string games 32, 37

structural equation modeling (SEM) 121, 123–4, 126

Stubs, Mr 7

subculture: hospitalized children 36–7

Subculture of a Children's Hospital, The (Russell) 36–7

support: from teachers 52, 56, 58

surgery 30

symbolic mediation 10–12, 13

symbolism 10–12, 13, 14

taboos 10

talk: reflective 48, 51

INDEX

teachers 45–6, 48; perspective of 47–8; play experiences 47; support from 52, 56, 58
teasing 88
television 103
tether lengths 72–3
theatre: applied 19, 21, 23
theatre artists 16–17, 18; mutual recognition 18; paediatric clowns 13
therapeutic clowning 7–8, 13, 14
therapeutic humour 141
therapeutic value 41, 44
therapists: child life 81, 85; play 141
therapy: family 46; occupational 80, 84, 85, 91, 92; play 45, 46, 47, 141
Thornimat 36
Thornton, C. 140, **140**
Three little pigs, The 141
three tries rule 37
top spinning 37
Tops, Tales and Granny's False Teeth project 29, 30–41, 41n
Toronto's Hospital for Sick Children 7
toys 81, 83, 86
traditional games 30–1, 32, **33**
traumatic experiences 44; behaviour 45; children 58; earthquakes 47–8; literature on 46; pretend play 55; teacher assistance 58
trust 22
tuberculosis 29
typhoid 29

United States of America (USA) 8–9, 97, 100, 119
University of Melbourne 31
university students 117–18, 119; life satisfaction 121, 124, 126; playfulness 120, 124, 125
urban development 72

value: therapeutic 41, 44
verbal interaction 24
Very Hungry Caterpillar, The (Carle) 35, **36**
video recordings 88, 91
video technology 17
videos: pre-admission 84
visiting hours 82

Warren, B. 19
We are the World (Jackson) 11, 12
wellness promotion 63
Wesley Mission Brisbane 17, 19
wheelchairs 32, 33
whole-child approach 30
Wilcoxon-signed rank tests 88, 89
Williams, Robin 6
World Health Organization (WHO): Global Strategy on Diet, Physical Activity and Health (2009) 63
world unity 12, 13

Yarnal, C.: Chang, Po-Ju and Qian, X. 115–27
Yen, A. 18, 20; *et al.* 16–28
Young Adult Playfulness Scale (Barnett) 120, 122